Christmas Cyclopedia

Christmas Cyclopedia

RUNNING PRESS
PHILADELPHIA · LONDON

© 2004 by Kris Kringle
All rights reserved under the Pan-American and International
Copyright Conventions
Printed in China

9   8   7   6   5   4   3   2   1
Digit on the right indicates the number of this printing
Library of Congress Control Number: 2004103055
ISBN 0-7624-2082-0

Cover design by Bill Jones
Interior design by Nova Graphic Services
Edited by Lindsay Powers (Running Press) and
Marta Steele (Nova Graphic Services)
Typography: (Palatino), (Balmoral ICG), and (Poetica ChanceryII)

This book may be ordered by mail from the publisher. Please include $2.50 for
postage and handling.
But try your bookstore first!

Running Press Book Publishers
125 South Twenty-second Street
Philadelphia, Pennsylvania 19103-4399

Visit us on the web!
www.runningpress.com

To Jeremy Zavell ~ For sharing the Christmas spirit with
family, friends, and even strangers 365 days a year . . .

Your kindness, generosity, and warmth are contagious.
You will always and forever be an inspiration for how to live life to the fullest.
Thank you.

Acknowledgments

*Thanks to children everywhere
for defining and embodying the Christmas spirit.*

$\mathcal{C}$ontents

Stories

Poems

Carols

Recipes

CONTENTS

Sweet Treats

Christmas Tips and Crafts

Santa Claus and Christmas Traditions around the World

Stories

Times was with most of us, when Christmas Day, encircling all our limited world like a magic ring, left nothing out for us to miss or seek; bound together all our home enjoyments, affections, and hopes; grouped everything and everyone round the Christmas fire, and made the little picture shining in our bright young eyes, complete.

—Charles Dickens

A Christmas Carol

by Charles Dickens

Introduction

When Charles Dickens wrote *A Christmas Carol* in 1843, he created a story for all ages, and for all time. His portrayal of the tight-fisted, mean-spirited mercenary who learns the true meaning of Christmas has such vitality that the name "Scrooge" has become a synonym for the ungenerous and unrelenting. More than one hundred fifty years later, no one wants to be called Scrooge. An extraordinary expression of the Christmas spirit, this brief novel is by turn jovial, nightmarish, and uplifting, but never pious or sentimental. *A Christmas Carol* is a fantasy grounded in reality, in which Dickens captures the worst and the best in human nature in ebullient, unforgettable prose.

I have endeavored in this Ghostly little book, to raise the Ghost of an Idea, which shall not put my readers out of humor with themselves, with each other, with the season, or with me. May it haunt their house pleasantly, and no one wish to lay it. —Their Faithful Friend and Servant, C.D.

December 1843

Chapter 1

Marley was dead to begin with. There is no doubt whatever about that. The register of his burial was signed by the clergyman, the undertaker, and the chief mourner. Scrooge signed it. Old Marley was dead as a doornail.

Scrooge knew he was dead? Of course he did. Scrooge and he were partners for I don't know how many years. Scrooge was his sole executor, his sole friend, and sole mourner. There is no doubt that Marley was dead. This must be distinctly understood, or nothing wonderful can come of the story I am going to relate.

Scrooge never painted out old Marley's name. There it stood years afterwards, above the warehouse door: Scrooge and Marley. Sometimes people called Scrooge Scrooge, and sometimes Marley, but he answered to both names, it was all the same to him.

Oh! but he was a tight fisted hand at the grind stone, Scrooge! A squeezing, wrenching, grasping, scraping, clutching, covetous old sinner! Hard and sharp as flint! Secret and solitary as an oyster. The cold within him froze his old features, nipped his pointed nose, shriveled his cheek, made his thin lips blue, and spoke out shrewdly in his grating voice. He carried his own low temperature always about him; he iced his office in the dog-days; and didn't thaw it one degree at Christmas.

External heat and cold had little influence on Scrooge. No warmth could warm him, nor wintry weather chill him. No wind that blew was bitterer than he, no falling snow was more intent upon its purpose, no pelting rain less open to entreaty.

Nobody ever stopped him in the street to say, with gladsome looks, "My dear Scrooge, how are you? When will you come to see me?" No beggars implored him to bestow a trifle, no children asked him what it was o'clock, no man or woman ever once in all his life inquired the way to such and such a place, of Scrooge. Even the blindmen's dogs appeared to know him; and when they saw him coming on, would tug their owners into doorways and up courts; and then would wag their tails as though they said, "No eye at all is better than an evil eye, dark master!"

Once upon a time—on Christmas Eve— old Scrooge sat busy in his counting-house. It was cold, bleak, biting weather, foggy withal, and he could hear the people in the court outside go wheezing up and down, beating their hands upon their breasts, and stamping their feet upon the pavement-stones to warm them. The city clocks had only just gone three, but it was quite dark already. It had not been light all day, and candles were flaring in the windows of the neighboring offices like ruddy smears upon the palpable brown air. The fog came pouring in at every chink and keyhole, and was so dense without that although the court was of the narrowest, the houses opposite were mere phantoms. To see the dingy cloud come drooping down, obscuring everything, one might have thought that Nature lived hard by, and was brewing on a large scale.

The door of Scrooge's counting-house was open that he might keep his eye upon his clerk, who in a dismal little cell beyond, a sort of tank, was copying letters.

Scrooge had a small fire, but the clerk's fire was so very much smaller that it looked like one coal. But he couldn't replenish it, for Scrooge kept the coalbox in his own room, and so surely as the clerk came in with the shovel, the master predicted that it would be necessary for them to part.

"A Merry Christmas, Uncle," cried a cheerful voice. It was Scrooge's nephew, who came in the door unnoticed.

"Bah!" said Scrooge, "Humbug!" This nephew of Scrooge's was ruddy and handsome, all aglow from rapid walking.

"Christmas a humbug, uncle!" said Scrooge's nephew. "You don't mean that?"

"I do," said Scrooge. "Merry Christmas! What reason have you to be merry? You're poor enough."

"What right have you to be dismal?" returned his nephew gaily. "You're rich enough."

Scrooge, having no better answer ready, said, "Bah!" again, and followed it up with, "Humbug."

"Don't be cross," said the nephew.

"What else can I be," returned the uncle, "when I live in such a world of fools as this? Merry Christmas! What's Christmas time to you but a time for paying bills without money, a time for finding yourself a year older, and not an hour richer? If I could work my will," said Scrooge, indignantly, "every idiot who goes about with 'Merry Christmas' on his lips should be boiled with his own pudding and buried with a stake of holly through his heart. He should!"

"Uncle!" pleaded the nephew.

"Nephew!" returned the uncle, "Keep Christmas in your own way, and let me keep it in mine."

"Keep it!" repeated Scrooge's nephew. "But you don't keep it."

"Let me leave it alone, then," said Scrooge. "Much good it has ever done you!"

"There are many things from which I might have derived good, but from which I have not profited," returned the nephew. "I have always thought of Christmas as a good time—a kind, charitable, pleasant time; the only time when men open their shut-up hearts freely and think of people below them as if they really were fellow-passengers to the grave, and not another race of creatures bound on other journeys. Therefore, though it has never put a scrap of gold or silver in my pocket, I believe that it has done me good, and will do me good; and I say, God bless it!"

The clerk in the rank involuntarily applauded.

"Let me hear another sound from you," said Scrooge, "and you'll keep your Christmas by losing your situation!"

"Don't be angry, uncle. Come! Dine with us tomorrow."

"Good afternoon," said Scrooge, ignoring the invitation.

"I want nothing from you. I ask nothing of you; why cannot we be friends?"

"Good afternoon," said Scrooge.

"I am sorry with all my heart to find you so resolute. But I have made the trial in homage to Christmas, so a Merry Christmas, uncle!"

His nephew left without an angry word, and as he departed, two other people came in.

They were pleasant gentlemen, who stood with their hats off, in, Scrooge's office.

"Scrooge and Marley's, I believe," said one of the gentlemen. "Have I the pleasure of addressing Mr. Scrooge, or Mr. Marley?"

"Mr. Marley has been dead these seven years," Scrooge replied. "He died seven years ago, this very night."

"We have no doubt his generosity is well represented by his surviving partner," said the gentleman.

Marley was well represented, all right, for they had been two kindred spirits. At the ominous word "generosity," Scrooge frowned.

"At this festive season, Mr. Scrooge," said the gentleman, "a few of us are endeavoring to raise a fund to buy the poor some meat and drink, and means of warmth. What shall I put you down for?"

"Nothing!" Scrooge replied. "Are there no prisons? No workhouses for these people?"

"Many can't go there; and many would rather die."

"If they would rather die," said Scrooge, "they had better do it, and decrease the surplus population. Besides, excuse me, I don't know that."

"But you might know it," observed the gentleman.

"It's not my business," Scrooge returned. "It's enough for a man to understand his own business, and not to interfere with other people's. Mine occupies me constantly. Good afternoon, gentlemen!"

Seeing that it would be useless to pursue their point, the gentlemen withdrew. Scrooge resumed his labors with an improved opinion of himself and a better temper than was usual.

Meanwhile, the fog and darkness thickened. The ancient church tower, whose old bell was always peeping slyly down at Scrooge out of a gothic window in the wall, became invisible, and struck the hours in the clouds, with tremulous vibrations afterwards as if its teeth were chattering in its frozen head. The piercing, biting cold became intense.

A boy, gnawed and numbed by the hungry cold, as bones are gnawed by dogs, stooped down at Scrooge's keyhole to regale him with a Christmas carol; but at the first sound of—

"God bless you merry gentlemen!" Scrooge seized the ruler with such energy of action that the singer fled in terror.

At length, the hour of shutting up the counting-house arrived. With an ill-will, Scrooge dismounted from his stool and tacitly admitted the fact to the expectant clerk in the tank, who instantly snuffed his candle out and put on his hat.

"You'll want all day tomorrow, I suppose?" said Scrooge.

"If quite convenient, sir."

"It's not convenient," said Scrooge, "and it's not fair. If I was to stop half-a-crown for it, you'd think yourself ill used. I'll be bound?"

The clerk smiled faintly.

"And yet," said Scrooge, "you don't think me ill used, when I pay a day's wages for no work."

The clerk observed that it was only once a year.

"A poor excuse for picking a man's pocket every twenty-fifth of December!" said Scrooge, buttoning his coat. "But I suppose you must have the whole day. Be here all the earlier the next morning!"

The clerk promised that he would, and Scrooge walked out with a growl. The office was closed in a twinkling; and the clerk, with the long ends of his white comforter dangling below his waist (for he wore no great-coat), went down with a slide on Cornhill, at the end of a lane of boys, twenty times, in honor of it being Christmas-eve, and then ran home to Camden Town as fast as he could to play blindman's-buff.

Scrooge took his melancholy dinner in his usual melancholy tavern; and having read all the newspapers, and beguiled the rest of the evening with his banker's book, went home to bed. He lived in chambers which had once belonged to his deceased partner. They were a gloomy suite of rooms, in a lowering pile of buildings, up a dilapidated yard. The yard was so dark that even Scrooge, who knew its every stone, was fain to grope with his hands. The fog and frost so hung about the old gateway of the house that it seemed as if the Genius of the Weather sat in mournful meditation on the threshold.

Now it is a fact that there was nothing at all particular about the knocker on the door, except that it was very large. It is also a fact that Scrooge had seen it night and morning during his whole residence in that place; also that Scrooge had as little of what is called fancy about him as any man in London. Let it also be remembered that Scrooge had not bestowed one thought on Marley since his last mention of his seven years' dead partner that afternoon. And then let any man explain to me, if he can, how it happened that Scrooge, having his key in the lock of the door, saw in the knocker, without its undergoing any intermediate process of change, not a knocker, but Marley's face.

Marley's face. It was not in impenetrable shadow as the other objects in the yard were, but had a dismal light about it. It was not angry, but looked at Scrooge as Marley used to look, with ghostly spectacles turned up upon its ghostly forehead. The hair was curiously stirred, as if by breath or hot-air, and though the eyes were wide open, they were perfectly motionless. That, and its livid color, made it horrible.

As Scrooge looked fixedly at this phenomenon, it was a knocker again.

To say that he was not startled, or that his blood was not conscious of a terrible sensation to which it had been a stranger from infancy, would be untrue. But he put his hand upon the key, turned it sturdily, walked in, and lighted his candle.

He did pause before he shut the door, and he did look cautiously behind it, as if he half expected to be terrified with the sight of Marley's pig-tail sticking out the back of the door. But there was nothing there except the screws and nuts that held the knocker on, so he said, "Pooh, pooh!" and closed it with a bang.

The sound resounded through the house like thunder. Scrooge was not a man to be frightened by echoes. He fastened the door and walked across the hall and up the stairs, slowly, too, trimming his candle as he went.

Up Scrooge went, not caring a button for the darkness of the staircase; darkness is cheap, and Scrooge liked it. But before he shut his heavy door, he walked through his rooms to see that all was right.

Sitting room, bedroom, lumber-room. All as they should be. Nobody under the table, nobody under the sofa, a small fire in the grate, spoon and basin ready, and the little saucepan of gruel (Scrooge had a cold in his head) upon the hob. Nobody under the bed, nobody in the closet, nobody in his dressing-gown which was hanging up against the wall.

Quite satisfied, he closed his door and locked himself in—double-locked himself in, which was not his custom. Thus secured against surprise, he took off his cravat, put on his dressing-gown, slippers, and his night-cap, and sat down before the fire to take his gruel.

His gaze wandered and his glance rested upon a bell that hung in the room. It was with great astonishment, and with a strange, inexplicable dread, that he saw this bell begin to swing. It swung so softly in the outset that it scarcely made a sound, but soon it rang loudly, and so did every bell in the house.

This might have lasted half a minute, but it seemed an hour. They were succeeded by a clanking noise, deep down below, as if some person were dragging a heavy chain. Scrooge then remembered to have heard that ghosts in haunted houses were described as dragging chains.

The cellar-door flew open with a booming sound and then he heard the noise much louder, on the floors below; then coming up the stairs; then coming straight toward his door.

42

"It's humbug still!" said Scrooge. "I won't believe it."

His color changed, though, when without a pause it came on through the door and passed into the room before his eyes. Upon its coming, the dying flame in the fireplace leaped up, as though it cried, "I know him! Marley's Ghost!" and fell again.

The same face—the very same. Marley in his pig-tail, usual waistcoat, tights, and boots; the tassels on the latter bristling like his pig-tail and coat-skirts, and the hair upon his head. The chain he drew was clasped about his middle. It was long and wound about him like a tail, and it was made of cash-boxes, keys, padlocks, ledgers, deeds, and heavy purses wrought in steel. His body was transparent, so that Scrooge, observing him and looking through his waistcoat, could see the buttons on his coat behind.

Scrooge refused to believe it even now. Though he looked the phantom through and through, and saw it standing before him—though he felt the chilling influence of its death-cold eyes and marked the texture of the kerchief bound about its head and chin, which wrapper he had not observed before—he was still incredulous, and fought against his senses.

"How now!" said Scrooge, caustic and cold as ever. "What do you want with me?"

"Much"—Marley's voice, no doubt about it.

"Who are you?"

"In life I was your partner, Jacob Marley. You don't believe in me," observed the Ghost. "Do not your senses convince you of my reality?"

"No," said Scrooge, "the littlest thing affects them. A slight disorder of the stomach makes them cheat. You may be an undigested bit of beef or a crumb of cheese. There's more of gravy than of grave about you, whatever you are!"

Scrooge was not much in the habit of cracking jokes. The truth is that he tried to be smart as a means of distracting his own attention and keeping down his terror, for the specter's voice disturbed the very marrow in his bones.

"You see this toothpick?" said Scrooge. "I have but to swallow this, and be for the rest of my days persecuted by a legion of goblins, all of my own creation. Humbug, I tell you, humbug!"

At this, the spirit raised a frightful cry and shook its chain with such an appalling

noise that Scrooge held on tight to his chair
to save himself from falling in a swoon.
But how much greater was his horror
when the Phantom, taking off the bandage
round its head as if it were too warm to wear
indoors, dropped its lower jaw down upon
its breast!

Scrooge fell upon his knees and clasped
his hands before his face.

"Mercy!" he said. "Dreadful apparition,
why do you trouble me!"

"Do you believe in me or not?" replied
the Ghost.

"I do," said Scrooge. "But why do spirits
walk the earth, and why do they come to me?"

"It is required of every man," the Ghost
returned, "that the spirit within him should
walk abroad among his fellow men and travel
far and wide, and if that spirit goes not forth

in life, it is condemned to do so after death. It is doomed to wander through the world—oh, woe is me!—and witness what it cannot share, but might have shared on earth, and turned to happiness!"

Again the specter raised a cry, and shook its chain and wrung its shadowy hands.

"Why are you fettered?" said Scrooge, trembling.

"I wear the chain I forged in life," replied the Ghost. "I made it link by link—I girded it on of my own free will, and of my own free will I wore it. Is its pattern strange to you?"

Scrooge trembled more and more.

"Do you not know," pursued the Ghost, "the weight and length of the coil you bear yourself?"

"Jacob," he implored, "Old Jacob Marley, speak comfort to me."

"I have none to give," the Ghost replied. "I cannot stay, I cannot linger anywhere. My spirit never walked beyond our counting-house. Mark me!—in life my spirit never roved beyond the narrow limits of our money-changing hole, and weary journeys lie before me!"

"Seven years dead!" gasped Scrooge. "And traveling all the time?"

"The whole time," said the Ghost. "No rest, no peace. Incessant torture of remorse."

Then the Ghost set up another cry and clanked its chain hideously.

"Oh! Captive, bound, and double-ironed," cried the phantom. "Not to know that any Christian spirit working kindly in its little sphere, whatever that may be, will find its mortal life too short for its vast means of usefulness. Not to know that no space of regret can make amends for one life's opportunity misused! Yet such was I!"

"But you were always a good man of business, Jacob," faltered Scrooge, who now began to apply this to himself.

"Business! Mankind was my business. The common welfare was my business—charity, mercy, forbearance, and benevolence, were all my business. The dealings of my trade were but a drop of water in the ocean of my business!"

It held up its chain and flung it heavily upon the ground again.

"At this time of the year," the specter said, "I suffer most. Why did I walk through crowds of fellow beings with my eyes turned down, and never raise them to that blessed star which led the Wise Men to a poor abode? Were there no poor homes to which its light would have conducted me!"

Scrooge was much dismayed at what the specter said and began to quake exceedingly.

"Hear me!" cried the Ghost. "My time is nearly gone."

"I will," said Scrooge. "Don't be hard upon me, Jacob!"

"How it is that I appear before you in a shape that you can see, I may not tell. I am here to warn you, that you have yet a chance and hope of escaping my fate. A chance and hope of my procuring, Ebenezer."

"Oh, thank'ee," said Scrooge.

"You will be haunted," resumed the Ghost, "by three Spirits."

Scrooge's countenance fell.

"Is that the chance and hope you mentioned, Jacob?" he demanded in a faltering voice.

"Expect the first tomorrow when the bell tolls once. Expect the second on the next night at the same hour. The third upon the next night when the last stroke of twelve has ceased to vibrate. Look to see me no more, and, for your own sake, remember what has passed between us!"

When it had said these words, the specter took its wrapper and bound it round its head, as before. The apparition walked backward from Scrooge, and at every step it took the window opened a little, so that when the specter reached it, it was wide open.

Scrooge became sensible of noises in the air, incoherent sounds of lamentation and regret, wailings inexpressibly sorrowful and self-accusatory. The specter joined in the mournful dirge, and then floated out upon the bleak, dark night.

Scrooge rushed to the window and looked out.

The air filled with phantoms wandering in restless haste, and moaning as they went. Everyone wore chains. Many had been personally known to Scrooge in their lives. An old ghost with a monstrous iron safe attached to its ankle cried at being unable to assist a wretched woman with an infant, whom it saw below, upon a doorstep. The misery with them all was clearly that they sought to interfere, for good, in human matters, and had lost the power forever.

The creatures disappeared. Scrooge closed the window and examined the door by which the Ghost had entered. It was double-locked. He tried to say: "Humbug!" but stopped. He went straight to bed, without undressing, and fell asleep upon the instant.

Chapter 2

When Scrooge awoke, it was terribly dark and the chimes of a neighboring church struck the four quarters. So he listened for the hour.

To his great astonishment the heavy bell tolled twelve. Twelve! It was past two when he went to bed. The clock was wrong. An icicle must have got into the works. Twelve!

"Why, it isn't possible," said Scrooge, "that I can have slept through a whole day and into another night."

The idea being an alarming one, he scrambled out of bed to the window. But all he could make out was that it was still foggy and extremely cold and there were no people running to and fro on the street. Scrooge went to bed again, and thought and thought it over and could make nothing of it. The more he thought, the more perplexed he was. Marley's ghost bothered him exceedingly. Every time he resolved within himself that it was all a dream, his mind flew back again, like a strong spring released, to its first position. "Was it a dream or not?"

Scrooge lay in this state until the chimes had gone three quarters more when he remembered, on a sudden, that the Ghost had warned him of a visitation when the bell tolled one. He waited. The quarter was interminably long.

"Ding, dong!"

"A quarter past," said Scrooge, counting.

"Ding, dong!"

"Half past!" said Scrooge.

"Ding, dong!"

"A quarter to it," said Scrooge.

"Ding, dong!"

"The hour itself," said Scrooge, triumphantly, "and nothing else!"

He spoke before the hour bell sounded, which it now did with a deep, dull, hollow, melancholy ONE. Light flashed up in the room upon the instant, and the curtains of his bed were drawn.

The curtains of his bed were drawn aside, I tell you, by a hand. And Scrooge found himself face to face with the unearthly visitor who drew them. It was a strange figure, like a child, yet not so like a child as like an old man viewed through some supernatural medium, which gave him the appearance of having receded from view and being diminished in a child's proportions. Its hair was white as if with age, and yet the face had not a wrinkle in it. It wore a tunic of the purest white, and round its waist was bound a lustrous belt, the sheen of which was beautiful. But the strangest thing about it was that from the crown of its head there sprung a bright, clear jet of light, and under its arm was a cap which was doubtless used as a great extinguisher.

Even this, though, when Scrooge looked at it with increasing steadiness, was not its strangest quality. For the figure fluctuated in distinctness, being now a thing with one arm, now with one leg, now with twenty legs, now a pair of legs without a head, now a head without a body; of which dissolving parts, no outline would be visible in the dense gloom wherein they melted away. And in the wonder of this, it would be itself again, distinct and clear.

"Are you the Spirit whose coming was foretold to me?" asked Scrooge.

"I am!" The voice was soft and gentle.

"Who and what are you?"

"I am the Ghost of Christmas Past."

"Long past?" inquired Scrooge.

"No. Your past."

Perhaps Scrooge could not have told anybody why, but he had a special desire to see the Spirit in his cap, and begged him to be covered.

"What!" exclaimed the Ghost, "Would you so soon put out, with worldly hands, the light I give?"

Scrooge reverently disclaimed all intention to offend and then made bold to inquire what business brought him there.

"Your welfare!" said the Ghost. "Your reclamation! Take heed!"

It put out its strong hand and clasped Scrooge gently by the arm. "Rise! And walk with me!"

As these words were spoken, they passed through the wall, and stood upon an open country road. The city and fog completely vanished, for it was a clear winter day with snow upon the ground.

"Good Heavens!" said Scrooge, clasping his hands together, as he looked about him. "I was bred in this place. I was a boy here!" He was conscious of a thousand thoughts and hopes and joys long forgotten!

They walked along the road; Scrooge recognizing every gate, and post, and tree. Some ponies now were seen trotting towards them with boys upon their backs, who shouted to each other in great spirits until the fields were so full of merry music, that the crisp air laughed to hear it.

"These are but shadows of things that have been," said the Ghost. "They have no consciousness of us."

The jocund travelers came nearer and Scrooge knew every one. Why was he rejoiced beyond all bounds to see them? Why was he filled with gladness when he heard them say, "Merry Christmas"? What was "Merry Christmas" to Scrooge? What good had it ever done to him?

"That school is not quite deserted," said the Ghost. "A solitary child, neglected by his friends, is left there still."

Scrooge said he knew it. And he sobbed.

They left the road and approached the school, an ancient mansion, crumbling with disrepair. They entered the great cold hall of the building. There was an earthy savor in the air, a chilly bareness in the place, which associated itself somehow with too much getting up by candlelight, and not too much to eat.

They walked, the Ghost and Scrooge, to a room at the back of the house, a long, bare, melancholy room lined with desks. At one of these, a lonely boy was reading near a feeble fire, and Scrooge sat down upon a seat and wept to see his poor forgotten self as he had used to be.

Not a latent echo in the house, not a squeak or scuffling from the mice behind the paneling, not a drip from the half-thawed water-spout in the dull yard behind, not a sigh among the leaf-less boughs of one despondent poplar, not the idle swinging of an empty store-house door—no, not a clicking in the fire, but fell upon the heart of Scrooge with a softening influence, and gave a freer passage to his tears.

"Poor boy!" Scrooge exclaimed and cried again. "I wish," Scrooge muttered, drying his eyes with his cuff. "But it's too late now."

"What is the matter?" asked the Spirit.

"Nothing," said Scrooge. "Nothing. There was a boy singing a Christmas carol at my door last night. I should like to have given him something. That's all."

The Ghost smiled thoughtfully, and waved its hand saying, "Let us see another Christmas!"

Scrooge's former self grew larger at the words, and the room became darker and more dirty. There he was, alone again, when all the other boys had gone home for the holidays.

He was not reading now, but walking up and down despairingly. Scrooge looked at the Ghost, and with a mournful shaking of his head, glanced anxiously towards the door.

It opened, and a little girl, much younger than the boy, came darting in, and putting her arms about his neck and kissing him, addressed him as her "Dear, dear brother."

"I have come to bring you home!" said the child, clapping her hands and laughing.

"Home, little Fan?" returned the boy.

"Yes!" said the child, brimful of glee. "Home, for good, for ever and ever. Father is so much kinder than he used to be, that home's like Heaven! He spoke so gently to me one night that I asked him once more if you might come home, and he said yes. He sent me in a coach to bring you home and you're never to come back here. But first, we're to be together all the Christmas long, and have the merriest time."

"You are quite a woman, little Fan!" exclaimed the boy.

She stood on tiptoe to embrace him. Then she began to drag him, in her childish eagerness, towards the door; and he, nothing loathe to go, accompanied her.

"Always a delicate creature," said the Ghost. "But she had a large heart!"

"So she had," cried Scrooge. "You're right. I'll not gainsay it, Spirit!"

"She died a woman," said the Ghost, "and had, as I think, children."

"One child," Scrooge returned.

"True," said the Ghost. "Your nephew!"

Scrooge seemed uneasy in his mind and answered briefly, "Yes."

Although they had but that moment left the school behind them, they were now in the busy thoroughfares of a city. It was made plain enough by the dressing of the shops that here, too, it was Christmas time again, but it was evening, and the streets were lighted up.

The Ghost stopped at a certain warehouse door, and asked Scrooge if he knew it.

"Knew it!" said Scrooge. "Was I apprenticed here?"

They went in. At the sight of an old gentleman in a Welsh wig, sitting behind such a high desk, Scrooge cried to great excitement.

"Why it's old Fezziwig! Bless his heart; it's Fezziwig alive again!"

Old Fezziwig laid down his pen, looked up at the clock, and called out in a rich, jovial voice: "Yo ho, there! Ebenezer! Dick!"

Scrooge's former self, now grown a young man, came briskly in, accompanied by his fellow 'prentice.

"Dick Wilkins!" said Scrooge to the Ghost.

"He was very much attached to me, was Dick. Poor Dick! Dear!"

"Yo ho, my boys!" said Fezziwig. "No more work tonight. Christmas Eve, Ebenezer! Let's have the shutters up. Hilli-ho, my lads! Clear away, and let's have lots of room here!"

In came a fiddler with a music-book, and went up to the lofty desk, and made an orchestra of it, and tuned like fifty stomach-aches. In came Mrs. Fezziwig, one vast substantial smile. In came the three Miss Fezziwigs, beaming and lovable. In came the six young followers whose hearts they broke. In came all the young men and women employed in the business. In came the housemaid, with her cousin, the baker. In came the cook, with her brother's particular friend, the milkman. In came the boy from over the way, who was suspected of not having board enough from his master, trying to hide himself behind the girl from next door, who was proved to have had her ears pulled by her Mistress. In they all came, one after another, some shyly, some boldly, some gracefully, some awkwardly, some pushing, some pulling; in they all came, anyhow and everyhow. Away they all went, twenty couples at once, hands half round and back again the other way, down the middle and up again, round and round in various stages of affectionate grouping. There were more dances and they dined on cakes and roasts and mince pies, and they drank more than plenty of beer.

When the clock struck eleven, this domestic ball broke up. Mr. and Mrs. Fezziwig took their stations, one on either side the door, and shaking hands with every person, wished him or her a Merry Christmas until the cheerful voices died away. At last, they wished the two 'prentices a warm, Merry Christmas and the lads were left to their beds.

During the whole of this time, Scrooge had acted like a man out of his wits. His heart and soul were in the scene and with his former self. He recalled everything, enjoyed everything, and underwent the strangest agitation. It was not until now that he remembered the Ghost, and became conscious that it was looking full upon him, while the light upon its head burnt very clear.

"A small matter," said the Ghost, "to make these silly folks so full of gratitude."

"Small!" echoed Scrooge.

"Why! Is it not?" the Ghost questioned him. "Fezziwig has spent but a few pounds of your mortal money for his party. Is that so much that he deserves great praise?"

"It isn't that," said Scrooge, heated by the remark and speaking unconsciously like his former, not his latter, self. "He has the power to render us happy or unhappy; to make our service a pleasure or a toil. Say that his power lies in words and looks, in things so slight and insignificant that it is impossible to add and count 'em up; what then? The happiness he gives is quite as great as if it cost a fortune."

He felt the Spirit's glance and stopped.

"What is the matter?" asked the Ghost.

"I should like to be able to say a word or two to my clerk just now!" said Scrooge. "That's all."

His former self turned down the lamps and Scrooge and the Ghost again stood in the open air.

"My time grows short," observed the Spirit. "Quick!"

This was not addressed to Scrooge, but it produced an immediate effect. For again Scrooge saw himself. He was older now, a man in the prime of life. His face had not the harsh and rigid lines of later years, but it had begun to wear the signs of care and avarice. There was an eager, greedy, restless motion in his eye which showed the passion that had taken root.

He was not alone, but sat by a fair young girl in a mourning dress, in whose eyes there were tears which sparkled in the light that shone out of the Ghost of Christmas past.

"Our contract is an old one," she said. "It was made when we were both poor and content to be so, until, in good season, we could improve our fortune by our patient industry. You are changed. I have seen your nobler aspirations fall off one by one, until the master-passion, gain, engrosses you. When our contract was made you were another man."

"I was a boy," he said impatiently.

"How often and how keenly I have thought of this, I will not say. It is enough that I have thought of it, and can release you."

"Have I ever sought release?"

"In words, no. Never."

"In what, then?"

"In an altered spirit; in another atmosphere of life; another hope as its great end. In everything that made my love of any worth in your sight. If this contract had never been between us," said the girl, "tell me, would you seek me out now? Ah, no!"

He seemed to yield to the justice of this supposition, in spite of himself. But he said, with a struggle, "You think not?"

"I would gladly think otherwise if I could," she answered. "But if you were free today, can even I believe that you would choose a dowerless girl, you who weigh everything by gain. Or, if you chose her, in a moment of false to your guiding principle, do I not know that your repentance and regret would surely follow? I do, and I release you. May you be happy in the life you have chosen!"

She left him, and they parted.

"Spirit!" said Scrooge, "Show me no more!" Conduct me home. Why do you delight to torture me?"

"One shadow more!" exclaimed the Ghost.

"No more!" cried Scrooge. "No more. I don't wish to see it. Show me no more!"

But the relentless Ghost pinioned him in both his arms, and forced him to observe what happened next.

They were in another scene and place, a room, not large or handsome, but full of comfort. Near the fire sat a beautiful young girl, so like the last that Scrooge believed it was the same, until he saw her, now a comely matron, sitting opposite her daughter. The noise in this room was tumultuous, for there were more children there than Scrooge could count, all cavorting about gaily. The mother and daughter laughed heartily, enjoying themselves very much.

Then a knocking at the door was heard and a rush immediately ensued to greet the father, who came home laden with Christmas toys and presents. What joy and ecstasy!

And now Scrooge looked on more attentively than ever, when the master of the house, having his daughters leaning fondly on him, sat down with her and her mother at his own fireside, and when he thought that such another creature, quite as lovely, might have called him father, and been a spring-time in the haggard winter of his life, his sight grew very dim indeed.

"Belle," said the husband, "I saw an old friend of yours this afternoon."

"Who was that?" she asked.

"Mr. Scrooge. I passed his office window and saw him inside. His partner lies upon the point of death, I hear, and there he sat alone. Quite alone in the world, I do believe."

"Spirit!" said Scrooge, in a broken voice, "Remove me from this place."

"I told you these were shadows of the things that have been," said the Ghost. "That they are what they are, do not blame me!"

"Remove me!" Scrooge exclaimed. "I cannot bear it!"

He turned upon the Ghost, and seeing that it looked upon his with a face in which in some strange way there were fragments of all the faces it had shown him, wrestled with it.

"Leave me! Haunt me no longer!"

In the struggle, Scrooge observed that the Ghost's light was burning high and bright, and dimly connecting that with its influence over him, he seized the extinguisher-cap, and by a sudden action pressed it down upon its head.

The Spirit dropped beneath it, so that the extinguisher covered its whole form; but though Scrooge pressed it down, he could not hide the light which streamed from under it in an unbroken flood upon the ground.

He was conscious of being exhausted, and overcome by an irresistible drowsiness and of being in his own bedroom. He had barely time to reel to bed, before he sank into a heavy sleep.

Chapter 3

Awaking in the middle of a prodigiously tough snore, and sitting up in bed to get his thoughts together, Scrooge had no occasion to be told that the bell was again upon the stroke of One. He felt that he was restored to consciousness in the nick of time, for the especial purpose of holding a conference with the second messenger dispatched to him through Jacob Marley's intervention. Now, being prepared for almost anything, he was still not prepared for nothing and, consequently, when the bell struck one and no shape appeared, he was taken with a violent fit of trembling. Five, ten minutes, a quarter of an hour went by, yet nothing came. All this time, he lay upon his bed, the very core and center of a blaze of ruddy light which streamed upon it when the clock proclaimed the hour, and which being only light, was more alarming than a dozen ghosts, as he was powerless to make out what it meant. At last, however, he began to think that the source of the ghostly light might be in the adjoining room, from whence it seemed to shine. So, tremulously, he got up and shuffled to the door.

The moment Scrooge's hand was on the lock, a strange voice called him by his name, and bade him enter. He obeyed.

It was his own room. There was no doubt about that. But it had undergone a surprising transformation. The walls and ceiling were so hung with living green that it looked a perfect grove, from every part of which bright gleaming berries glistened. The crisp leaves of holly, mistletoe, and ivy reflected back the light, as if so many little mirrors had been scattered there, and a mighty blaze went roaring up the chimney. Heaped up on the floor, to form a kind of throne, were turkeys, geese, game, poultry, brawn, great joints of meat, suckling pigs, long wreaths of sausages, mince pies, plum puddings, barrels of oysters, red hot chestnuts, cherry cheeked apples, juicy oranges, luscious pears, immense twelfth cakes, and seething bowls of punch that made the chamber dim with their delicious steam. Upon this couch there sat a jolly giant, glorious to see, who bore a glowing torch in the shape not unlike Plenty's horn, and held it up to shed its light to Scrooge as he came peeping round the door.

"Come in!" exclaimed the Ghost. "Come in!"

"And know me better, man!"

Scrooge entered timidly and hung his head before this Spirit. He was not the stubborn Scrooge he had been, and though the Spirit's eyes were clear and kind, he did not like to meet them.

"I am the Ghost of Christmas Present," said the Spirit. "Look upon me!"

Scrooge reverently did so. It was clothed in one simple green robe, bordered with white fur. This garment hung so loosely on the figure that its capacious breast was bare. Its feet were also bare, and on its head it wore a holly wreath, set with shining icicles. Its dark brown curls were long and free, free as its genial face, its sparkling eyes, its open hand, its cheery voice, its unconstrained demeanor, and its joyful air.

The Ghost of Christmas Present rose.

"Spirit," said Scrooge submissively, "conduct me where you wish. I went forth last night on compulsion, and I learned a lesson which is working now. Tonight, if you have aught to reach me, let me profit by it."

"Touch my robe!"

Scrooge did as he was told, and held it fast.

Holly, mistletoe, red berries, ivy, turkeys, geese, game, poultry, brawn, meat, pigs, sausages, oysters, pies, pudding, fruit, and punch—all vanished instantly. So did the room, the fire, the ruddy glow, the hour of night, and they stood in the city streets on Christmas morning, where people made a rough music scraping the snow from the pavement in front of their dwellings and from the tops of their houses, whence it was mad delight to the boys to see it come plumping down into the road below and splitting into artificial little snow-storms.

The house fronts looked black enough, and the windows blacker, contrasting with the smooth white sheet of snow upon the roofs and with the dirtier snow upon the ground. The sky was gloomy and the streets were choked with a dingy mist as if all the chimneys in Great Britain were blasting away at once. There was nothing cheerful in the climate or the town, and yet there was an air of cheerfulness abroad that the clearest summer air and brightest sun might have endeavored to diffuse in vain.

For the people who were shoveling away on the housetops were jovial and full of glee, calling out to one another. The poulterers' shops were still half open, and the fruiterers' were radiant in their glory. There were potbellied baskets of chestnuts, pyramids of pears and apples, and bunches of grapes dangling from conspicuous hooks.

The Grocers! Oh, the Grocers! were nearly closed, but through the gaps between the shutters such glimpses of raisins, almonds, and candied fruits, so caked and spotted with molten sugar as to make the coldest lookers-on feel faint. The customers were all eager in the hopeful promise of the day that they tumbled against each other at the door.

But soon the steeples called good people all to church, and away they came, flocking through the streets in their best clothes and gayest faces. And at the same time there emerged from scores of by-lanes and nameless streets innumerable people carrying their dinners to the bakers' shops. The sight of these poor revelers interested the Spirit very much, for he stood with Scrooge beside him in a baker's doorway, and sprinkled incense on their dinners from his torch. And it was a very uncommon kind of torch, for at times, when there were angry words between some dinner carriers who had jostled each other, he shed a few drops of water on them from it and their good humor was restored directly. For they said it was a shame to quarrel upon Christmas Day. And so it was! God love it, so it was!

"Is there a peculiar flavor in what you sprinkle from your torch?" asked Scrooge.

"There is. My own."

"Would it apply to any kind of dinner on this day?"

"To any kindly given. To a poor one most."

"Why to a poor one most?" asked Scrooge.

"Because it needs it most."

Then they went on into the suburbs of the town. Perhaps it was the Spirit's own kind, generous nature, and his sympathy with all poor men, that led him straight to Scrooge's clerk's. For there he went, and took Scrooge with him, holding to his robe, and on the threshold of the door, the Spirit stopped to bless Bob Cratchit's dwelling with the sprinkling of his torch. Think of that! The Ghost of Christmas Present blessed Bob's poor four-roomed house!

Then up rose Mrs. Cratchit dressed poorly in a twice-turned gown, but brave in ribbons which are cheap but make a goodly show. She laid the cloth, assisted by Belinda Cratchit, second of her daughters, while Master Peter Cratchit stood proudly with his thin neck swallowed in his father's shirt. And now two smaller Cratchits, boy and girl, came tearing in, screaming that outside the baker's they had smelt the goose and known it for their own. Basking in luxurious thoughts of sage and onion, these young Cratchits danced about the table and exalted Master Peter Cratchit to the skies, while he (not proud, although his collars nearly choked him) blew the fire until the slow potatoes, bubbling up, knocked loudly at the saucepan-lid to be let out and peeled.

"Where is your father then," said Mrs. Cratchit. "And your brother, Tiny Tim, and Martha, your sister?"

"Here's Martha!" said a girl, appearing as she spoke.

"How late you are, my dear!" said Mrs. Cratchit, kissing her a dozen times.

"We'd still a deal of work to do this morning, mother," replied the girl.

"Sit down before the fire, dear, and have a warm," said Mrs. Cratchit.

"No! There's father coming," cried the two young Cratchits. "Hide Martha, hide!"

So Martha hid herself, and in came Bob, the father, his thread-bare clothes darned up and brushed to look seasonable, and Tiny Tim upon his shoulder. Alas for Tiny Tim, he bore a little crutch, and his limbs supported by an iron frame!

"Where's our Martha?" cried Bob Cratchit looking around.

"Not coming," said Mrs. Cratchit.

"Not coming upon Christmas Day!" said Bob, with a sudden declension in his high spirits.

Martha didn't like to see him disappointed, even if it were only in joke; she came out from behind the door and ran into his arms.

Master Peter and the two young Cratchits went to fetch the goose, with which they soon returned in high procession.

Such a bustle ensued that you might have thought a goose the rarest of all birds, and in truth it was something like it in that house. Mrs. Cratchit made the gravy sizzling hot; Master Peter mashed the potatoes; Miss Belinda sweetened the applesauce. Bob took Tiny Tim beside him in a tiny corner at the table. At last everyone sat down and grace was said. It was succeeded by a breathless pause, as Mrs. Cratchit prepared to plunge the carving knife into the breast of the goose. But when she did, and when the long expected gush of stuffing issued forth, one murmur of delight arose all round the board, and even Tiny Tim, excited by the two young Cratchits, beat on the table and feebly cried,

"Hurrah!" There never was such a goose. Bob said he didn't believe there ever was such a goose cooked. Eked out by the applesauce and mashed potatoes, it was a sufficient dinner for the whole family. Then Mrs. Cratchit disappeared into the kitchen and emerged, smiling proudly, with the pudding, like a speckled cannon-ball, blazing in ignited brandy with Christmas holly stuck into the top. At last the dinner was all done and the Cratchit family drew round the hearth. Bob concocted a hot drink of lemon and gin and passed the jug to everyone while chestnuts crackled on the fire. Bob proposed a toast: "A Merry Christmas to us all, my dears. God bless us!" Which all the family echoed. "God bless us every one!" said Tiny Tim, the last of all.

He sat close to his father's side, upon his stool. Bob held his withered little hand in his, as if he loved the child and wished to keep him by his side, and dreaded that he might be taken from him.

"Spirit," said Scrooge, with an interest he had never felt before, "tell me if Tiny Tim will live."

"I see a vacant seat," replied the Ghost, "in the chimney corner, and a crutch without an owner, carefully preserved. If these shadows remain unaltered by the future, the child will die."

"No!" said Scrooge. "Oh no, kind Spirit! Say he will be spared."

"If these shadows remain unaltered by the future, none other of my race," returned the Ghost, "will find him here. What then? If he be like to die, he had better do it, and decrease the surplus population."

Scrooge hung his head to hear his own words quoted by the spirit, and was overcome with penitence and grief.

'"Man," said the Ghost, "if man you be in heart, not adamant, forbear that wicked cant until you have discovered what the surplus is, and where it is. Will you decide what men shall live, what men shall die? It may be that in the sight of Heaven you are more worthless and less fit to live than millions like this poor man's child."

Scrooge bent before the Ghost's rebuke, and trembling, cast his eyes upon the ground. But he raised them speedily, on hearing his own name.

"Mr. Scrooge!" said Bob. "I'll give you Mr. Scrooge, the founder of the feast!"

"The founder of the feast indeed!" cried Mrs. Cratchit, reddening. I wish I had him here. I'd give him a piece of my mind to feast upon, and I hope he'd have a good appetite for it."

"My dear," said Bob, "the children; Christmas Day."

"It should be Christmas Day, I am sure," said she, "on which one drinks the health of such an odious, stingy, hard, unfeeling man as Mr. Scrooge. You know he is, Robert! Nobody knows it better than you do, poor fellow!"

"My dear," was Bob's mild answer, "Christmas Day."

"I'll drink his health for your sake and the Day's," said Mrs. Cratchit, "not for his. Long life to him! A Merry Christmas and a happy New Year!—He'll be merry and happy, I have no doubt!"

The children drank the toast after her. It was the first of their proceedings which had no heartiness in it. Tiny Tim drank it last of all, but he didn't care two pence for it. Scrooge was the ogre of the family. His name cast a shadow on the party, which was not dispelled for several minutes.

After it passed away, they were ten times merrier than before, from the mere relief of Scrooge the Baleful being done with. All this time the chestnuts and the jug went round, and bye and bye they had a song from Tiny Tim about a lost child traveling in the snow. He had a plaintive little voice and sang it very well indeed.

There was nothing of high mark in this. They were not a handsome family, nor well off. But they were happy, grateful, pleased with one another, and contented. And when they faded from sight and looked happier yet in the bright sprinklings of the Spirit's torch at parting, Scrooge had his eye upon them, and especially on Tiny Tim, until the last.

By this time it was getting dark and snowing heavily, and as Scrooge and the Spirit went along the streets, the brightness of the fires in kitchens and parlors was wonderful. Here, the blaze showed preparations for a dinner, with hot plates baking through before the fire. There, the children of the house were running out to meet their married sisters, brothers, cousins, and be the first to greet them.

If you had judged from the numbers of people on their way to friendly gatherings, you might have thought that no one was at home to give them welcome when they got there. Blessings on it, how the Ghost exulted!

How it bared its breast and opened its capacious palm, and floated on, outpouring with a generous hand its bright and harmless mirth on everything within its reach!

And now, without a word of warning from the Ghost, they stood upon a bleak and desert moor, where monstrous masses of rude stone were cast about as though it were the burial-place of giants. Nothing grew on the icy ground but moss and coarse grass. Down in the west the setting sun had left a streak of fiery red which glared upon the desolation for an instant like a sullen eye, and frowning lower, lower, lower yet, was lost in the thick gloom of darkest night.

"What place is this?" asked Scrooge.

"A place where miners live, who labor in the bowels of the earth," returned the spirit. "But they know me. See!"

A light shone through the window of a hut, and swiftly they advanced towards it. Passing through the wall of mud and stone, they found a cheerful company assembled round a glowing fire. An old, old man and woman, with their children and their children's children, and another generation beyond that, all decked out gaily in their holiday attire. The old man, in a voice that seldom rose above the howling of the wind, was singing them an old Christmas song, and from time to time they all joined in the chorus.

The Spirit did not tarry here, but bade Scrooge hold his robe, and passing on above the moor, sped out to sea. To Scrooge's horror, looking back, he saw the last of the land, a frightful range of rocks behind them, and his ears were deafened by the thundering of water as it rolled, and roared, and raged.

Built upon a dismal reef of sunken rocks, there stood a solitary lighthouse. Grea heaps of seaweed clung to its base, and storr birds rose and fell about it, like the waves they skimmed.

But even here, two men who watched th light had made a fire that, through the loophole in the thick stone wall, shed out a r of brightness on the awful sea. Joining their worn hands over the rough table at which th sat, they wished each other Merry Christmas in their can of grog.

Again the Ghost sped on, above the blac and heaving sea, until they lighted on a ship They stood beside the helmsman at the whee the look-out in the bow, the officers who had the watch; dark, ghostly figures in their sever stations; but every man among them humme a Christmas tune, or had a Christmas though or spoke to his companion of some past Christmas Day. Every man on board had a kinder word for another on that day than on any day in the year, and had remembered those he cared for at a distance, and had known that they delighted to remember him.

It was a great surprise to Scrooge, while listening to the moaning of the wind, to hear a loud and hearty laugh. It was an even greater surprise to Scrooge to recognize it as his own nephew's, and to find himself in a bright gleaming room with the Spirit standing smiling by his side, and looking at that same nephew with approving affability!

"Ha, ha!" laughed Scrooge's nephew. "Ha, ha, ha! If you should happen, by an unlikely chance, to know a man more blest in a laugh than Scrooge's nephew, all I can say is, I should like to know him, too. Scrooge's niece, by marriage, laughed as heartily as his nephew. And their assembled friends being a bit behind-hand, roared out lustily.

"Ha, ha! Ha, ha, ha, ha!"

"He said that Christmas was a humbug, as I live!" cried Scrooge's nephew. "He believed it, too!"

"More shame for him, Fred!" said Scrooge's niece, indignantly.

She was exceedingly pretty, with a dimpled, capital face. Oh, perfectly satisfactory!

"He's a comical old fellow," said Scrooge's nephew, "that's the truth, and not so pleasant as he might be. However, his offenses carry their own punishment, and I have nothing to say against him."

"I'm sure he is very rich, Fred," hinted Scrooge's niece.

"What of that, my dear!" said Scrooge's nephew. "His wealth is of no use to him. He doesn't do any good with it. He doesn't make himself comfortable with it. He hasn't the satisfaction of thinking—ha, ha, ha—that he is ever going to benefit us with it.

"I have no patience with him," observed Scrooge's niece.

"I have!" said Scrooge's nephew. "I am sorry for him; I couldn't be angry with him if I tried. Who suffers by his ill whims! Himself, always. Here he takes it into his head to dislike us, and he won't come and dine with us. What's the consequence? He loses some pleasant moments, which could do him no harm. I mean to give him the same chance every year, whether he likes it or not, for I pity him. He may rail at Christmas till he dies, but he can't help thinking better of it—I defy him—if he finds me going there year after year and saying Uncle Scrooge, 'how are you?' If it only puts him in a mind to leave his poor clerk fifty pounds, that's something; and I think I shook him yesterday."

It was their turn to laugh now, at the notion of his shaking Scrooge. But being good-natured and not much caring what they laughed at, he encouraged them in their merriment and passed the bottle, joyously.

After tea, they had some music. The songs that Scrooge's niece played upon the harp reminded him of tunes he had known in his childhood. When this strain of music sounded, all the things the Ghost of Christmas Past had shown Scrooge came upon his mind; he softened more and more; and thought that if he could have listened to it often, years ago, he might have cultivated the kindnesses of life for his own happiness, with his own hands.

The evening then progressed to games and there might have been twenty people there, young and old, but they all played, and so did Scrooge. Wholly caught up in what was going on, and forgetting that his voice made no sound in their ears, he sometimes came out with answers to the games' questions, and often guessed right, too.

The Ghost was greatly pleased to find him in this mood, and looked upon him with such favor that Scrooge begged like a boy to be allowed to stay until the guests departed. But this the Spirit said could not be done, and without warning, he and the Spirit were again upon their travels.

Much they saw, and far they went, and many homes they visited, but always with a happy end. The Spirit stood beside sick beds, and they were cheerful; by struggling men, and they were patient in their greater hope; by poverty, and it was rich. In almshouse, hospital, and jail, in misery's every refuge, where vain man in his little brief authority had not made fast the door and barred the Spirit out, he left his blessing and taught Scrooge his precepts.

It was a long night, if it were only a night. It was strange, too, that the Ghost grew older, clearly older, and his hair grew gray. Scrooge could not help but notice.

"Are spirits' lives so short?" asked Scrooge.

"My life upon this globe is very brief," replied the Ghost. "It ends tonight."

"Tonight!" cried Scrooge.

"Tonight at midnight. Hark! The time is drawing near."

The chimes were ringing the three quarters past eleven at the moment.

"Forgive me if I am not justified in what I ask, said Scrooge, looking intently at the Spirit's robe, "but I see something strange protruding from your skirts."

"Oh, Man! Look here," was the Spirit's sorrowful reply.

From the foldings of its robe, it brought two children, wretched, ragged, frightful, miserable. Where graceful youth should have filled their features out, a stale and shriveled hand, like that of age, had pinched and twisted them and pulled them into shreds. Where angels might have sat enthroned, devils lurked and glared out menacing. Scrooge started back, appalled.

"Spirit! Are they yours?" He could say no more.

"They are Man's," said the Spirit. "This boy is Ignorance. This girl is Want."

"Have they no refuge or resource?" cried Scrooge.

"Are there no prisons?" said the Spirit, turning on him for the last time with his own words. "Are there no workhouses?"

The bell struck twelve.

Scrooge looked about him for the Ghost, and saw it not. As the last stroke ceased to vibrate, he remembered the prediction of old Jacob Marley, and lifting up his eyes beheld a solemn Phantom, draped and hooded, coming like a mist along the ground towards him.

Chapter 4

The Phantom slowly, gravely, silently, approached. When it came near him, Scrooge bent down upon his knee, for in the very air through which this Spirit moved it seemed to scatter gloom and mystery.

It was shrouded in a deep black garment which concealed its head, its face, its form, and left nothing of it visible, save one outstretched hand. But for this, it would have been difficult to separate its figure from the darkness which surrounded it.

When it came beside Scrooge, its mysterious presence filled him with dread. The Spirit neither spoke nor moved.

"I am in the presence of the Ghost of Christmas Yet to Come?" said Scrooge.

The Spirit answered not, but pointed onward.

"You are about to show me shadows of things that have not happened, but will happen in the time before us," Scrooge pursued. "Is that so, Spirit?"

The garment moved slightly as if the Spirit had inclined its head.

Although well used to ghostly company by now, Scrooge feared this silent shape so much that his legs trembled and he could hardly stand when he prepared to follow it. It thrilled him with a vague uncertain horror to know that behind the dusky shroud there were ghostly eyes intently fixed upon him, while he could see nothing but a spectral hand.

"Ghost of the future!" he exclaimed, I fear you more than any Specter I have seen. But as I know your purpose is to do me good, and as

I hope to live to be another man from what I was, I am prepared to bear your company and do it with a thankful heart. Will you not speak to me?"

It gave him no reply. The hand was pointed straight before them.

"Lead on!" said Scrooge. "The night is waning fast, and it is precious time to me, I know."

The city seemed to spring up around them. There they were, in the heart of it, amongst the merchants who chinked the money in their pockets and conversed in groups. Scrooge had seen them often.

The Spirit stopped beside one knot of businessmen and pointed. Scrooge advanced to listen to their talk.

"I don't know much," said a man with a monstrous chin. "I only know he died last night."

"Why, I thought he'd never die," said another.

"What has he done with his money?" asked a red-faced gentleman.

"I haven't heard," said the man with the large chin. "He hasn't left it to me. That's all I know."

This pleasantry was received with a general laugh.

"It's likely to be a very cheap funeral," said the same speaker, "for I don't know of anybody to go to it."

"I'll go if lunch is provided," observed the red-faced gentleman.

"I'll go, if anybody else will," said the first speaker. "When I come to think of it, I'm not sure that I wasn't his most particular friend, for we used to stop and speak whenever we met."

The group strolled away. Scrooge knew these men, and looked towards the Spirit for an explanation.

There was none.

Scrooge was at first surprised that the Spirit should attach importance to conversations so trivial, but feeling assured that they must have some hidden purpose, he considered what it was likely to be. He could not think of anyone connected with himself to whom he could apply them. But not doubting that they had some latent moral for his own improvement, he resolved to treasure up every word and everything he saw, and especially to observe the shadow of himself when it appeared. For he expected that the conduct of his future self would give him the clue he missed and render the solution of these riddles easy.

He looked about for his own image; but another man stood in his accustomed corner and he saw no likeness of himself among the multitudes.

The Phantom stood beside him with outstretched hand. Scrooge felt the unseen eyes were looking at him keenly. It made him shudder and feel very cold. They left the busy scene and went into an obscure part of town, where the ways were foul and narrow and the shops and houses wretched. The whole quarter reeked with crime, filth, and misery.

Far in this den of infamous resort there was a low-browed shop where iron, old rags, bottles, and refuse were bought. Upon the floor within were piled up heaps of rusty keys, nails, chains, hinges, files, scales, weights, and refuse iron of all kinds. Secrets that few would like to scrutinize were hidden in mountains of unseemly rubbish here. Sitting among the wares he dealt in, by a charcoal-stove made of old bricks, was a gray-haired rascal, Old Joe, who had screened himself from the cold air without and smoked his pipe in all the luxury of calm retirement.

Scrooge and the Phantom came into the presence of this person just as two women and a black-suited man came in, each carrying a bundle.

"Come into the parlor," Joe said to them.

The parlor was behind a screen of rags, a curtaining of miscellaneous tatters.

"Let's have a look," directed Joe, and the man, an undertaker's apprentice, came forward and produced his plunder. It was not extensive. A seal, a pencil case, a pair of sleeve buttons, and a cheap brooch. They were appraised by old Joe, who chalked the sums he was disposed to give for each upon the wall.

"That's your account," said Joe. "Nothing more. Who's next?"

Mrs. Dilber, the laundress, was next. Sheets and towels, some wearing apparel, two old-fashioned silver teaspoons, a few boots. Her account was stated on the wall in the same manner.

"And now undo my bundle, Joe," said the first woman.

Joe unwound the knots, and dragged out a heavy roll of some dark stuff.

"Bed curtains!" cried the woman, laughing.

"You don't mean to say you took 'em down, rings and all, with him lying there?" said Joe.

"Yes, I do," replied the woman. "Why not?

"You were born to make your fortune," said Joe, and you certainly will."

"I certainly shan't hold back my hand when I can get something by reaching out, for the sake of such a man as he was, I promise you," returned the woman coolly. Then she held up her prize.

"Look at this shirt till your eyes ache," she said. "You won't find a threadbare place. It's the best he had, and a fine one, too. They'd have wasted it, if it hadn't been for me."

"What do you call wasting it?" asked Joe.

"Somebody was fool enough to put it on him to be buried in," replied the woman with a laugh.

"But I took it off again and changed to an old calico one, good enough for the purpose."

Scrooge listened to this dialogue in horror. As they sat grouped about their spoil, he viewed them with a detestation which could hardly have been greater if they had been demons, marketing the corpse itself.

"Ha, ha!" laughed the same woman, when Joe, producing a flannel bag of money, told out their several gains upon the ground.

"This is the end of it, you see. He frightened everyone away from him when he was alive," she said. "If he had somebody to look after him when he was struck with Death, instead of lying gasping out his last alone, we never would have had these things. But it's our profit, now he's dead. Everyone has a right to take care of themselves. He always did! Ha, Ha!"

"Spirit!" said Scrooge, shuddering from head to foot. "I see. The case of this unhappy man might be my own. My life tends that way, now. Merciful Heaven! What is this!"

He recoiled in terror, for the scene had changed, and now he almost touched a bed; a bare uncurtained bed, on which beneath a ragged sheet, there lay a something covered up, which, though, it was dumb, announced itself in awful language.

The room was dark, too dark to be observed with any accuracy, though Scrooge glanced round anxiously. A pale light fell upon the bed, and on it, plundered and bereft, unwatched, unwept, uncared for, was the body of this man.

Scrooge glanced towards the Phantom. Its steady hand was pointed to the head. The cover was so carelessly adjusted that the slightest raising of it, the motion of a finger upon Scrooge's part, would have disclosed the face. Scrooge longed to do it, but could not. He had no more power to withdraw that veil than to dismiss the specter at his side.

Still the Ghost pointed with an unmoved finger to the head.

He lay, in the dark empty house, with not a man, a woman, or a child to say that he was kind to me in this or that, and for the memory of one kind word I will be kind to him. A cat was tearing at the door, and there was a sound of gnawing rats beneath the hearth stone. What they wanted in the room of death, and why they were so restless and disturbed, Scrooge did not dare to think.

"Spirit!" he said, "this is a fearful place. In leaving it, I shall not leave its lesson, trust me. Let us go!" Still the Ghost pointed with an unmoved finger to the head.

"I understand," Scrooge returned, "and I would do it, if I could. But I have not the power, Spirit." Again it seemed to look upon him.

"If there is any person in the town who feels emotion caused by this man's death," said Scrooge quite agonized, "show that person to me, Spirit, I beseech you!"

The Phantom spread its dark robe before him and withdrawing it, revealed a room by daylight, where a mother and her children were.

She was expecting someone with anxious eagerness, for she paced the room and glanced at the clock.

At length, the long-expected knock was heard. She hurried to meet her husband, a man whose face was care-worn and depressed, though he was young. There was a remarkable expression in it now, a kind of serious delight of which he felt ashamed and struggled to repress.

He sat down to his dinner and she asked him faintly, what news. He appeared embarrassed how to answer.

"Bad," he answered.

"We are quite ruined?"

"No. There is hope yet, Caroline."

"If he relents," she said, amazed, "there is! Nothing is past hope, if such a miracle has happened."

"He is dead," said her husband.

She was a patient creature if her face spoke truth, but she was thankful in her soul to hear it, and she said so, with clasped hands. She prayed forgiveness the next moment and was sorry, but the first was the emotion of her heart.

"To whom will our debt be transferred?" she asked.

I don't know. But before that time, we shall be ready with the money. And even if we were not, it would be unlikely to find so merciless a creditor in his successor. We may sleep tonight with light hearts, Caroline!"

Yes, their hearts were lighter and it was a happier house for this man's death! The only emotion that the Ghost could show him caused by the event was one of pleasure.

"Let me see some tenderness connected with a death," said Scrooge, "or that dark chamber, Spirit, which we left just now, will be forever present to me."

The Ghost conducted him through familiar streets, and as they went along, Scrooge looked here and there to find himself, but nowhere was he to be seen. They entered poor Bob Cratchit's house and found the mother and the children seated round the fire.

Quiet. Very quiet. The noisy little Cratchits were as still as statues and sat looking at Peter, who had a book before him. The mother and her daughters were sewing.

"And He took a child, and set him in the midst of them."

Where had Scrooge heard those words? The boy must have read them, as he and the Spirit entered.

The mother laid down her work and put her hand up to her face.

"The color hurts my eyes," she said.

The color? Ah, poor Tiny Tim!

"They're better now," said Cratchit's wife. I wouldn't show weak eyes to your father when he comes home. He's late tonight."

"He's walked slower these few last evenings," Peter said.

They became very quiet again. At last she said, in a steady, cheerful voice that only faltered once: "He has walked with, he walked with Tiny Tim upon his shoulder, fast indeed.

But he was very light to carry, and his father loved him so, that it was no trouble. And there is your father at the door!"

Bob, poor fellow, came in. They all rushed to greet him. The two young Cratchits got upon his knees and leaned against him as if to say, "Don't mind it, Father. Don't be grieved!"

Bob was very cheerful with them. He looked at the sewing and praised the industry and speed of Mrs. Cratchit. They would be done long before Sunday, he said.

"Sunday! You went today, then, Robert?" said his wife.

"Yes, dear," returned Bob. "I wish you could have gone. But you'll see it often. I promised him that I would walk there on a Sunday. My little, little child!" cried Bob. "My little child!"

He broke down all at once. He couldn't help it.

He went upstairs into the room which above was lighted cheerfully and hung with Christmas. There was a chair set close beside the child, and poor Bob sat down. When he had thought a little and composed himself, he kissed the little face. He was reconciled to what had happened, and went down again quite happy.

They drew about the fire and talked. Bob told them of the extraordinary kindness of Mr. Scrooge's nephew, whom he had scarcely seen but once, and who, meeting him in the street, had said, "I am heartily sorry for it, Mr. Cratchit. If I can be of any service to you, pray, come to me."

Then Bob Cratchit spoke to his family with earnestness.

"You will all be growing up and on your own some day," he said. "But I am sure we shall none of us forget poor Tiny Tim, shall we?"

"Never, Father!" cried they all.

"I am very happy," said Bob.

Mrs. Cratchit kissed him, his daughters kissed him, the two young Cratchits kissed him, and Peter and himself shook hands. Spirit of Tiny Tim, thy childish essence was from God!

"Specter, " said Scrooge, "something informs me that our parting moment is at hand. Tell me what man that was whom we saw lying dead?"

The Ghost of Christmas Yet to Come conveyed him to an iron gate. A church-yard. Here, then, the wretched man whose name he had now to learn lay underneath the ground. It was a worthy place. Walled in by houses, overrun by grass and weeds, the growth of vegetation's death, not life, choked up with too much burying, fat with repleted appetite. A worthy place!

The Spirit stood among the graves and pointed down to one.

"Before I draw nearer to that stone," said Scrooge, "answer me one question. Are these the shadows of the things that will be, or are they shadows of things that may be, only?"

The Ghost pointed still.

"Men's courses will foreshadow certain ends," said Scrooge. "But if the courses be departed from, the ends will change. Say it is thus with what you show me!"

The Spirit was immovable as ever.

Scrooge crept towards it, trembling and following the finger, read upon the stone of

the neglected grave his own name,
EBENEZER SCROOGE.

"Am I that man whose death I have heard of tonight?" he cried, upon his knees.

The finger pointed from the grave to him, and back again.

"No, Spirit! Oh, no, no!"

"Spirit!" he cried. "Hear me! I am not the man I was. Why show me this, if I am past all hope!" For the first time the hand appeared to shake.

"Good Spirit," he pursued, "assure me that I yet may change these shadows you have shown me, by an altered life."

The kind hand trembled.

"I will honor Christmas in my heart, and try to keep it all the year. I will not shut out the lessons of the Past, Present, and Future.

Oh, tell me I may sponge away the writing on this stone!"

In his agony, he caught the spectral hand. It sought to free itself, but he was strong in his entreaty. The Spirit, stronger yet, repulsed him.

Holding up his hands in a last prayer to have his fate reversed, he saw an alteration in the Phantom's hood and dress. It shrunk, collapsed, and dwindled down into a bedpost.

Chapter 5

Yes! And the bedpost was his own. The bed was his own, the room was his own. Best and happiest of all, the time before him was his own, to make amends in!

"I will live in the Past, the Present, and the Future!" Scrooge repeated, as he scrambled out of bed. "The Spirits of all three shall strive within me. Oh, Jacob Marley! Heaven, and the Christmas time be praised for this! I say it on my knees, old Jacob!"

He was so fluttered with his good intentions, that he could barely speak. He had been sobbing violently in the conflict with the Spirit, and his face was wet with tears.

"They are not torn down," cried Scrooge, folding one of his bed curtains in his arms. "They are here. I am here. The shadows of the things that would have been may be dispelled. They will be! I know they will!"

His agitation was so great he hopped about putting his clothes on inside out and upside down.

"I don't know what to do!" cried Scrooge, laughing and crying in the same breath. I am light as a feather. Happy as an angel. Merry as a school boy.

"A Merry Christmas to everybody! Hallo! Whoop!

"Hallo!

"There's the saucepan the gruel was in!" cried Scrooge, frisking round the fireplace. "There's the door by which the Ghost of Jacob Marley entered! There's the corner whence the Ghost of Christmas Present sat! It all happened. Ha, ha, ha!"

For a man who had been out of practice for so many years, it was a splendid laugh.

"I don't know what day of the month it is!" said Scrooge. I don't know how long I've been among the Spirits. I'm quite a baby. Never mind. I don't care Whoop! Hallo there!"

He was checked in his transports by the churches ringing out the lustiest peals he had ever heard. Clash, clang, hammer, ding, dong, bell. Bell, dong, ding, hammer, clang, clash! Oh, glorious, glorious! Running to the window, he opened it and put out his head. No fog—clear, stirring cold. Golden sunlight, sweet air. Glorious!

"What's today?" cried Scrooge, calling down to a boy below.

"Today!" replied the boy. "Why, CHRISTMAS DAY."

"It's Christmas Day!" said Scrooge to himself. "I haven't missed it. The Spirits have done it all in one night. Of course, they can do anything they like."

"Hallo!" he called to the boy. "Do you know the poulterer's on the corner?"

"I should hope I did," replied the lad.

"An intelligent boy!" said Scrooge. "Do you know whether they've sold the prize turkey that was hanging there?"

"It's hanging there now," replied the boy.

"Go and buy it for me," said Scrooge. "Tell 'em to bring it here, so I may give them directions where to take it. Come back with the man and I'll give you a shilling. Come back in less than five minutes and I'll give you half a crown!"

The boy was off like a shot.

"I'll send it to Bob Cratchit's!" whispered Scrooge, laughing. "He shan't know who sends it. It's twice the size of Tiny Tim!"

The hand in which he wrote the address was not a steady one, but write it he did, and went downstairs to wait for the poulterer's man. As he stood there, the knocker caught his eye.

"I shall love it, as long as I live!" cried Scrooge, patting it with his hand. "I never looked at it before. What an honest expression it has in its face! Hallow! Here's the turkey, Merry Christmas!"

It was a turkey! He never could have stood upon his legs, that bird. He would have snapped 'em short off in a minute, like sticks of sealing wax.

"Why, it's impossible to carry that to Cratchit's," said Scrooge. "You must have a cab."

The chuckles with which he paid for the turkey, and the chuckle with which he paid for the cab, and the chuckle with which he recompensed the boy, were only exceeded by the chuckle with which he sat down breathless in his chair again and cried.

He dressed himself "all in his best" and went out into the streets. The people were pouring forth as he had seen them with the Ghost of Christmas Present. Walking with his hands behind him, Scrooge regarded everyone with a delighted smile.

He had not gone far, when he beheld the gentleman who had walked into his counting-house the day before and said, "Scrooge and Marley's, I believe?"

"Dear sir," Scrooge said, taking the gentleman by both his hands. "I hope you succeeded yesterday. A Merry Christmas to you!"

"Mr. Scrooge?"

"Yes, said Scrooge. "Allow me to ask your pardon. And will you have the goodness . . ." Here Scrooge whispered in his ear.

"My dear Mr. Scrooge," cried the gentleman, "are you serious?"

"Not a farthing less," said Scrooge. "A great many back payments are included in it, I assure you."

"I don't know what to say to such munifi—" said the other, shaking his head.

"Don't say anything," Scrooge returned. "I am obliged to you. Bless you!"

He went to church and walked about the streets. He watched people hurrying about, and patted children on the head. He had never dreamed that any walk—that any-thing—could give him so much happiness. In the afternoon, he turned towards his nephew's house.

He passed the door a dozen times before he had the courage to knock. But knock he did.

"Is your master home?" said Scrooge to the girl. Nice girl!

"Yes, sir," she answered. "He's in the dining room along with mistress. I'll show you in."

"Thankee. He knows me," said Scrooge, with his hand already on the dining room lock. "I'll go in here."

He turned it gently and sidled his face in, round the door.

"Fred!" said Scrooge.

"Why bless my soul!" cried Fred, "Who's that?"

"It's I. Your uncle Scrooge. I have come to dinner. Will you let me in, Fred?"

My, how his niece by marriage started!

Let him in! It is a mercy he didn't shake his arm off. He was at home in five minutes. Wonderful party, wonderful games, wonderful happiness!

But he was early at the office next morning. If he could only be there first and catch Bob Cratchit coming late! That was what he had set his heart upon.

And he did it. The clock struck nine. No Bob. He was full eighteen minutes behind his time. Scrooge sat with his door open, so he might see him come into the tank.

Poor Bob was in the door and on his stool in a jiffy, driving away with his pen.

"Hallo!" growled Scrooge, in his accustomed voice. "What do you mean by coming here at this time?"

"I am very sorry, sir," pleaded Bob. "It's only once a year, sir. It shall not be repeated. I was making rather merry yesterday."

"I'll tell you what, my friend," said Scrooge. "I am not going to stand this sort of thing any longer. And therefore . . ." he continued, leaping from his stool, "I am about to raise your salary!"

Bob trembled and got a little nearer to the ruler. He had a momentary idea of knocking Scrooge down with it; holding him up, and calling people in the court for help and a straight-jacket.

"A Merry Christmas, Bob!" said Scrooge, with an earnestness that could not be mistaken, as he clapped him on the back. "A Merrier Christmas than I have given you for many a year! I'll raise your salary, and endeavor to assist your struggling family, Bob! Make up the fires, and buy another coal scuttle before you dot another 'i', Bob Cratchit!"

Scrooge was better than his word. He did it all, and infinitely more. And to Tiny Tim, who did *not* die, he was a second father. He became as good a friend, as good a master, and as good a man as the good old city knew. Some people laughed to see the alteration in him, but he let them laugh, and little heeded them. His own heart laughed, and that was quite enough for him.

He had no further intercourse with Spirits. And it was always said of him that he knew how to keep Christmas well, if any man alive possessed the knowledge. May that be truly said of us, and all of us! And so, as Tiny Tim observed, "God bless us, every one!"

The Nutcracker

Adapted by Daniel Walden
from the Story by E. T. A. Hoffman

Introduction

Have you ever loved a toy so much you wished it came to life? Did you dream of the exciting adventures you would have with your special friend? If so, you are not the only one. Nearly two hundred years ago, in 1815, the German writer E. T. A. Hoffman wrote a story called *The Nutcracker and the Mouse King*, telling how a little girl's love brought to life her cherished Nutcracker, an enchanted Christmas gift from her mysterious godfather.

The tale charmed readers of all ages, including the French writer Alexandre Dumas, who published a retelling of the story in 1847. From that adaptation, the Russian composer Peter Ilich Tchaikovsky and the choreographer Lev Ivanov created their ballet, *The Nutcracker*. First performed in St. Petersburg in 1892, it is now a classic performed throughout the world every holiday season.

Why has *The Nutcracker* remained so popular? As the story itself explains, "If you love something very much, it is always alive." Pure love of this extraordinary story has kept the words alive for nearly two hundred years, so they can dance for you across these colorful pages.

Chapter 1

It had been snowing all day, and the gray city of Frankfurt was transformed. From her bedroom window Maria Stahlbaum watched the white flakes falling across the chimneys and tiled roofs, whirling against dark windows, and laying a thick carpet down every street and alley. The wind was rising, frequently blowing the snow in layers so dense as to hide the houses opposite. Then the layers would open and you could see every lintel and cornice growing bigger with the snow.

Presently lamps were lighted in the windows next door, and in the bright beams the driven snowflakes surged up like a crowd of elfin dancers in ballet dress. Waltzing and following fast behind each other, they moved on in a mighty leap straight across the space toward Maria's window. She heard the tinkle of tiny diamonds upon the panes. She saw the fairylike figures, just for a moment, before a great blast of wind shook the old house and threw a blanket of snow against the glass.

Luckily, Maria thought, the fir tree had been brought to the door that morning—for it was Christmas Eve—the party gifts had all been wrapped and the good things to eat prepared or delivered. But how would the guests ever get here through such a storm? There was to be a dance in the big room at the back of the house, and Maria could not bear to miss any of the ladies in their evening dresses.

And what of old Papa Drosselmeyer? He was godfather to both Maria and her brother Fritz. Christmas would not be Christmas without Godfather Drosselmeyer! Such a strange old man, so wise and so clever. So severe at times, in his black formal clothes, his old-fashioned manners, and grave voice. For years he had worn a dark patch over one eye—but the other eye was as staring and sharp as an owl's. And yet Maria and Fritz loved him completely. No one else could tell such exciting stories, or bring such a feeling of wonder to every part of the festivities. And his presents were fantastic beyond belief—and each one made by himself. It was almost as if he were a magician!

Last year he had brought them a toy castle on a hill above a moat, and when you turned a crank a troop of knights rode up to the gate. Then the drawbridge was lowered, the great door opened, and out came a princess to receive her guests. Before that, one year, there had been a magic theater with two scenes from *Sleeping Beauty* acted out by tiny figures. And other inventions so precious that Father had a special cupboard built to keep them safe behind glass doors. That cupboard, too, stood in the big room downstairs where the Christmas party always took place.

Maria unlatched the window and pushed it open against the snow piled on the sill. The icy, white powder rushed up into her face, but as she leaned out a little she could see people with lanterns coming down the street. There were four grown-ups and several children. All of them were bundled tight in heavy coats. They looked funny because their feet were almost buried in the soft snow. Beyond them was another group of people. Surely that was her Aunt Lisa in the scarlet greatcoat! All of them were coming toward Maria's house. Soon she and Fritz would be summoned to the big room, and the wonderful Christmas party would begin.

Suddenly Maria felt herself lifted from behind by two strong arms. She struggled and kicked backward and came down in the room with a thud. She had scooped up a fistful of snow and now she held it menacingly toward her brother Fritz. He was always playing tricks like that. But he let her go, to dodge the snowball, which broke on the carpet behind him.

"Ria," he said, "Mr. and Mrs. Kretchmas have come, and Mr. and Mrs. Krone, with all their children, and the whole Zimmerman family. Come down the back stairs! You can see the grown-ups trimming the tree through the keyhole of the side door. The tree is the best we've ever had . . . and I think I have a real cannon . . . and you have a doll with a big moustache!"

"You're making it up! No doll has a moustache."

"This one does, and a blue hat with a plume. It's a man doll, I guess, and I think he has a long sword . . . he must be a general."

"You're crazy! Who ever heard of a general doll?"

"I saw it," Fritz said. "And at any rate there is a table loaded with food—chocolate cake, ginger cookies, and heaps of peppermint stripes and all-colored bonbons. Come on!"

"Has Godfather come?"

"Godfather never comes at the beginning. Don't you remember?"

"But will he come through this storm? He's so old and wrinkled . . . and then he has only one good eye."

"He'll come all right . . . with some mad present that has to be kept locked up. The snow won't keep him away. You know, I think he can fly like an owl and see in the dark.

How he scares me sometimes! I'll bet he could fly right through that window. . . . Look out, here he comes!"

"Whoo—whoo," the blizzard shrieked against the windowpane. A chunk of solid snow dropped unexpectedly from the roof like a white owl upon the ledge outside. Fritz ran and locked the window tight, then grabbed his sister's hand, and the children rushed laughing out of the room.

A mouse scurried out of sight as Maria and Fritz hurried down the hall. Dr. Stahlbaum's house was old and huge and there were a number of mice in the walls, but he was too kind-hearted to trap them. Fritz did not mind them at all. But ever since Maria had seen one running off with a little rug from her doll house she did not like them. They were big, blackish mice, too, and having such kind-hearted people to live with had made them very bold. Sometimes at night, most often when the moon was shining, Maria would be wakened by the faint but persistent *cranch, cranch* of a mouse gnawing a hole in the wall behind her bureau.

There was a broad, steep stairway going down to the family rooms on the floors below. On the ground floor, running out like a wing into the garden, was the largest room in the house. It was a kind of drawing-room and play-room combined. You could reach it through the main hall and you could also reach it by way of the back stairs, which was the way Fritz and Maria now took.

When this house was built, long ago, doors often had keyholes as big as your middle finger, and since this door was a double one, the keyhole was extra large. At first, as Maria looked, everything was blurred by people moving back and forth as busy as squirrels, each one adding some bit to the preparations. The carpet had been rolled back for dancing. Along the right side was a long table spread with platters and raised dishes of all kinds of food.

Behind and above the people, in front of one window and nearly as tall, rose the Christmas tree. Its dark and beautiful branches curved out into the room, layer above layer, adorned with marvelous little toys, with fairy-tale angels and birds, with flowers of spun glass, and with amusing cotton kittens and gnomes and animals of all kinds—so many that you could not possibly count them. And, in much the way that snow might lie on a fir tree in the forest, a frosting of silver tinsel dripped from bough to bough in even curves, growing smaller as the tree narrowed upward. Near the top was a figure of Father Christmas, and at the very top a star.

"Isn't the tree wonderful!" Maria exclaimed.

Clara and Karl were only two of several cousins who had come to the Christmas Eve party here. But they also knew about the side door to the great room and now came running in upon Fritz and Maria.

"Merry Christmas!" they called. "Oh, you're peeking! Let me look. Let me look."

And, pushing and shoving, as overhasty people do, they all tried to look through the keyhole, no one having time enough to catch more than a blurred image before another child was close upon him trying to see, and finally all of them falling on top of one another in a mad scramble of giggles and acrobatics. They would have rolled in a heap, right into the room, had the door been suddenly opened.

Just then the clock struck seven and the children heard Mrs. Stahlbaum calling: "Children, Father Christmas has come!"

They had just managed to disentangle themselves, to stand up and smooth out their party clothes when the doors were thrown open wide. Maria's mother stood inside with her arms extended.

"Merry Christmas, my darlings," she said.

The tree had been lighted. Its glow and its fragrance filled the room. At the top of the tree the star shone; every ornament twinkled.

"Merry Christmas," the children said softly.

Chapter 2

It was the custom for the children to have a little dance first, and then for the grown-ups to have a waltz, and then for young and old to dance together. Between dances they had glasses of punch, and Maria helped her mother pass the little cups around.

She did not see Godfather Drosselmeyer. She kept looking, too, for the strange man doll that Fritz had described—but there was nothing like that among her many presents. And now she was far too busy passing the cold meat and sandwiches and little cakes to think about her gift. But quite suddenly, as she offered a slice of cake to old Mrs. Gumpel, who was sitting close to the tree, Maria saw the most remarkable thing.

Fritz had been telling the truth. Standing stiffly on a little table, as if at attention, was a little soldier. He wore highly polished boots, red trousers with a blue stripe, a white vest crossed by two bands of crimson, a deep blue general's coat, and an impressive hat with a plume. He must be made out of some kind of metal, Maria thought, for he looked so sturdy and strong. He had a high-arched nose, a jutting chin, and round and brave-looking eyes. A rather extra-large moustache grew from his upper lip. He held a long sword at his left side, and his eyes had such a trusting and noble expression—brave and gentle at the same time—that Maria lost her heart to him at once.

Why, he is like a little prince! she thought. The soldier looked up at her steadily. His painted eyelashes gave him a very alert and appealing expression, like a big dog begging for a piece of your cake. How could anyone resist him? He made you feel protective and brave yourself.

". . . Thank you, child," she heard Mrs. Gumpel saying. "The almond torte is delicious. . . ."

The clock struck again, and as it did so the door to the big hall opened slowly, and there stood Godfather Drosselmeyer. He was dressed all in black, with a gold chain around his neck. His white cravat and his hair like spun silver made the black suit look very somber. He always wore a black patch over his left eye, but his other eye was so bright and piercing that it well served him for two. His usually white face was flushed with a rosy glow from the snowy night. When he came forward, he was followed by two tiny, little menservants, each carrying a Christmas package nearly as big as a big boy. No one had seen such large packages before. When the greetings were over, the two servants untied and opened the packages. Out of one box they took a huge cabbage; out of the other a very pink cake. Everyone crowded around in astonishment and curiosity.

The servants then lifted the cabbage and the cake, and underneath each was a doll nearly three feet tall, and almost real-looking. They were dressed as a shepherd and shepherdess. Then they seemed to come alive! The dolls rose and bowed to the audience and then to each other, and executed a most graceful and charming dance. They ended by bowing low and sitting again in position ready for the green cabbage and pink cake to cover them. Everyone was delighted and charmed by the performance.

When they had vanished under the covers, Godfather Drosselmeyer came over to Maria and Fritz. He kissed each of them and said:

"My dear godchildren, these creations were made for you. They come to wish you a Happy Christmas, to give you old Drosselmeyer's love."

"Thank you, Godfather," they said together, "and Merry Christmas to you."

Drosselmeyer took Maria's hand affectionately. "I sent you and Fritz another little gift," he said. "Have you seen it? No? Well, look here!"

He went across toward the tree, past old Mrs. Gumpel, who was still munching sweet cakes, and picked up the brave, iron soldier.

"Oh, I love him, Godfather!" Maria cried.

"He is a nutcracker," said Papa Drosselmeyer, "Look! His jaws are so strong that he can crack the hardest nut without hurting his teeth at all."

Papa Drosselmeyer held the soldier with one hand and with his other raised the soldier's long sword backward. As he did so the mouth opened wide, revealing two rows of very white teeth. Then Drosselmeyer placed a walnut in the nutcracker's mouth, pressed down the sword, and the jaw closed, cracking the shell into four even pieces. He handed the cracked nut to Maria. Then he tried a hazelnut, an almond, and a Brazil nut, each time giving the opened nut to one little girl or another. The boys, too, had crowded around to see this curious fellow. But Fritz was not much impressed.

"Didn't I tell you, Maria?" he said. "Now you have a doll with a big, black moustache!"

"He's not a doll. He's a magic nutcracker."

"What's so magic about him?" Fritz asked. He had never seen a nutcracker shaped like a soldier, but he had seen silver ones and wooden ones with springs.

"Let me have him," he demanded. "I'll bet he can't crack every nut."

"No, you'll hurt him. Godfather, please don't give Nutcracker to Fritz."

"But I brought him for both of you my dear. There Fritz . . . and be careful. He'll crack your nuts for years, but you must not abuse him."

Thereupon Godfather Drosselmeyer turned away to speak with some older friends. Fritz held the little soldier high in the air and started putting nuts in his mouth and crushing them, one right after another. *Crack, crack, crack, crack* went the little jaws, and nut after nut fell out perfectly bitten into four pieces. Then Fritz became annoyed and took an exceptionally large and heavy hickory nut, the toughest he could find, and pushed it far back into the soldier's mouth. *Crack, crack, crack, . . .* Fritz banged the sword up and down. The nut fell out, its shell broken in four even pieces, but there was a loose, clanking sound. The little mouth fell open again, though no one had lifted the sword. Nutcracker was badly hurt.

"Fritz, you did it on purpose! You hurt him on purpose! How unhappy he looks now!"

Maria was dreadfully upset. Fritz laughed, to cover his shame, and turned away. But Maria took Nutcracker up in her arms and tried again and again to get his lower jaw into position. For Nutcracker seemed more real to her than did any of her dolls, and she felt certain he was in pain. What would she do now?

Papa Drosselmeyer had been watching her from across the room. He came over and shook his head. Gently he took up Nutcracker and tried to set the broken jaw, but it was no use.

"He is badly hurt, Maria," he said. "But perhaps we can heal the wound in time. Let us bandage it well and give him some rest."

Taking a large linen handkerchief from his coat pocket, Drosselmeyer bound it firmly around the jaw, holding it in position as he did so.

"With love and good care he should recover. Now put him down and enjoy the rest of the party."

Maria went to the toy cupboard, where one of her doll's beds stood on the lowest shelf. It was just the right size for Nutcracker.

Gently, she made him comfortable in the bed, and she was not at all surprised when his eyes closed as she laid him down. He had no fever, she could tell. He could sleep now. In the morning she would come to look after him and bring him some nourishment.

Meanwhile the party had become very merry. People were laughing and talking gaily. Coming back from the cupboard, Maria saw that the presents had just been given. For each girl a handsomely dressed doll, with a doll's blanket and pillow. For each boy a little rifle, and either a drum or a fife. Soon the girls were rocking their new babies in their arms, and the boys, led by Fritz, formed into a platoon of well-drilled troops and went parading back and forth across the room. Shrill fifes pierced the air and drum rolls thundered out over all conversation. On they came, in full battle array, and suddenly making a left-march, they plunged head-on into the group of girls with their dolls. Maria started scolding Fritz, and in two minutes there was more noise in the room than in the wild storm outside.

At length Fritz's father could tolerate it no longer. "Stop it, stop it!" he cried. "This is a party for everyone, not just for boys and girls. Come all of you and take partners. We need another dance."

Aunt Lisa sat at the square piano, and soon they were all off in a lively polka. It was great fun, and had to be followed by an easier waltz. Then the ices and rich mocha cake were served, with hot chocolate for the children. Some of the grown people had wine, and they offered toasts to each other and to Christmas itself. They stood in front of the tree and sang the carol of Christmas Night.

And then it was time to be going. Old Mrs. Gumpel was already nodding, and several boys were struggling to keep from yawning. The warm room, the rich food, and the dancing had made everyone tired. So into their winter wraps and out into the snowy night they went, with such fond farewells that you would have thought there is no time so wonderful as Christmas time—and you would have been right.

The last to come was the last to leave. Long after the children were in their beds, Mother and Father stood in the front hall saying good-night to the lingering guests. It was getting chilly from the constant opening of the outer door. Only when everyone else had gone did Godfather Drosselmeyer appear—at the far end of the hall, not from the cloak room, although he was covered from shoulders to shoes in an immense gray fur coat. There was a crafty glint in his eye and a smile on his face.

"Well, you have made an old man feel young again," Papa Drosselmeyer said to his hosts. "What a splendid and joyous party! I have not spent a more enjoyable evening in many a year. Truly, a spell was put upon this house tonight."

He shook hands with Dr. Stahlbaum, put on his tall fur hat, and stood on the top step. The snowstorm swirled down around him and he seemed to vanish in it like a wizard.

Days later a maid, who had come back into the empty party room that night to tidy up a bit after all the guests had gone, said she had been badly frightened by finding an old man there in the corner, bending over a doll's bed. He had a slender shining object in one hand, like a medicine dropper or a small screwdriver. When she called out to him he just raised one finger to his lips and made the sign of silence. In the dim room the maid was too startled to know if it was one of the guests—she thought it could not possibly be.

Chapter 3

Cranch, cranch . . . cranch . . . there was that sound in the walls again. Maria sat up in bed, holding the quilt around her. How cold it was. She leaned from her bed to look at the sky. The snow had stopped falling and the moon had come out. She could see it glinting on the tiny, tinsel wrapper of a candy on her bed table. She had brought it up for a goodnight snack and had been too sleepy to eat it. She felt wide awake now, though she could not have slept very long, for it was deep night.

Cranch, cranch—they were louder than ever. Were they bigger mice? Or were there more of them? She thought of the Christmas tree and of Nutcracker lying in his little bed with its thin cover. She wished she had brought him up here. Surely she should have given him more covers, for the party room would be bitterly cold by now.

Maria slid out of bed, and into her slippers and wrapper. When she lighted her bedside candle-lamp, the sound in the walls stopped abruptly. She opened the door quietly and went down the long, dark hall towards the stairs. Maria's velvet slippers muffled her steps. The stairs were carpeted and firm and she went down them in complete silence.

Even going into the big room made no sound, for the door was ajar and she could pass through. Most of the room lay in shadow; her candle beam lighted only a narrow strip of the floor. As she came in it followed across the wall, up the tall owl-clock. It picked out the dial and then both golden hands pointing together to the owl's head on top.

The owl stirred and opened its eyes, and at that very instant, the clock spoke—a loud, deep, and hollow *O-o-o-o* that echoed from wall to wall. The owl raised itself up and began beating its wings. The clock struck again, and again, as Maria went on to the toy cupboard. In front of it was the doll's bed. And there was Nutcracker sound asleep. To her great joy, his mouth was peacefully closed and the bandage had slipped off. He would get well!

She started to take him up in her arms . . . and there came that sound, faintly, *cranch, cranch, cranchety-cranch.*

The sound came again, closer and louder: *cranch, cranch!* It was followed by the rattle of tiny running feet.

A mouse's face appeared under the Christmas tree, and vanished. Then another one, much nearer. Oh what a big and ugly mouse! He seemed to be getting larger and coming straight for Maria.

At this moment her candle went out. A score of wicked little mouse eyes danced around the room. Terrified, Maria threw herself on the sofa and buried her face in the pillows.

When she looked out again there was a strange dim light all over the room. She could not tell where it came from. Mice—large, fat, and nearly black mice, with long and stringy tails—were moving back and forth in a kind of planned activity, as if following orders. They had sharp, little knives like swords, and they were assembling on the side of the room opposite the toy cupboard.

Then Maria noticed the strangest thing. The mice and the sofa and the table and chairs were getting larger and larger. The Christmas tree boughs reached out into the room, the needles growing much longer, and all the ornaments blowing out like balloons but keeping their various forms. The tinsel garlands were thick ropes of silver and gold. The doll's bed—and Nutcracker in it—were becoming nearly life-size. The room itself was expanding.

Or was Maria growing smaller and smaller? She felt the sofa rising beneath her. The seat was already about six feet from the floor. She had better get off right away. She slid down the curving leg, and touched the floor just a few feet from her doll's bed, which was now roomy enough for Maria herself. Nutcracker was gone!

The room was in a great commotion. The mice, as large as big dogs, were crowding together across the room, lining up in regular rows. One of them gave a high shriek, flourished his knife, and the whole band came charging toward the cupboard. Their wiry black feet made that scratchy sound Maria knew so well.

In another second the mice would have been upon her. But a bugle sounded, the cupboard door opened, and a troop of wooden soldiers as large as the mice rushed out to engage them. Cannons were wheeled into position, and ball after ball—red, pink, white, and blue—was sent in showers against the mice. But how strangely soft they were, more like big gumdrops. They seemed only to bounce off the fat mice's fur.

The bugle sounded again. A noble figure suddenly appeared at the head of the troops, in red trousers, blue coat, and plumed head dress. It was Nutcracker.

He had drawn his sword. He turned halfway round to the first line of troops, gave a command, and led them straight into the front ranks of the mouse army. What fierce hand-to-hand combat followed! The soldiers stood there bravely, but their tin swords were no match for the knives and sharp teeth of the mice.

Cranch, cranch, sounded the mouse battle-cry.

Nutcracker signaled again, and the second line of soldiers ran into the fight. Pausing a few feet from their huddled foes, they fell to their knees and took aim with their rifles. The savage mouse horde came on then, eyes and teeth flashing. The riflemen fired. Their courage was not matched by arms of sufficient power, and the shots only tickled the tough skins of the mice. One or two squealed in pain. The rest were only made more angry.

Nutcracker now summoned his last defenses. The third rank came on at a run, guns lowered and sharp steel bayonets thrust forward. The mouse villains did not move and were about to be pierced through and through when they dropped on all fours. They scampered cunningly between the soldiers' legs, unbalancing many of them, which they then carried off as prisoners.

It seemed certain now that the toy cupboard, with all its treasures, would fall victim to the mouse army. At this moment a horrible creature appeared, largest of all the mice, his terrible eyes flashing from left to right, his whiskers vibrating with rage. He wore a headdress of seven crowns. He was the Mouse King. He put himself at the front of his cutthroat band, puffed himself up with pride and prepared to lead them to the cupboard.

Nutcracker, rather badly beaten, was directly in the Mouse King's path. He stood as usual, feet planted together, holding his long, strong sword.

The Mouse King had a club—black and dreadful to look at. And he had his very large, very sharp teeth.

There has never been such a strange and furious encounter. The Mouse King feigned a terrific blow with his club and then darted under his raised weapon to give his foe a savage bite. But Nutcracker was made of iron, and the Mouse King hurt his teeth so severely that he became enraged. Taking his black club in both hands, he began beating Nutcracker mercilessly. But the brave soldier warded off the club with his sword. Quickly, Nutcracker followed that with a sharp thrust at his enemy's fat belly.

But for all his fatness, the Mouse King was the quickest of the mice, and so expert at twisting and dodging and leaping and ducking this way and that, that Nutcracker could barely touch him lightly here and there. All the time he had to fend off the blows of that terrible club. Down, down, the blows kept falling on Nutcracker's head and shoulders.

Maria had been watching the combat from her place at the sofa. She saw that Nutcracker could not last much longer. But she had no gun and no sword. What could she do? Her fear for Nutcracker made her both cunning and bold. She took off one velvet slipper. No longer afraid, she ran up to the Mouse King, and as he lifted his club high over his head, she threw the slipper right in his face.

Astonished and enraged, the Mouse King deserted his opponent and raced after

Maria. And that was just what she wanted. Immediately, Nutcracker came up behind the Mouse King and struck down the monster with his sword. Maria bounced into her doll's bed. She was not hurt at all.

Nutcracker stood perfectly still for a moment. He was overcome with weariness and relief. His deep-drawn breathing was the only sound in the entire room—or was it the thudding of his heart? He put away his sword. Suddenly he toppled over, without bending, like a toy.

The horde of mice, who had thought their monarch invincible, fell down in grief and terror at his death. In another moment they gathered up his swollen body in their arms, and fled. You could hear the scampering of their wiry feet, even after the last one had disappeared. Where they went, or how they went, is a mystery. All we know is that their wicked little eyes were never seen in that house again.

Chapter 4

Nutcracker stirred and opened his eyes. He raised himself on one arm. Then he stood up, restored. Restored not only to his full strength but to his true self. He was no longer dressed like a soldier; he was no longer made of iron; he no longer had a moustache and a high-arched nose. He was a handsome youth dressed in long, blue hose, a jacket and slippers of silver, and a little cloak lined with crimson. His hair was cut close, of a ruddy blond color almost matching his belt and scabbard of gold. Only his gentle eyes had not changed. They were as deep and round and confident as before.

Nutcracker crossed to the far corner of the room and found that velvet slipper that had saved his life, and then to the opposite side, where Maria's wrapper hung over the foot of the bed. He put the wrapper around her and the slipper on her foot.

"Is it you, Nutcracker?" Maria said, so astonished she could only stand and stare. "What does it all mean?"

He smiled at her very tenderly.

"It means," he said, "that the spell has been broken. I was a young boy who did not appreciate his good fortune. I had health and friends and work to do—but I was so foolish as to be discontented and to complain of this and that all the time. An enchanter deprived me of speech and turned me into a nutcracker so that my mouth would no longer whine, but would serve some kind of purpose until I should learn to be glad of living and being of use. The spell would only be broken when someone realized how much I had changed and believed that I had a new heart under my funny costume of painted iron. It was you, Maria, who broke the enchantment—or rather, completed it. For you see, it was a lucky enchantment, since now I do know that it is good and wonderful to be alive."

The room became illuminated as the moon began to shine on the snow outside the window. It shone on Maria's slipper and on the golden sword at Nutcracker's side. It shone on all the twinkling ornaments on the Christmas tree.

"What is your real name?" Maria asked.

"My name is Prince Nikita, but now I like Nutcracker better."

"And what are you going to do now?"

"I think I shall go on being a nutcracker," he said. "That is as good a job as any, at least for a while."

"But if you are a prince you must live far away, Nutcracker. Will you go there?"

"No, I want to stay here with you, Maria. Where I live is quite far away, if you think it is far away. But it is only a few steps really. Come, I will show you."

One of the tall French windows blew open. Nutcracker lifted his beautiful sword and walked out into the night. Maria was spellbound for a moment. And then as she was about to rise and follow him, her little bed began to move like a sleigh toward the window. She tucked the wrapper and coverlet close around her. She was quite warm. Without a sound her bed glided on, under the yellow curtains, through the window, and out of doors.

Have you ever been in a forest in deep winter? With the snow frozen so hard that you can walk on its glassy surface, and green fir and pine trees wearing edgings of snow like white fur? With little tracks of rabbits and birds criss-crossing on the white floor, and tiny crystals of ice blinking on and off like winter fireflies? When it is so still that you can hear the least movement of twig or shifting snow?

Through such a forest Maria found herself moving in her sleigh-bed. Nutcracker strode on ahead, his red cloak like a beckoning torch. It was no longer night, and it was snowing again—large flakes that circled around the bed and came rushing toward it in a great throng at every new turn in the path. Then Maria saw what she had only glimpsed from the window hours ago—the Snow Fairies soaring through the air and dancing down the aisles of the forest. They were extraordinarily lovely with their costumes of silver hoarfrost and diadems of snowflakes more brilliant than diamonds. They surrounded the sleigh-bed whirling and leaping so close together that it was quite dizzying. Then at the height of their wild dance, the forest and all its spirits seemed to melt into air.

The snow was gone. The path had become a little canal of water bordered with green plants and colorful flowers. The bed was a boat upon it. Far down the canal, Maria could see a flight of stairs at one side, with Nutcracker waiting on the lowest step. As the little boat-bed drew up, he stepped aboard beside Maria, and they sailed on.

In the distance, a castle seemed to rise out of the water. It gleamed like a giant party cake. Its walls were made of icing; over the windows were candy flowers; and peppermint stripes spiraled up the tall towers. At intervals stood statues carved out of marzipan.

An archway of golden taffy spanned the canal, and under it the boat glided into the castle. It stopped at a flight of broad steps, in a great hall made entirely of rock candy in soft pinks and yellows. A stately lady dressed in gleaming white satin stood at the top of the stairs to receive them, and beyond were many men and women dressed as if for a ball.

Nutcracker said the lady was the Sugar Plum Fairy and that this was the Fortress of Sweets. He introduced Maria, and then he told everyone how Maria had saved his life and broken the magic spell. Everyone said she had been very brave.

The Sugar Plum Fairy escorted the two children to a table overlooking the rock-candy hall.

People brought in many delicious and unusual foods. For, after their battle with the mice and their trip through the forest, Nutcracker and Maria were very hungry. Each kind of refreshment was so prettily decorated that you could not tell just what it was. But it was better than ice cream, or cherry pie, or any birthday cake.

While they were eating this delectable feast, the court entertained them with music and a series of dances, each representing something good to eat or drink. Two women in ruffled skirts and two men in flaring trousers did the dance of Chocolate, which was really a Spanish dance because so much chocolate comes, or used to come, from Spain.

A stern Arab did a slow and rather sleepy dance on a rug. The music and his languid movements made you see the hot and lonely desert at night. Servants gave him tiny cups of coffee now and then, for the Arabians are great coffee drinkers.

Two Chinese girls brought in a big box of bamboo, like a tea chest. Out of it vaulted two Asian acrobats. Around and around the candy hall they turned cartwheels and flip-flops. One of them vaulted right over the table where Nutcracker and Maria were sitting. This dance was called the Dance of Tea, because the Chinese love that drink especially.

Next came a number of muscular young men dressed in red and white stripes, and carrying hoops. This was a dance of great agility and speed. The men seemed to fly through the air as they dove through their whirling hoops. It was the most brilliant dance of all.

The music changed to an airy and soaring waltz. A troop of dancers looking like flowers floated softly down from balconies and windows between the clear-sugar columns. They danced as if borne up by a breeze, and made you think of a mountain meadow. Finally, like dandelion seeds, they were wafted up, one after the other, and out between the columns.

But now came the most amusing one. How Fritz would have liked it! A very tall woman came jerkily in, wearing the most tremendous skirt, like a huge round candy box. Suddenly she lifted one part of her skirt, and out came the tiniest children, who tumbled and tripped about, just like dainty bonbons. They were dressed in pink and lavender, pale green and yellow, and there were so many of them! But somehow they all managed to crowd back under the big skirts again, and the candy-box lady sidled off.

Now the Sugar Plum Fairy came forward with a handsome man to show what they could do. And this was best of all, dancing so wonderful that Nutcracker and Maria forgot their caramel sherbet and sat enraptured.

Only a dancer could describe the grandeur and charm of those figures, responding to the music in perfect unison, creating a pattern of motion that seemed to fill the vast room with advances and retreats, vigor and grace, till you were hypnotized by its splendor. At the climax the Sugar Plum Fairy spun like a top at a furious speed all the length of the room and was caught and lifted up triumphantly by her partner.

When the applause had subsided the dancers smiled and beckoned for Nutcracker and Maria to come down. All of the court gathered around, and the children thanked them, bowing low.

Chapter 5

As Maria raised her head she knew that the court was not there. The light was different and the ballroom floor was the quilt of her bed at home. She opened her eyes wide. The clear light of the morning was streaming into her room. An icicle glittered outside the window pane, and beyond, the sky was intensely blue. There was a faint smell of toast and coffee from downstairs.

Then she saw, near the fireplace, her doll's bed. And Nutcracker lying in it, in his General's uniform. He seemed to have just awakened, too, and he was looking right at her. She thought that he smiled.

The door to the hall opened, and Maria's mother came in with a tray of food.

"How late you have slept! And on Christmas morning! The storm is over, and the whole world is washed clean. You never saw such a beautiful Christmas Day."

She came over and kissed Maria.

"I've brought you breakfast in bed, for we are all through downstairs. . . . Are you feeling well?"

"Yes, Mother, I am, and thank you for breakfast. What a party it was! . . . I was so excited I don't remember bringing Nutcracker upstairs."

"No, darling, I brought him up early this morning. And one of your slippers. The big room was in such a state . . . there were gumdrops all over the floor!"

"Mother, is Godfather Drosselmeyer a magician?"

"Of course not. He is just a clever and ingenious man who is very fond of you."

"But how did he bring Nutcracker alive?"

"If Nutcracker came alive, it was because you like him so well. If you love something very much it is always alive. . . . What a funny child you are today! Now get washed and dressed and have your breakfast. I'll light the fire."

The Gift of the Magi

by O. Henry

One dollar and eighty-seven cents. That was all. And 60 cents of it was in pennies. Pennies saved one and two at a time by bulldozing the grocer and the vegetable man and the butcher until one's cheeks burned with the silent imputation of parsimony that such close dealing implied. Three times Della counted it. One dollar and eighty-seven cents. And the next day would be Christmas.

There was clearly nothing to do but flop down on the shabby little couch and howl. So Della did it. Which instigates the moral reflection that life is made up of sobs, sniffles, and smiles, with sniffles predominating.

While the mistress of the home is gradually subsiding from the first stage to the second, take a look at the home. A furnished flat at $8 per week. It did not exactly beggar description, but it certainly had that word on the lookout for the mendicancy squad.

In the vestibule below, belonged to this flat a letter-box into which no letter would go, and an electric button from which no mortal finger could coax a ring. Also appertaining thereunto was a card bearing the name "Mr. James Dillingham Young."

The "Dillingham" had been flung to the breeze during a former period of prosperity when its possessor was being paid $30 per week. Now, when the income was shrunk to $20, the letters of "Dillingham" looked

blurred, as though they were thinking seriously of contracting to a modest and unassuming
D. But whenever Mr. James Dillingham Young
came home and reached his flat above he was
called "Jim" and greatly hugged by Mrs. James
Dillingham Young, already introduced to you
as Della. Which is all very good.

Della finished her cry and attended to her
cheeks with the powder rag. She stood by the
window and looked out dully at a gray cat
walking a gray fence in a gray backyard.
Tomorrow would be Christmas Day, and she
had only $1.87 with which to buy Jim a
present. She had been saving every penny she
could for months, with this result. Twenty
dollars a week doesn't go far. Expenses had
been greater than she had calculated. They
always are. Only $1.87 to buy a present for
Jim. Her Jim. Many a happy hour she had

spent planning for something nice for him.
Something fine and rare and sterling—
something just a little bit near to being worthy
of the honor of being owned by Jim.

There was a pier-glass between the
windows of the room. Perhaps you have seen
a pier-glass in an $8 flat. A very thin and very
agile person may, by observing his reflection in
a rapid sequence of longitudinal strips, obtain
a fairly accurate conception of his looks. Della,
being slender, had mastered the art.

Suddenly she whirled from the window
and stood before the glass. Her eyes were
shining brilliantly, but her face had lost its color
within twenty seconds. Rapidly she pulled
down her hair and let it fall to its full length.

Now, there were two possessions of the
James Dillingham Youngs in which they both
took a mighty pride. One was Jim's gold

watch that had been his father's and his grandfather's. The other was Della's hair. Had the Queen of Sheba lived in the flat across the airshaft, Della would have let her hair hang out the window some day to dry and mocked at Her Majesty's jewels and gifts. Had King Solomon been the janitor, with all his treasures piled up in the basement, Jim would have pulled out his watch every time he passed, just to see him pluck at his beard from envy.

So now Della's beautiful hair fell about her, rippling and shining like a cascade of brown waters. It reached below her knee and made itself almost a garment for her. And then she did it up again nervously and quickly. Once she faltered for a minute and stood still while a tear or two splashed on the worn red carpet.

On went her old brown jacket; on went her old brown hat. With a whirl of skirts and with the brilliant sparkle still in her eyes, she fluttered out the door and down the stairs to the street.

Where she stopped the sign read: "Mme. Sofronie. Hair Goods of All Kinds." One flight up Della ran, and collected herself, panting, before Madame, large, too white, chilly and hardly looking the "Sofronie."

"Will you buy my hair?" asked Della.

"I buy hair," said Madame. "Take yer hat off and let's have a sight at the looks of it."

Down rippled the brown cascade.

"Twenty dollars," said Madame, lifting the mass with a practiced hand.

"Give it to me quick," said Della.

Oh, and the next two hours tripped by on rosy wings. Forget the hashed metaphor. She was ransacking the stores for Jim's present.

She found it at last. It surely had been made for Jim and no one else. There was none other like it in any of the stores, and she had turned all of them inside out. It was a platinum fob chain simple and chaste in design, properly proclaiming its value by substance alone and not by meretricious ornamentation—as all good things should do. It was even worthy of The Watch. As soon as she saw it she knew that it must be Jim's. It was like him. Quietness and value—the description applied to both. Twenty-one dollars they took from her for it. And she hurried home with the 87 cents. With that chain on his watch Jim might be properly anxious about the time in any company. Grand as the watch was, he sometimes looked at it on the sly on account of the old leather strap that he used in place of a chain.

When Della reached home her intoxication gave way a little to prudence and reason. She got out her curling irons and lighted the gas and went to work repairing the ravages made by generosity added to love. Which is always a tremendous task, dear friends—a mammoth task.

Within forty minutes her head was covered with tiny, close-lying curls that made her look wonderfully like a truant schoolboy. She looked at her reflection in the mirror long, carefully, and critically.

"If Jim doesn't kill me," she said to herself, "before he takes a second look at me, he'll say I look like a Coney Island chorus girl.

But what could I do—oh, what could I do with a dollar and eighty-seven cents!"

At 7 o'clock the coffee was made and the frying-pan was on the back of the stove hot and ready to cook the chops.

Jim was never late. Della doubled the fob chain in her hand and sat on the corner of the table near the door that he always entered. Then she heard his step on the stair away down on the first flight, and she turned white for just a moment. She had a habit for saying little silent prayers about the simplest everyday things, and now she whispered: "Please, God, make him think I am still pretty."

The door opened and Jim stepped in and closed it. He looked thin and very serious. Poor fellow, he was only twenty-two—and to be burdened with a family! He needed a new overcoat and he was without gloves.

Jim stopped inside the door, as immovable as a setter at the scent of quail. His eyes were fixed upon Della, and there was an expression in them that she could not read, and it terrified her. It was not anger, nor surprise, nor disapproval, nor horror, nor any of the sentiments that she had been prepared for. He simply stared at her fixedly with that peculiar expression on his face.

Della wriggled off the table and went for him.

"Jim, darling," she cried, "don't look at me that way. I had my hair cut off and sold because I couldn't have lived through Christmas without giving you a present. It'll grow out again—you won't mind, will you? I just had to do it. My hair grows awfully fast. Say 'Merry Christmas!' Jim, and let's be happy. You don't know what a nice—what a beautiful, nice gift I've got for you."

"You've cut off your hair?" asked Jim, laboriously, as if he had not arrived at that patent fact yet even after the hardest mental labor.

"Cut it off and sold it," said Della. "Don't you like me just as well, anyhow? I'm me without my hair, ain't I?"

Jim looked about the room curiously.

"You say your hair is gone?" he said, with an air almost of idiocy.

"You needn't look for it," said Della. "It's sold, I tell you—sold and gone, too. It's Christmas Eve, boy. Be good to me, for it went for you. Maybe the hairs of my head were numbered," she went on with sudden serious sweetness, "but nobody could ever count my love for you. Shall I put the chops on, Jim?"

Out of his trance Jim seemed quickly to wake. He enfolded his Della. For ten seconds let us regard with discreet scrutiny some inconsequential object in the other direction. Eight dollars a week or a million a year—what is the difference? A mathematician or a wit would give you the wrong answer. The magi brought valuable gifts, but that was not among them. This dark assertion will be illuminated later on.

Jim drew a package from his overcoat pocket and threw it upon the table.

"Don't make any mistake, Dell," he said, "about me. I don't think there's anything in the way of a haircut or a shave or a shampoo that could make me like my girl any less. But if you'll unwrap that package you may see why you had me going a while at first."

White fingers and nimble tore at the string and paper. And then an ecstatic scream of joy;

and then, alas! a quick feminine change to hysterical tears and wails, necessitating the immediate employment of all the comforting powers of the lord of the flat.

For there lay The Combs—the set of combs, side and back, that Della had worshipped and longed for in a Broadway window. Beautiful combs, pure tortoise shell, with jeweled rims—just the shade to wear in the beautiful vanished hair. They were expensive combs, she knew, and her heart had simply craved and yearned over them without the least hope of possession. And now, they were hers, but the tresses that should have adorned the coveted adornments were gone.

But she hugged them to her bosom, and at length she was able to look up with dim eyes and a smile and say: "My hair grows so fast, Jim!"

And then Della leaped up like a little singed cat and cried, "Oh, oh!"

Jim had not yet seen his beautiful present. She held it out to him eagerly upon her open palm. The dull, precious metal seemed to flash with a reflection of her bright and ardent spirit.

"Isn't it a dandy, Jim? I hunted all over town to find it. You'll have to look at the time a hundred times a day now. Give me your watch. I want to see how it looks on it."

Instead of obeying, Jim tumbled down on the couch and put his hands under the back of his head and smiled.

"Dell," said he, "let's put our Christmas presents away and keep 'em a while. They're too nice to use just at present. I sold the watch to get the money to buy your combs. And now suppose you put the chops on."

The magi, as you know, were wise men—wonderfully wise men—who brought gifts to the Babe in the manger. They invented the art of giving Christmas gifts. Being wise, their gifts were no doubt wise ones, possibly bearing the privilege of exchange in case of duplication. And here I have lamely related to you the uneventful chronicle of two foolish children in a flat who most unwisely sacrificed for each other the greatest treasures of their house. But in a last word to the wise of these days let it be said that of all who give gifts these two were the wisest. Of all who give and receive gifts, such as they are wisest. Everywhere they are wisest. They are the magi.

Yes, Virginia, There Is a Santa Claus

by Francis P. Church

In 1897, a young girl wrote to the *New York Sun* asking whether Santa Claus truly existed.

The paper's response, written by Francis P. Church, appeared in *The Sun* on Sept. 21, 1897.

Virginia, your little friends are wrong. They have been affected by the skepticism of a skeptical age. They do not believe except what they see. They think that nothing can be which is not comprehensible by their little minds.

All minds, Virginia, whether they be men's or children's, are little. In this great universe of ours man is a mere insect, an ant, in his intellect, as compared with the boundless world about him, as measured by the intelligence capable of grasping the whole of truth and knowledge.

Yes, Virginia, there is a Santa Claus. He exists as certainly as love and generosity and devotion exist, and you know that they abound and give to our life its highest beauty and joy.

Alas! how dreary would be the world if there were no Santa Claus. It would be as dreary as if there were no Virginias.

There would be no childlike faith then, no poetry, no romance, to make tolerable this existence. We should have no enjoyment, except in sense and sight. The eternal light with which childhood fills the world would be extinguished.

Not believe in Santa Claus! You might as well not believe in fairies! You might get your papa to hire men to watch in all the chimneys on Christmas Eve to catch Santa Claus, but even if they did not see Santa Claus coming down, what would that prove?

Nobody sees Santa Claus, but that is no sign that there is no Santa Claus.

The most real things in the world are those that neither children nor men can see. Did you ever see fairies dancing on the lawn? Of course not, but that's no proof that they are not there. Nobody can conceive or imagine all the wonders there are unseen or unseeable in the world.

You may tear apart the baby's rattle and see what makes the noise inside but there is a veil covering the unseen world which not the strongest man, nor even the united strength of all the strongest men that ever lived, could tear apart. Only faith, fancy, poetry, love, romance, can push aside that curtain and view and picture the supernal beauty and glory beyond. Is it all real? Ah, Virginia, in all this world there is else nothing real and abiding.

No Santa Claus! Thank God he lives, and he lives forever. A thousand years from now, Virginia, nay ten times ten thousand years from now, he will continue to make glad the heart of childhood.

A Child's Christmas in Wales

by Dylan Thomas

Introduction

Renowned as perhaps the greatest lyric poet of the twentieth century, Dylan Thomas left a legacy of captivating tales and timeless reminiscence. Born in South Wales in 1914, Thomas devoted his life to writing. His romantic prose and passionate poetry have been widely published in *Portrait of the Artist as a Young Dog*, *Quite Early One Morning*, *Letters to Vernon Watkins*, and other works.

Of all of his writings, however, the most widely celebrated is *A Child's Christmas in Wales*. Set in a small town and inspired by Thomas's own boyhood, this vivid tale magically recreates the innocent, "tinseled" world of a child.

Originally titled "Memories of Christmas," this work was scheduled to be read by Thomas in a live radio broadcast on "The Welsh Children's Hour" in 1945. However, the show was cancelled by the producer, who distrusted Thomas's mercurial nature.

In 1950 the work resurfaced in the United States, this time published as *A Child's Christmas in Wales* in *Harper's Bazaar* magazine. It immediately became Thomas's most popular prose work and has remained a cherished Christmas gift that is both familiar and new with each reading.

One Christmas was so much like another, in those years around the sea-town corner now and out of all sound except the distant speaking of the voices I sometimes hear a moment before sleep, that I can never remember whether it snowed for six days and six nights when I was twelve or whether it snowed for twelve days and twelve nights when I was six.

All the Christmases roll down toward the two-tongued sea, like a cold and headlong moon bundling down the sky that was our street; and they stop at the rim of the ice-edged, fish-freezing waves, and I plunge my hands in the snow and bring out whatever I can find. In goes my hand into that wool-white bell-tongued ball of holidays resting at the rim of the carol-singing sea, and out come Mrs. Prothero and the firemen.

It was on the afternoon of the day of Christmas Eve, and I was in Mrs. Prothero's garden, waiting for cats, with her son Jim. It was snowing. It was always snowing at Christmas. December, in my memory, is white as Lapland, though there were no reindeer. But there were cats. Patient, cold and callous, our hands wrapped in socks, we waited to snowball the cats. Sleek and long as jaguars and horrible-whiskered, spitting and snarling, they would slink and sidle over the white back-garden walls, and the lynx-eyed hunters, Jim and I, fur-capped and moccasined trappers from Hudson Bay, off Mumbles Road, would hurl our deadly snowballs at the green of their eyes.

The wise cats never appeared. We were so still, Eskimo-footed arctic marksmen in the muffling silence of the eternal snows—eternal, ever since Wednesday—that we never heard Mrs. Prothero's first cry from her igloo at the bottom of the garden. Or, if we heard it at all, it was, to us, like the far-off challenge of our enemy and prey, the neighbor's polar cat. But soon the voice grew louder. "Fire!" cried Mrs. Prothero, and she beat the dinner-gong.

And we ran down the garden, with the snowballs in our arms, toward the house; and smoke, indeed, was pouring out in the dining-room and the gong was bombilating, and Mrs. Prothero was announcing ruin like a town crier in Pompeii. This was better than all the cats in Wales standing on the wall in a row. We bounded into the house, laden with snowballs, and stopped at the open door of the smoke-filled room.

Something was burning all right; perhaps it was Mr. Prothero, who always slept there after midday dinner with a newspaper over his face. But he was standing in the middle of the room, saying, "A fine Christmas!" and smacking at the smoke with a slipper.

"Call the fire brigade," cried Mrs. Prothero as she beat the gong.

"They won't be there," said Mr. Prothero, "it's Christmas."

There was no fire to be seen, only clouds of smoke and Mr. Prothero standing in the middle of them, waving his slipper as though he were conducting.

"Do something," he said.

And we threw all our snowballs into the smoke—I think we missed Mr. Prothero—and ran out of the house to the telephone box.

"Let's call the police as well," Jim said.

"And the ambulance."

"And Ernie Jenkins, he likes fires."

215

But we only called the fire brigade, and soon the fire engine came and three tall men in helmets brought a hose into the house and Mr. Prothero got out just in time before they turned it on. Nobody could have had a noisier Christmas Eve. And when the firemen turned off the hose and were standing in the wet, smoky room, Jim's aunt, Miss Prothero, came downstairs and peered in at them. Jim and I waited, very quietly, to hear what she would say to them. She said the right thing, always. She looked at the three tall firemen in their shining helmets, standing among the smoke and cinders and dissolving snowballs, and she said: "Would you like anything to read?"

Years and years and years ago, when I was a boy, when there were wolves in Wales, and birds the color of red-flannel petticoats whisked past the harp-shaped hills, when we sang and wallowed all night and day in caves that smelt like Sunday afternoons in damp front farmhouse parlors, and we chased, with the jawbones of deacons, the English and the bears, before the motor car, before the wheel, before the duchess-faced horse, when we rode the daft and happy hills bareback, it snowed and it snowed. But here a small boy says: "It snowed last year, too. I made a snowman and my brother knocked it down and I knocked my brother down and then we had tea."

"But that was not the same snow," I say. "Our snow was not only shaken from whitewash buckets down the sky, it came shawling out of the ground and swam and drifted out of the arms and hands and bodies of the trees; snow grew overnight on the roofs of the houses like a pure and grandfather moss, minutely whiteivied the walls and settled on the postman,

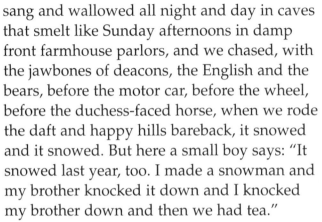

opening the gate, like a dumb, numb thunder-storm of white, torn Christmas cards."

"Were there postmen then, too?"

"With sprinkling eyes and wind-cherried noses, on spread, frozen feet they crunched up to the doors and mittened on them manfully. But all that the children could hear was a ringing of bells."

"You mean that the postman went rat-a-tat-tat and the doors rang?"

"I mean that the bells that the children could hear were inside them."

"I only hear thunder sometimes, never bells."

"There were church bells, too."

"Inside them?"

"No, no, no, in the bat-black, snow-white belfries, tugged by bishops and storks. And they rang their tidings over the bandaged town, over the frozen foam of the powder and ice-cream hills, over the crackling sea. It seemed that all the churches boomed for joy under my window; and the weathercocks crew from Christmas, on our fence."

"Get back to the postmen."

"They were just ordinary postmen, fond of walking and dogs and Christmas and the snow. They knocked on the doors with blue knuckles. . . ."

"Ours has got a black knocker. . . ."

"And then they stood on the white Welcome mat in the little, drifted porches and huffed and puffed, making ghosts with their breath, and jogged from foot to foot like small boys wanting to go out."

"And then the Presents?"

"And then the Presents, after the Christmas box. And the cold postman, with a rose on his button-nose, tingled down the tea-tray-slithered run of the chilly glinting hill. He went in his ice-bound boots like a man on fish-monger's slabs.

"He wagged his bag like a frozen camel's hump, dizzily turned the corner on one foot, and, by God, he was gone."

"Get back to the Presents."

"There were the Useful Presents: engulfing mufflers of the old coach days, and mittens made for giant sloths, zebra scarfs of a substance like silky gum that could be tug-o'-warred down to the galoshes; blinding tam-o'-shanters like patchwork tea cozies and bunny-suited busbies and balaclavas for victims of head-shrinking tribes; from aunts who always wore wool next to the skin there were mustached and rasping vests that made you wonder why the aunts had any skin left at all; and once I had a little crocheted nose bag from an aunt now, alas, no longer whinnying with us. And pictureless books in which small boys, though warned with quotations not to, *would* skate on Farmer Giles' pond and did and drowned; and books that told me everything about the wasp, except why."

"Go on to the Useless Presents."

"Bags of moist and many-colored jelly babies and a folded flag and a false nose and a tram-conductor's cap and a machine that punched tickets and rang a bell; never a catapult; once, by mistake that no one could explain, a little hatchet; and a celluloid duck that made, when you pressed it, a most unducklike sound, a mewing moo that an ambitious cat might make who wished to be a cow; and a painting book in which I could make the grass, the trees, the sea and the animals any color I pleased, and still the dazzling sky-blue sheep are grazing in the red field under the rainbow-billed and pea-green birds. Hardboileds, toffee, fudge and allsorts, crunches, cracknels, humbugs, glaciers, marzipan, and butter-welsh for the Welsh. And troops of bright tin soldiers who, if they could not fight, could always run. And Snakes-and-Families and Happy Ladders. And Easy Hobbi-Games for Little Engineers, complete with instructions. Oh, easy for Leonardo! And a whistle to make the dogs bark to wake up the old man next door to make him beat on the wall with his stick to shake our picture off the wall. And a packet of cigarettes: you put one in your mouth and you stood at the corner of the street and you waited for hours, in vain, for an old lady to scold you for smoking a cigarette, and then with a smirk you ate it. And then it was breakfast under the balloons."

"Were there Uncles like in our house?"

"There are always Uncles at Christmas. The same Uncles. And on Christmas mornings, with dog-disturbing whistle and sugar fags, I would scour the swatched town for the news of the little world, and find always a dead bird by the white Post Office or by the deserted swings; perhaps a robin, all but one of his fires out. Men and women wading or scooping back from chapel, with taproom noses and wind-bussed cheeks, all albinos, huddled their stiff black jarring feathers against the irreligious snow. Mistletoe hung from the gas brackets in all the front parlors; there was sherry and walnuts and bottled beer and crackers by the dessert spoons; and cats in their fur-abouts watched the fires; and the high-heaped fire spat, all ready for the chestnuts and the mulling pokers. Some few large men sat in the front parlors, without their collars, Uncles almost certainly, trying their new cigars, holding them out judiciously at arms' length returning them to their mouths, coughing, then holding them out again as though waiting for the explosion; and some few small aunts, not wanted in the kitchen, not anywhere else for that matter, sat on the very edges of their chairs, poised and brittle, afraid to break, like faded cups and saucers."

Not many those mornings trod the piling streets: an old man always, fawn-bowlered, yellow-gloved and, at this time of year, with spats of snow, would take his constitutional to the white bowling green and back, as he would take it wet or fine on Christmas Day or Doomsday, sometimes two hale young men, with big pipes blazing, no overcoats and wind-blown scarfs, would trudge, unspeaking, down to the forlorn sea, to work up an appetite, to blow away the fumes, who knows, to walk into the waves until nothing of them was left but the two curling smoke clouds of the inextinguishable briars. Then I would be slap-dashing home, the gravy smell of the dinners of others, the bird smell, the brandy, the pudding and mince, coiling up to my nostrils, when out of a snow-clogged side lane would come a boy the spit of myself, with a pink-tipped cigarette and the violet past of a black eye, cocky as a bullfinch, leering all to himself.

I hated him on sight and sound, and would be about to put my dog whistle to my lips and blow him off the face of Christmas when suddenly he, with a violet wink, put *his* whistle to *his* lips and blew so stridently, so high, so exquisitely loud, that gobbling faces, their cheeks bulged with goose, would press against their tinseled windows, the whole length of the white echoing street. For dinner we had turkey and blazing pudding, and after dinner the Uncles sat in front of the fire, loosened all buttons, put their large moist hands over their watch chains, groaned a little and slept. Mothers, aunts and sisters scuttled to and fro, bearing tureens. Auntie Bessie, who had already been frightened, twice, by a clock-work mouse, whimpered at the sideboard and had some elderberry wine. The dog was sick. Auntie Dosie had to have three aspirins, but Auntie Hannah, who liked port, stood in the middle of the snowbound back yard, singing like a big-bosomed thrush. I would blow up balloons to see how big they would blow up to; and, when they burst, which they all did, the Uncles jumped and rumbled. In the rich and heavy afternoon, the Uncles breathing like dolphins and the snow descending. I would sit among festoons and Chinese lanterns and nibble dates and try to make a model man-o'-war, following the Instructions for Little Engineers, and produce what might be mistaken for a sea-going tramcar.

Or I would go out, my bright new boots squeaking, into the white world, on to the seaward hill, to call on Jim and Dan and Jack and to pad through the still streets, leaving huge deep footprints on the hidden pavements.

"I bet people will think there's been hippos."

"What would you do if you saw a hippo coming down our street?"

"I'd go like this, bang! I'd throw him over the railings and roll him down the hill and then I'd tickle him under the ear and he'd wag his tail."

"What would you do if you saw *two* hippos?"

Iron-flanked and bellowing he-hippos clanked and battered through the scudding snow toward us as we passed Mr. Daniel's house.

"Let's post Mr. Daniel a snowball through his letter box."

"Let's write things in the snow."

"Let's write, 'Mr. Daniel looks like a spaniel' all over his lawn."

Or we walked on the white shore. "Can the fishes see it's snowing?"

The silent one-clouded heavens drifted on to the sea. Now we were snow-blind travelers lost on the north hills, and vast dewlapped dogs, with flasks round their necks, ambled and shambled up to us, baying "Excelsior." We returned home through the poor streets where only a few children fumbled with bare red fingers in the wheel-rutted snow and cat-called after us, their voices fading away, as we trudged uphill, into the cries of the dock birds and the hooting of ships out in the whirling bay. And then, at tea the recovered Uncles would be jolly; and the ice cake loomed in the center of the table like a marble grave. Auntie Hannah laced her tea with rum, because it was only once a year.

Bring out the tall tales now that we told by the fire as the gaslight bubbled like a diver. Ghosts whooed like owls in the long nights when I dared not to look over my shoulder; animals lurked in the cubby-hole under the stairs where the gas meter ticked. And I remember that we went singing carols once, when there wasn't the shaving of a moon to light the flying streets. At the end of a long road was a drive that led to a large house, and we stumbled up the darkness of the drive that night, each one of us afraid, each one holding a stone in his hand in case, and all of us too brave to say a word. The wind through the trees made noises as of old and unpleasant and maybe webfooted men wheezing in caves. We reached the black bulk of the house.

"What shall we give them? Hark the Herald?"

"No," Jack said, "Good King Wenceslas. I'll count three."

One, two, three, and we began to sing, our voices high and seemingly distant in the snow-felted darkness round the house that was occupied by nobody we knew. We stood close together, near the dark door.

Good King Wenceslas looked out On the Feast of Stephen . . .

And then a small, dry voice, like the voice of someone who has not spoken for a long time, joined our singing: a small, dry, eggshell voice from the other side of the door: a small dry voice through the keyhole. And when we stopped running we were outside *our* house; the front room was lovely; balloons floated under the hot-water-bottle-gulping gas; everything was good again and shone over the town.

"Perhaps it was a ghost," Jim said.

"Perhaps it was trolls," Dan said, who was always reading.

"Let's go in and see if there's any jelly left," Jack said. And we did that.

Always on Christmas night there was music. An uncle played the fiddle, a cousin sang "Cherry Ripe," and another uncle sang "Drake's Drum." It was very warm in the little house. Auntie Hannah, who had got on to the parsnip wine, sang a song about Bleeding Hearts and Death, and then another in which she said her heart was like a Bird's Nest; and then everybody laughed again; and then I went to bed. Looking through my bedroom window, out into the moonlight and the unending smoke-colored snow, I could see the lights in the windows of all the other houses on our hill and hear the music rising from them up the long, steadily falling night. I turned the gas down, I got into bed. I said some words to the close and holy darkness, and then I slept.

The First Christmas

Luke 2:1-17

And it came to pass in those days, that there went out a decree from Caesar Augustus that all the world should be taxed. . . . And all went to be taxed, every one to his own city. And Joseph also went up from Galilee from the city of Nazareth, into Judaea to the city of David, which is called Bethlehem (because he was of the house and lineage of David), to be taxed with Mary his espoused being great with child. And so it was, that, while they were there the days were accomplished that she delivered. And she brought forth her firstborn and wrapped him in swaddling clothes, and laid him in a manger; because there was no room for them in the inn.

And there were in the same country shepherds abiding in the field, keeping watch over their flock by night. And, lo, the angel of the Lord came upon them, and the glory of the Lord shone around about them, and they were sore afraid. And the angel said unto them, Fear not: for, behold, I bring you good tidings of great joy, which shall be to all people. For unto you is born this day in the city of David a Saviour, which is Christ the Lord. And this *shall* be a sign unto you; Ye shall find the babe wrapped in swaddling clothes, lying in a manger. And suddenly there was with the angel a multitude of the heavenly host praising God, and saying, Glory to God in the highest, and on earth peace, good will toward men.

And it came to pass, as the angels were gone aways from them into heaven, the shepherds said one to another, Let us now go even unto Bethlehem, and see this thing which is come to pass, which the Lord hath made known unto us. And they came with haste, and found Mary, and Joseph, and the babe lying in a manger. And when they had seen *it*, they made known abroad the saying which was told them concerning this child.

A Merry Christmas

by Louisa May Alcott, from Little Women

Jo was the first to wake in the gray dawn of Christmas morning. No stockings hung at the fireplace, and for a moment she felt as much disappointed as she did long ago, when her little sock fell down because it was so crammed with goodies. Then she remembered her mother's promise, and slipping her hand under her pillow, drew out a little crimson-covered book. She knew it very well, for it was that beautiful old story of the best life ever lived, and Jo felt that it was a true guide-book for any pilgrim going the long journey. She woke Meg with a "Merry Christmas," and bade her see what was under her pillow. A green-covered book appeared, with the same picture inside, and a few words written by their mother, which made their one present very precious in their eyes. Presently Beth and Amy woke, to rummage and find their little books also—one dove-colored, the other blue; and all sat looking at and talking about them, while the East grew rosy with the coming day.

In spite of her small vanities, Margaret had a sweet and pious nature, which unconsciously influenced her sisters, especially Jo, who loved her very tenderly, and obeyed her because her advice was so gently given.

"Girls," said Meg, seriously, looking from the tumbled head beside her to the two little night-capped ones in the room beyond, "mother wants us to read and love and mind these books, and we must begin at once.

We used to be faithful about it; but since father went away, and all this war trouble unsettled us, we have neglected many things. You can do as you please; but *I* shall keep my book on the table here, and read a little every morning as soon as I wake, for I know it will do me good, and help me through the day."

Then she opened her new book and began to read. Jo put her arm round her, and, leaning cheek to cheek, read also, with the quiet expression so seldom seen on her restless face.

"How good Meg is! Come, Amy, let's do as they do. I'll help you with the hard words, and they'll explain things if we don't under-stand," whispered Beth, very much impressed by the pretty books and her sister's example.

"I'm glad mine is blue," said Amy; and then the rooms were very still while the pages were softly turned, and the winter sunshine crept in to touch the bright heads and serious faces with a Christmas greeting.

"Where is mother?" asked Meg, as she and Jo ran down to thank her for their gifts, half an hour later.

"Goodness only knows. Some poor creeter come a-beggin', and your ma went straight off to see what was needed. There never *was* such a woman for givin' away vittles and drink, clothes, and firin'," replied Hannah, who had lived with the family since Meg was born, and was considered by them all more as a friend than a servant.

"She will be back soon, I guess; so do your cakes, and have everything ready," said Meg, looking over the presents which were collected in a basket and kept under the sofa, ready to be produced at the proper time. "Why, where is Amy's bottle of Cologne?" she added, as the little flask did not appear.

"She took it out a minute ago, and went off with it to put a ribbon on it, or some such notion," replied Jo, dancing about the room to take the first stiffness off the new army-slippers.

"How nice my handkerchiefs look, don't they? Hannah washed and ironed them for me, and I marked them all myself," said Beth, looking proudly at the somewhat uneven letters which had cost her such labor.

"Bless the child, she's gone and put 'Mother' on them instead of 'M. March;' how funny!" cried Jo, taking up one.

"Isn't it right? I thought it was better to do it so, because Meg's initials are 'M. M.,' and I don't want any one to use these but Marmee," said Beth, looking troubled.

"It's all right, dear, and a very pretty idea; quite sensible, too, for no one can ever mistake now. It will please her very much, I know," said Meg, with a frown for Jo, and a smile for Beth.

"There's mother; hide the basket, quick!" cried Jo, as a door slammed, and steps sounded in the hall.

Amy came in hastily, and looked rather abashed when she saw her sisters all waiting for her.

"Where have you been, and what are you hiding behind you?" asked Meg, surprised to see, by her hood and cloak, that lazy Amy had been out so early.

"Don't laugh at me, Jo, I didn't mean any one should know till the time came. I only meant to change the little bottle for a big one, and I gave *all* my money to get it, and I'm truly trying not to be selfish any more."

As she spoke, Amy showed the handsome flask which replaced the cheap one; and looked so earnest and humble in her little effort to forget herself, that Meg hugged her on the spot, and Jo pronounced her "a trump," while Beth ran to the window, and picked her finest rose to ornament the stately bottle.

"You see I felt ashamed of my present, after reading and talking about being good this morning, so I ran round the corner and changed it the minute I was up; and I'm *so* glad, for mine is the handsomest now."

Another bang of the street-door sent the basket under the sofa, and the girls to the table eager for breakfast.

"Merry Christmas, Marmee! Lots of them! Thank you for our books; we read some, and mean to every day," they cried, in chorus.

"Merry Christmas, little daughters! I'm glad you began at once, and hope you will keep on. But I want to say one word before we sit down. Not far away from here lies a poor woman with a little new-born baby. Six children are huddled into one bed to keep from freezing, for they have no fire. There is nothing to eat over there; and the oldest boy came to tell me they were suffering hunger and cold. My girls, will you give them your breakfast as a Christmas present?"

They were all unusually hungry, having waited nearly an hour, and for a minute no one spoke, only a minute, for Jo exclaimed impetuously, "I'm so glad you came before we began!"

"May I go and help carry the things to the poor little children?" asked Beth, eagerly.

"*I* shall take the cream and the muffins," added Amy, heroically giving up the articles she most liked.

Meg was already covering the buckwheats, and piling the bread into one big plate.

"I thought you'd do it," said Mrs. March, smiling as if satisfied. "You shall all go and help me, and when we come back we will have bread and milk for breakfast, and make it up at dinner-time."

They were soon ready, and the procession set out. Fortunately it was early, and they went through back streets, so few people saw them, and no one laughed at the funny party.

A poor, bare, miserable room it was, with broken windows, no fire, ragged bed-clothes, a sick mother, wailing baby, and a group of pale, hungry children cuddled under one old quilt, trying to keep warm. How the big eyes stared, and the blue lips smiled, as the girls went in!

"Ach, mein Gott! It is good angels come to us!" cried the poor woman, crying for joy.

"Funny angels in hoods and mittens," said Jo, and set them laughing.

In a few minutes it really did seem as if kind spirits had been at work there. Hannah, who had carried wood, made a fire, and stopped up the broken panes with old hats, and her own shawl. Mrs. March gave the mother tea and gruel, and comforted her with promises of help, while she dressed the little baby as tenderly as if it had been her own. The girls, meantime, spread the table, set the children round the fire, and fed them like so many hungry birds; laughing, talking, and trying to understand the funny broken English.

"Das ist gute!" "Der angel-kinder!" cried the poor things, as they ate, and warmed their purple hands at the comfortable blaze. The girls had never been called angel children before, and thought it very agreeable, especially Jo, who had been considered "a Sancho" ever since she was born. That was a very happy breakfast, though they didn't get any of it; and when they went away, leaving comfort behind, I think there were not in all the city four merrier people than the hungry little girls who gave away their breakfasts, and contented themselves with bread and milk on Christmas morning.

"That's loving our neighbor better than ourselves, and I like it," said Meg, as they set out their presents, while their mother was up stairs collecting clothes for the poor Hummels.

Not a very splendid show, but there was a great deal of love done up in the few little bundles; and the tall vase of roses, white chrysanthemums, and trailing vines, which stood in the middle, gave quite an elegant air to the table.

"She's coming! Strike up, Beth, open the door, Amy. Three cheers for Marmee!" cried Jo, prancing about, while Meg went to conduct mother to the seat of honor.

Beth played her gayest march, Amy threw open the door, and Meg enacted escort with great dignity. Mrs. March was both surprised and touched; and smiled with her eyes full as she examined her presents, and read the little notes which accompanied them. The slippers went on at once, a new handkerchief was slipped into her pocket, well scented with Amy's Cologne, the rose was fastened in her bosom, and the nice gloves were pronounced "a perfect fit."

There was a good deal of laughing, and kissing, and explaining, in the simple, loving fashion which makes these home-festivals so pleasant at the time, so sweet to remember long afterward.

Christmas Every Day

by William Dean Howells

Well, once there was a little girl who liked Christmas so much that she wanted it to be Christmas every day in the year; and as soon as Thanksgiving was over she began to send postal cards to the old Christmas Fairy to ask if she mightn't have it. In about three weeks—or just the day before Christmas, it was—she got a letter from the Fairy, saying she might have it Christmas every day for a year, and then they would see about having it longer.

The little girl was a good deal excited already, preparing for the old-fashioned, once-a-year Christmas that was coming the next day, and perhaps the Fairy's promise didn't make such an impression on her as it would have made at some other time. She just resolved to keep it to herself, and surprise everybody with it as it kept coming true: and then it slipped out of her mind altogether.

She had a splendid Christmas. She went to bed early, so as to let Santa Claus have a chance at the stockings, and in the morning she was up the first of anybody and went and felt them, and found hers all lumpy with packages of candy, and oranges and grapes, and pocketbooks and rubber balls and all kinds of small presents just as they always had every Christmas. Then she waited around till the rest of the family were up, and she was the first to burst into the library, when the doors were opened, and look at the large presents laid out on the library table—books, and dolls, and little stoves, and dozens of handkerchiefs, and ink stands, and skates, and snow shovels, and photograph frames, and little easels, and boxes of watercolors, and candied cherries, and doll's houses, and the big Christmas tree, lighted and standing in the middle.

She had a splendid Christmas all day. She ate so much candy that she did not want any breakfast; and the whole forenoon the presents kept pouring in and she went 'round giving the presents she had got for other people, and came home and ate turkey and cranberry for dinner, and plum-pudding and nuts and raisins and oranges and more candy, and then went and coasted and came in with a stomachache, crying; and they had a light supper, and pretty early everybody went to bed cross.

The little girl slept very heavily, and she slept very late, but she was wakened at last by the other children dancing 'round her bed with their stockings full of presents in their hands.

"What is it?" said the little girl, and she rubbed her eyes and tried to rise up in bed.

"Christmas! Christmas! Christmas!" they all shouted, and waved their stockings.

"Nonsense! It was Christmas yesterday."

Her brothers and sisters just laughed. "We don't know about that. It's Christmas today, any way. You come into the library and see."

Then all at once it flashed on the little girl that the Fairy was keeping her promise, and her year of Christmases was beginning. She was dreadfully sleepy, but she sprang up like a lark—a lark that had overeaten itself and gone to bed cross—and darted into the library. There it was again! The Christmas tree blazing away, and the family picking out their presents, but looking pretty sleepy, and her father perfectly puzzled, and her mother ready to cry.

"I'm sure I don't see how I'm to dispose of all these things," said her mother, and her father said it seemed to him they had had something just like it the day before, but he must have dreamed it. Well, the next day, it was just the same thing over again, but everybody getting crosser; and at the end of a week's time so many people had lost their tempers that they perfectly strewed the ground. Even when people tried to recover their tempers they usually got somebody else's, and it made the most dreadful mix.

The little girl began to get frightened, keeping the secret all to herself; she wanted to tell her mother, but she didn't dare to; and she was ashamed to ask the Fairy to take back her gift, it seemed ungrateful, and she thought she would try to stand it, but she hardly knew how she could, for a whole year. So it went on and on, and it was Christmas on St. Valentine's Day, and Washington's Birthday just the same as any day, and it didn't skip even the First of April, though everything was counterfeit that day, and that was some *little* relief.

After a while, turkeys got to be so scarce that they were about a thousand dollars apiece, and they got to passing off almost anything for turkey. And the cranberries— well, they asked a diamond apiece for cranberries. All the woods and orchards were cut down for Christmas trees and where the woods and orchards used to be, it looked just like a stubblefield, with the stumps. After a while they had to make Christmas trees out of rags, and stuff them with bran, like old-fashioned dolls; but there were plenty of rags, because people got so poor, buying presents for one another, that they couldn't get any new clothes, and they just wore their old ones to tatters. It was perfectly shameful.

Well, after it had gone on about three or four months, the little girl, whenever she came into the room in the morning and saw those great ugly lumpy stockings dangling at the fireplace, and the disgusting presents around everywhere, used to just sit down and burst out crying. In six months she was perfectly exhausted; she couldn't even cry any more, she just slammed her presents across the room.

By that time people didn't carry presents around nicely any more. They flung them over the fence, or through the window, or anything; and, instead of taking great pains to write "For dear Papa," or "Mamma," or "Brother," or "Sister," or "Susie," or "Sammie," or "Billie," or whoever it was, and troubling to get the spelling right, and then signing their names, and "Xmas, 188," they used to write in the gift books, "Take it, you horrid old thing!" and then go and bang it against the front door. Nearly everybody had built barns to hold their presents, but pretty soon the barns overflowed, and then they used to let them lie out in the rain, or anywhere. Sometimes the police used to come and tell them to shovel their presents off the sidewalk, or they would arrest them.

Well, before it came Thanksgiving, it had leaked out who had caused all these Christmases. The little girl had suffered so much that she had talked about it in her sleep; and after that, hardly anybody would play with her. People just perfectly despised her, because if it had not been for her greediness, it wouldn't have happened; and now, when it came Thanksgiving, and she wanted them to go to church, and have squash-pie and turkey, and show their gratitude, they said that all the turkeys had been eaten up for her old Christmas dinners, and if she would stop the Christmases, they would see about the gratitude. And the very next day the little girl began to send letters to the Christmas Fairy, and then telegrams, to stop it. But it didn't do any good; and then she got to calling at the Fairy's house, but the girl that came to the door always said "Not at home," or "Engaged," or "At dinner," or something like that; and so it went on till it came to the old once-a-year Christmas Eve. The little girl fell asleep, and when she woke up in the morning—it wasn't Christmas at last.

Well, there was the greatest rejoicing all over the country, and it extended clear up into

Canada. The people met together everywhere, and kissed and cried for joy. The city carts went around and gathered up all the candy and raisins and nuts, and dumped them into the river; and it made the fish perfectly sick; and the whole United States, as far out as Alaska, was one blaze of bonfires, where the children were burning their gift-books and presents of all kinds. They had the greatest time!

The little girl went to thank the old Fairy because she had stopped its being Christmas, and she said she hoped she would keep her promise, and see that Christmas never, never came again. Then the Fairy frowned, and asked her if she was sure she knew what she meant; and the little girl asked her, why not? And the old Fairy said that now she was behaving just a greedily as ever, and she'd better look out. This made the little girl think it all over carefully again, and she said she would be willing to have it Christmas about once in a thousand years; and then she said a hundred, and then she said ten, and at last she got down to one. Then the Fairy said that was the good old way that had pleased people ever since Christmas began, and she was agreed. Then the little girl said, "What're your shoes made of?" And the Fairy said, "Leather." And the little girl said, "Bargain's done forever," and skipped off, and hippity-hopped the whole way home.

The Little Blue Dishes

Retold by Elizabeth Amy Janke

Once upon a time, there was a poor woodcutter who lived with his wife and three children in a log cabin on the edge of town. The eldest boy in the family was named Nicholas, the middle brother was named Robert, and the youngest little sister, who was just five years old, was named Ilsa.

Soon it would be Christmas, so the children went into town to the toymaker's store to look at all the toys. There were dolls nestled in their dollhouses, spinning, colorful tops, toy soldiers lined in a row, and many other wonderful things.

"Ilsa," said Robert, "which toy is your favorite?"

"Oh, that little box of blue dishes," said Ilsa, "that is my favorite of them all!" She imagined how much fun it would be to have tea parties with these dishes, but she knew they were too much money for her family to buy them for her.

On Christmas Eve, the children hung up their stockings, even though they knew they were too poor to expect much this year. After supper, Nicholas went out to play with the other older children. Ilsa and Robert sat by the fire talking about the toys they had seen in town.

"I do so wish I had those little blue dishes," said Ilsa. Soon she became very sleepy and her father carried her off to bed.

As soon as Ilsa drifted off to sleep, Robert ran to his bank. He found only one penny inside, but still ran all the way to the toy store in town to buy his sister a gift.

"What can I buy for one penny?" he asked the toymaker.

"Only a little candy heart with a picture on it," replied the toymaker.

"But I want that set of blue dishes for my sister," said Robert.

"Those cost ten cents," said the man.

"Well, then I'll take the candy heart" said Robert. He hurried home with his package, put it in Ilsa's stocking, and went to bed.

Later that night, Nicholas came home. He was cold and hungry. As he sat by the fire, he noticed how bumpy the bottom of Ilsa's stocking looked. He reached inside the stocking, and pulled out the candy heart. Before he realized what he was doing, he ate the entire heart. "Oh my," he thought, "that was a gift for Ilsa. I must go and get her another present."

He ran to his bank and removed his savings of ten pennies. He raced to the toy store and found the toymaker ready to close his shop. "What can I buy for ten cents?"

"Well, I have very little left," said the man, "but there is still a little set of blue dishes for ten cents."

"I'll take them," said Nicholas. He hurried home and put the dishes in Ilsa's stocking.

Early Christmas morning, the children raced down the stairs to look in their stockings.

"Oh," cried Ilsa, "Look at my stocking!" She was so excited to see the blue dishes tucked inside her stocking.

Robert was amazed. He never understood how his little candy heart magically changed into the box of blue dishes.

Why the Chimes Rang

by Raymond MacDonald Alden

There was once, in a faraway country where few people have ever traveled, a wonderful church. It stood on a high hill in the midst of a great city; and every Sunday, as well as on sacred days like Christmas, thousands of people climbed the hill to its great archways, looking like lines of ants all moving in the same direction.

When you came to the building itself, you found stone columns and dark passages, and a grand entrance leading to a main room of the church. This room was so

264

long that one standing at the doorway could scarcely see to the other end, where the choir stood by the marble altar. In the farthest corner was the organ; and this organ was so loud that, sometimes when it played, the people for miles around would close their shutters and prepare for a great thunderstorm. Altogether, no such church as this was ever seen before, especially when it was lighted up for some festival, and crowded with people, you and old. But the strangest thing about the whole building was the wonderful chime of bells.

At one corner of the church was a great gray tower, with ivy growing over it as far up as one could see. I say as far as one could see, because the tower was quite great enough to fit the great church, and it rose so far into the sky that it was only in very fair weather that anyone claimed to be able to see the top.

Even then one could not be certain that it was in sight. Up, and up, and up climbed the stones and the ivy; and, as the men who built the church had been dead for hundreds of years, everyone had forgotten how high the tower was supposed to be.

Now all the people knew that at the top of the tower was a chime of Christmas bells. They had hung there ever since the church had been built, and were the most beautiful bells in the world. Some thought it was because a great musician had cast them and arranged them in their place; others said it was because of the great height, which reached up where the air was clearest and purest; however that might be, no one who had ever heard the chimes denied that they were the sweetest in the world. Some described them as sounding like angels far up in the sky; others, as sounding like strange winds singing throughout the trees.

But the fact was that no one had heard them for years and years. There was an old man living not far from the church, who said that his mother had spoken of hearing them when she was a little girl, and he was the only one who was sure of as much as that. They were Christmas chimes, you see, and were not meant to be played by men or on common days. It was the custom on Christmas Eve for all the people to bring to the church their offerings to the Christ child; and when the greatest and best offering was laid on the altar, there used to come sounding through the music of the choir the Christmas chimes far up in the tower. Some said that the wind rang them, and others that they were so high that the angels could set them swinging. But for many long years they had never been heard. It was said that people had been growing less careful of their gifts for the Christ child, and that no offering was brought, great enough to deserve the music of the chimes.

Every Christmas Eve the rich people still crowded to the altar, each one trying to bring some better gift than any other, without giving anything that he wanted for himself, and the church was crowded with those who thought that perhaps the wonderful bells might be heard again. But although the service was splendid, and the offerings plenty, only the roar of the wind could be heard, far up in the stone tower.

Now, a number of miles from the city, in a little country village, where nothing ould be seen of the great church but glimpses of the tower when the weather was fine, lived a boy named Pedro, and his little brother. They knew very little about the Christmas chimes, but they had heard of the service in the church on Christmas Eve, and had a secret plan, which they had often talked over when by themselves, to go to see the beautiful celebration.

"Nobody can guess, Little Brother," Pedro would say, "all the fine things there are to see and hear; and I have even heard it said that the Christ child sometimes comes down to bless the service. What if we could see Him?"

The day before Christmas was bitterly cold, with a few lonely snowflakes flying in the air, and a hard white crust on the ground. Sure enough, Pedro and Little Brother were able to slip quietly away early in the afternoon; and although the walking was hard in the frosty air, before nightfall they had trudged so far, hand in hand, that they saw the lights of the big city just ahead of them. Indeed, they were about to enter one of the great gates in the wall that surrounded it, when they saw something dark on the snow near their path, and stepped aside to look at it.

It was a poor woman, who had fallen just outside the city, too sick and tired to get in where she might have found shelter. The soft snow made of a drift a sort of pillow for her, and she would soon be so sound asleep, in the wintry air, that no one could ever waken her again.

All this Pedro saw in a moment, and he knelt down beside her and tried to rouse her, even tugging at her arm a little, as though he would have tried to carry her away. He turned her face toward him, so that he could rub some of the snow on it, and when he had looked at her silently a moment he stood up again, and said:

"It's no use, Little Brother. You will have to go on alone."

"Alone?" cried Little Brother. "And you not see the Christmas festival?"

"No," said Pedro, and he could not keep back a bit of a choking sound in his throat. "See this poor woman. Her face looks like the Madonna in the chapel window, and she will freeze to death if nobody cares for her. Everyone has gone to the church now, but when you come back you can bring someone to help her. I will rub her to keep her from freezing, and perhaps get her to eat the bun that is left in my pocket."

"But I cannot bear to leave you, and go on alone," said Little Brother.

"Both of us need not miss the service," said Pedro, "and it had better be I than you. You can easily find your way to the church; and you must see and hear everything twice, Little Brother—once for you and once for me. I am sure the Christ child must know how I should love to come with you and worship Him; and Oh if you get a chance, Little Brother, to slip up to the altar without getting in anyone's way, take this little silver piece of mine, and lay it down for my offering, when no one is looking. Do not forget where you have left me, and forgive me for not going with you."

In this way he hurried Little Brother off to the city, and winked hard to keep back the tears, as he heard the crunching footsteps sounding farther and farther away in the twilight. It was pretty hard to lose the music and splendor of the Christmas celebration that he had been planning for so long, and spend the time instead in that lonely place in the snow.

The great church was a wonderful place that night. Everyone said that it had never looked so bright and beautiful before. When the organ played and the thousands of people sang, the walls shook with the sound, and little Pedro, away outside the city wall, felt the earth tremble around him.

At the close of the service came the procession with the offerings to be laid on the altar. Rich men and great men marched proudly up to lay down their gifts to the Christ child. Some brought wonderful jewels, some baskets of gold so heavy that they could scarcely carry them down the aisle. A great writer laid down a book that he had been making for years and years. And last of all

walked the king of the country, hoping with all
the rest to win for himself the chime of the
Christmas bells. There went a great murmur
throughout the church, as the people saw the
king take from his head the royal crown, all set
with precious stones, and lay it gleaming on
the altar, as his offering to the Holy Child.
"Surely," everyone said, "we shall hear the
bells now, for nothing like this has ever
happened before."

But still only the cold old wind was heard
in the tower, and the people shook their heads;
and some of them said, as they had before,
that they never really believed the story of the
chimes, and doubted if they ever rang at all.

The procession was over, and the choir
began the closing hymn. Suddenly the organist
stopped playing as though he had been shot, and
everyone looked at the old minister, who was

standing by the altar, holding up his hand for silence. Not a sound could be heard from anyone in the church, but as all the people strained their ears to listen, there came softly, but distinctly, swinging through the air, the sound of the chimes in the tower. So far away, and yet so clear the music seemed—so much sweeter were the notes than anything that had been heard before, rising and falling away up there in the sky, that the people in the church sat for a moment as still as though something held each of them by the shoulders. Then they all stood up together and stared straight at the altar, to see what great gift had awakened the long-silent bells.

But all that the nearest of them saw was the childish figure of Little Brother, who had crept softly down the aisle when no one was looking, and had laid Pedro's little piece of silver on the altar.

Poems

Somehow, not only for Christmas,
But all the long year through,
The joy that you give to others,
Is the joy that comes back to you.

     —John Greenleaf Whittier

Christmas Greeting

Sing hey! Sing hey!
For Christmas Day;
Twine mistletoe and holly,
For friendship glows
In winter snows,
And so let's all be jolly.

—*Traditional*

Christmas Bells
by Henry Wadsworth Longfellow

I heard the bells on Christmas Day
Their old, familiar carols play,
And wild and sweet
The words repeat
Of peace on earth, good-will to men!

And thought how, as the day had come,
The belfries of all Christendom
Had rolled along
The unbroken song
Of peace on earth, good-will to men!

Till, ringing, singing on its way
The world revolved from night to day,
A voice, a chime,
A chant sublime
Of peace on earth, good-will to men!

Then from each black, accursed mouth
The cannon thundered in the South,
And with the sound
The Carols drowned
Of peace on earth, good-will to men!

And in despair I bowed my head;
'There is no peace on earth,' I said;
'For hate is strong,
And mocks the song
Of peace on earth, good-will to men!'

Then pealed the bells more loud and deep:
'God is not dead; nor doth he sleep!
The Wrong shall fail,
The Right prevail,
With peace on earth, good-will to men!'

A Hymn on the Nativity of My Savior

by Ben Jonson

I sing the birth was born tonight,
The Author both of life and light;
The angels so did sound it,
And like the ravished shepherds said,
Who saw the light, and were afraid,
Yet searched, and true they found it.

The Son of God, the eternal King,
That did us all salvation bring,
And freed the soul from danger;

He whom the whole world could not take,
The Word, which heaven and earth did make,
Was now laid in a manger.

The Father's wisdom willed it so,
The Son's obedience knew no "No,"
Both wills were in one stature;
And as that wisdom had decreed,
The Word was now made Flesh indeed,
And took on Him our nature.

What comfort by Him do we win?
Who made Himself the Prince of sin,
To make us heirs of glory?
To see this Babe, all innocence,
A Martyr born in our defense,
Can man forget this story?

A Bell
by Clinton Scollard

Had I the power
To cast a bell that should from some grand
   tower,
At the first Christmas hour,
Outring,
And fling
A jubilant message wide,
The forged metals should be thus allied:—
No iron Pride,
But soft Humility, and rich-veined Hope
Cleft from a sunny slope;
And there should be
White Charity,

And silvery Love, that knows not Doubt nor
  Fear,
To make the peal more clear;
And then to firmly fix the fine alloy,
There should be Joy!

A Child's Song of Christmas

by Marjorie L. C. Pickthall

My counterpane is soft as silk,
My blankets white as creamy milk.
The hay was soft to Him, I know,
Our little Lord of long ago.

Above the roofs the pigeons fly
In silver wheels across the sky.
The stable-doves they cooed to them,
Mary and Christ in Bethlehem.

Bright shines the sun across the drifts,
And bright upon my Christmas gifts.
They brought Him incense, myrrh, and gold,
Our little Lord who lived of old.

O, soft and clear our mother sings
Of Christmas joys and Christmas things.
God's holy angels sang to them,
Mary and Christ in Bethlehem.

Our hearts they hold all Christmas dear,
And earth seems sweet and heaven seems near,
O, heaven was in His sight, I know,
That little Child of long ago.

When Santa Claus Comes

A good time is coming, I wish it were here,
The very best time in the whole of the year;
I'm counting each day on my fingers and
    thumbs—
the weeks that must pass before Santa Claus
    comes.

Then when the first snowflakes begin to come
    down,
And the wind whistles sharp and the branches
    are brown,
I'll not mind the cold, though my fingers it numbs,
For it brings the time nearer when Santa Claus
    comes.

—*Author Unknown*

Santa Claus

He comes in the night! He comes in the night!
He softly, silently comes;
While the little brown heads on the pillows so
  white
Are dreaming of bugles and drums.
He cuts through the snow like a ship through
  the foam,
While the white flakes around him whirl;
Who tells him I know not, but he findeth the home
Of each good little boy and girl.

His sleigh it is long, and deep, and wide;
It will carry a host of things,
While dozens of drums hang over the side,
With the sticks sticking under the strings.

And yet not the sound of a drum is heard,
Not a bugle blast is blown,
As he mounts to the chimney-top like a bird,
And drops to the hearth like a stone.
The little red stockings he silently fills,
Till the stockings will hold no more;
The bright little sleds for the great snow hills
Are quickly set down on the floor.
Then Santa Claus mounts to the roof like a
   bird,
And glides to his seat in the sleigh;
Not a sound of a bugle or drum is heard
As he noiselessly gallops away.

He rides to the East, and he rides to the West,
Of his goodies he touches not one;
He eateth the crumbs of the Christmas feast
When the dear little folks are done.

Old Santa Claus doeth all that he can;
This beautiful mission is his;
Then, children be good to the little old man,
When you find who the little man is.

—*Author Unknown*

Christmas Song
by Eugene Field

Why do bells for Christmas ring?
Why do little children sing?

Once a lovely shining star,
Seen by shepherds from afar,
Gently moved until its light
Made a manger's cradle bright.

There a darling baby lay,
Pillowed soft upon the hay;
And its mother sang and smiled,
"This is Christ, the holy Child!"

Therefore bells for Christmas ring,
Therefore little children sing.

His Mother's Joy

by John White Chadwick

Little, I ween, did Mary guess,
As on her arm her baby lay,
What tides of joy would swell and beat,
Through ages long, on Christmas day.

And what if she had known it all,
The awful splendor of his fame?
The inmost heart of all her joy
Would still, methinks, have been the same:

The joy that every mother knows
Who feels her babe against her breast:
The voyage long is overpast,
And now is calm and peace and rest.

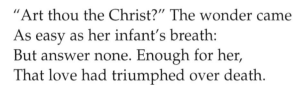

"Art thou the Christ?" The wonder came
As easy as her infant's breath:
But answer none. Enough for her,
That love had triumphed over death.

A Christmas Hymn

by John Charles McNeill

Near where the shepherds watched by night
And heard the angels o'er them,
The wise men saw the starry light
Stand still at last before them.
No armored castle there to ward
His precious life from danger,
But, wrapped in common cloth, our Lord
Lay in a lowly manger.
No booming bells proclaimed his birth,
No armies marshalled by,
No iron thunders shook the earth,
No rockets clomb the sky;
The temples builded in his name
Were shapeless granite then,
And all the choirs that sang his fame

Were later breeds of men.
But, while the world about him slept,
Nor cared that he was born,
One gentle face above him kept
Its mother watch till morn;
And, if his baby eyes could tell
What grace and glory were,
No roar of gun, no boom of bell
Were worth the look of her.
Now praise to God that ere his grace
Was scorned and he reviled
He looked into his mother's face,
A little helpless child;
And praise to God that ere men strove
About his tomb in war
One loved him with a mother's love,
Nor knew a creed therefor.

Long, Long Ago

Winds thro' the olive trees
Softly did blow,
Round little Bethlehem
Long, long ago.

Sheep on the hillside lay
Whiter than snow;
Shepherds were watching them,
Long, long ago.

Then from the happy sky,
Angels bent low,
Singin their songs of joy,
Long, long ago.

For in a manger bed,
Cradled we know,
Christ came to Bethlehem,
Long, long ago.

—*Author Unknown*

A Catch by the Hearth

Sing we all merrily
Christmas is here,
The day that we love best
Of the days in the year.

Bring forth the holly,
The box, and the bay,
Deck out our cottage
For glad Christmas-day.

Sing we all merrily
Draw around the fire,
Sister and brother,
Grandsire, and sire.

—*Traditional from England*

The Night Before Christmas
by Clement C. Moore

Introduction

In 1822, a New York clergyman named Clement Clark Moore spun together Christmas memories for his children. The poem he wrote featured a red-suited Santa in a reindeer-drawn sleigh, a never-empty sack of toys, and stockings hung expectantly above the fireplace. He called it "A Visit from St. Nicholas," and it was then published anonymously in a newspaper in Troy, New York. It captured the public's imagination. The poem's opening line—" 'Twas the night before Christmas"— soon replaced the original title.

One reason Moore's poem has endured is that it is a joy to read aloud. Beginning in hushed suspense, the poem builds to a dramatic crescendo as the rollicking verses usher in the mysterious midnight visitor.

A tale of anticipation and wonder, "The Night Before Christmas" has become a holiday tradition in itself for many families. So as you open these pages, whether for a first Christmas or to recall those past, celebrate and share the timeless joys of this enchanted holiday.

'Twas the night before Christmas,
when all through the house
Not a creature was stirring,
not even a mouse;

The stockings were hung
by the chimney with care,
In hopes that St. Nicholas
soon would be there.

The children were nestled
all snug in their beds,
While visions of sugarplums
danced in their heads;

And Momma in her kerchief
and I in my cap,
Had just settled down
for a long winter's nap—

When out on the lawn
there rose such a clatter,
I sprang from my bed
to see what was the matter.

Away to the window
I flew like a flash,
Tore open the shutters
and threw up the sash.

The moon on the breast
of the new-fallen snow,
Gave a luster of midday
to objects below;

When, what to my wondering eyes
should appear
But a miniature sleigh
and eight tiny reindeer,

With a little old driver
so lively and quick,
I knew in a moment
it must be St. Nick.

More rapid than eagles
his coursers they came,
And he whistled, and shouted,
and called them by name—

"Now, Dasher! Now, Dancer!
Now, Prancer and Vixen!
On, Comet! On, Cupid!
On, Donner and Blitzen!

To the top of the porch,
to the top of the wall!
Now, dash away! Dash away!
Dash away all!"

As dry leaves before
the wild hurricane fly,
When they meet with an obstacle,
mount to the sky,

So up to the housetop
the coursers they flew,
With sleigh full of toys—
and St. Nicholas too;

And then in a twinkling,
I heard on the roof
The prancing and pawing
of each little hoof.

As I drew in my head
and was turning around,
Down the chimney St. Nicholas
came with a bound.

He was dressed all in fur
from his head to his foot,
And his clothes were all tarnished
with ashes and soot.

A bundle of toys
he had flung on his back,
And he looked like a peddler
just opening his pack.

His eyes how they twinkled!
His dimples how merry!
His cheeks were like roses,
his nose like a cherry!

His droll little mouth
was drawn up like a bow,
And the beard on his chin
was as white as snow!

The stump of a pipe
he held in his teeth,
And the smoke it encircled
his head like a wreath.

He had a broad face
and a little round belly
That shook when he laughed
like a bowl full of jelly.

He was chubby and plump—
a right jolly old elf,
And I laughed when I saw him,
in spite of myself.

A wink of his eye
and a twist of his head,
Soon gave me to know
I had nothing to dread.

He spoke not a word,
but went straight to his work,
And filled all the stockings
then turned with a jerk,

And laying his finger
aside of his nose,
And giving a nod,
up the chimney he rose.

He sprang to his sleigh,
to his team gave a whistle
And away they all flew
like the down of a thistle.

But I heard him exclaim
as he drove out of sight,
"Merry Christmas to all
and to all a Good Night!"

Merry Christmas

M for the Music, merry and clear;
E for the Eve, the crown of the year;
R for the Romping of bright girls and boys;
R for the Reindeer that bring them the toys;
Y for the Yule-log softly aglow.

C for the Cold of the sky and the snow;
H for the Hearth where they hang up the hose;
R for the Reel which the old folks propose;
I for the Icicles seen through the pane;
S for the Sleigh bells, with tinkling refrain;
T for the Tree with gifts all abloom;
M for the Mistletoe hung in the room;
A for the Anthems we all love to hear;
S for **St. Nicholas**—joy of the year!

From *St. Nicholas* magazine

#

by *William Hamilton Hayne*

Out of the mighty Yule log came
The crooning of the lithe wood-flame,
A single bar of music fraught
With cheerful yet half pensive thought,
A thought elusive: out of reach,
Yet trembling on the verge of speech.

Bethlehem of Judea

A little child,
A shining star.
A stable rude,
The door ajar.

Yet in that place,
So crude, folorn,
The Hope of all
The world was born.

—*Author Unknown*

Christmas Carols

Christmas in Bethlehem. The ancient dream: a cold, clear night made brilliant by a glorious star, the smell of incense, shepherds and wise men falling to their knees in adoration of the sweet baby, the incarnation of perfect love.

—Lucinda Franks, "Pilgrimage," The New York Times, 23 December 1984

Introduction

The stamp of snowy shoes outside, a muffled giggle, silence, and then, a chorus of voices in the chill air, singing songs of the season. Caroling has a place at the heart of our holiday celebrations.

The tradition of caroling dates back five hundred years to the English "waits," groups of minstrels given the privilege of walking the town at Christmastime, singing at houses and receiving gifts from the townspeople. More recently, caroling was taken up by groups of boys, often unskilled in singing, but demanding a tip nonetheless! Caroling as we know it today began in Victorian times and continues little changed.

Through the years, songs other than carols have been sung at Christmastime. Some of the songs we call carols are hymns or popular songs that celebrate the holiday season. Others are traditional tunes sung with more contemporary lyrics.

The songs sung by carolers have changed as much as caroling itself, but the joy of singing together at Christmastime remains as great as ever!

A Christmas Carol,

Sung to the King in the
Presence at White-Hall
by Robert Herrick

[Chorus] What sweeter music can we
   bring,
Than a carol, for to sing
The birth of this our heavenly King?
Awake the voice! Awake the string!
Heart, ear, and eye, and everything.
Awake! the while the active finger
Runs division with the singer.

[Voice 1] Dark and dull night, fly hence
   away,
And give the honor to this day,
That sees December turned to May.

[2] If we may ask the reason, say
The why, and wherefore, all things here
Seem like the springtime of the year?

[3] Why does the chilling Winter's morn
Smile, like a field beset with corn?
Or smell, like to a mead new-short,
Thus on the sudden?

[4] Come and see
The cause, why things thus fragrant be:
'Tis He is born, whose quickening birth
Gives life and luster, public mirth,
To heaven, and the under-earth.

[Chorus] We see Him come, and know
    Him ours,
Who with His sunshine, and His showers,
Turns all the patient ground to flowers.

[1] The darling of the world is come,
And fit it is, we find a room
To welcome Him. [2] The nobler part
Of all the house here, is the heart,

[Chorus] which we will give Him and
  bequeath
This holly, and this ivy wreath,
To do Him honor; who's our King,
And Lord of all this reveling.

[The musical part was composed by Master Henry Lawes.]

The Friendly Beasts

Jesus, our brother, kind and good
Was humbly born in a stable rude.
And the friendly beasts around him stood,
Jesus, our brother, kind and good.

"I," said the donkey, shaggy and brown,
"I carried His mother uphill and down,
I carried her safely to Bethlehem town."
"I," said the donkey, shaggy and brown.

"I," said the cow, all white and red,
"I gave Him my manger for His bed,
I gave Him my hay to pillow His head."
"I," said the cow, all white and red.

320

"I," said the sheep with the curly horn,
"I gave Him my wool, for His blanket
     warm.
He wore my coat on Christmas morn."
"I," said the sheep with the curly horn.

"I," said the dove from the rafters high,
"Cooed Him to sleep, that He should not
     cry,
We cooed Him to sleep, my mate and I."
"I," said the dove from the rafters high.

So every beast by some good spell,
In the stable dark was glad to tell
Of the gift he gave Emmanuel.
The gift he gave Emmanuel.

—*An old English Christmas carol*

Angels We Have Heard on High

Angels we have heard on high,
Sweetly singing o'er the plains;
And the mountains, in reply,
Echoing their joyous strains:

Chorus:
Gloria in excelsis Deo,
Gloria in excelsis Deo!

Shepherds, why this jubilee?
Why your joyful strains prolong?
What the gladsome tidings be
That inspire your heav'nly song?

Come to Bethlehem and see
Him whose birth the angels sing.
Come adore on bended knee
Christ the Lord, our newborn King.

See Him in a manger laid,
Whom the choirs of angles praise.
Mary, Joseph, lend your aid
While our hearts in love we raise.

Repeat Chorus:
Gloria in excelsis Deo,
Gloria in excelsis Deo!

Away in a Manger

Away in a manger, no crib for his bed,
The little Lord Jesus laid down His sweet
head.
The stars in the heavens looked down
where He lay:
The little Lord Jesus, asleep in the hay.

The cattle are lowing, the baby awakes,
But little Lord Jesus, no crying He makes.
I love Thee, Lord Jesus! Look down from
the sky.
And stay by my cradle till morning is
nigh.

Be near me, Lord Jesus, I ask Thee to stay,
Close by me forever, and love me, I pray!
Bless all the dear children in Thy tender
    care
And take us to heaven, to live with Thee
    there.

Deck the Halls

Deck the halls with boughs of holly,
Fa la la la la, la la la la.
'Tis the season to be jolly,
Fa la la la la, la la la la.
Don we now our gay apparel,
Fa la la, la la la, la la la.
Troll the ancient Yuletide carol:
Fa la la la la, la la la la.

See the blazing Yule before us,
Fa la la la la, la la la la.
Strike the harp and join the chorus,
Fa la la la la, la la la la.
Follow me in merry measure,
Fa la la, la la la, la la la.

While I tell of Yuletide treasure,
Fa la la la la, la la la la.

Fast away the old year passes,
Fa la la la la, la la la la.
Hail the new, ye lads and lasses,
Fa la la la la, la la la la.
Sing we joyous, all together,
Fa la la, la la la, la la la.
Heedless of the wind and weather,
Fa la la la la, la la la la.

The First Noel

The First Noel, the angels did say
Was to certain poor shepherds in fields
   where they lay,
In fields where they lay, keeping their sheep,
On a cold winter's night that was so deep.

Chorus:
Noel, Noel, Noel, Noel,
Born is the King of Israel!

They looked up and saw a star,
Shining in the East, but beyond them far.
And unto the Earth it gave a great light,
And so it continued, both day and night.

And by the light of that same star

Three Wise Men came from country far.
To seek for a King was the intent,
And to follow the star wherever it went.

This star drew nigh to the northwest,
Over Bethlehem it took its rest,
And there it did both stop and stay
Right over the stable where Jesus lay.

Then they did know and in wonder
      confide
That within that house a King did reside.
One entered in then, with his own eyes to
      see
And discovered the Babe in poverty.

Between the stalls of the oxen, forlorn,
This Child on that cold night in truth was
      born.

And for want of a crib, Mary did Him lay
In the depths of a manger amongst the
   hay.

Then entered in all those Wise Men three,
Fell reverently upon bended knee,
And offered there, in His presence,
Gifts of gold and of myrrh and of
   frankincense.

Repeat Chorus:
Noel, Noel, Noel, Noel,
Born is the King of Israel!

God Rest Ye Merry, Gentlemen

God rest ye merry, gentlemen;
Let nothing you dismay.
Remember, Christ our Savior
Was born on Christmas Day,
To save us all from Satan's pow'r
When we had gone astray.

Chorus:
Oh, tidings of comfort and joy,
Comfort and joy,
Oh, tidings of comfort and joy!

'Twas in the town of Bethlehem
This blessed Babe was born.

They laid Him in a manger
Where oxen feed on corn,
And Mary knelt and prayed to God
Upon the blessed morn.

From God our Heav'nly Father
A host of angels came
Unto some certain shepherds
With tidings of the same:
That there was born in Bethlehem
The Son of God by name.

"Fear not," then said the angels,
"Let nothing you affright.
This day is born a Savior
Of virtue, pow'r, and might,
To ransom you from Sin and Death
And vanquish Satan quite."

The shepherds, at these tidings,
Rejoiced much in mind,
And on that windy plain they left
Their sleeping flocks behind,
And straight they went to Bethlehem,
Their newborn King to find.

Now when they came to Bethlehem,
Where our sweet Savior lay,
They found Him in a manger,
Where oxen fed on hay.
His blessed Mother, kneeling down,
Unto the Lord did pray.

With sudden joy and gladness
The shepherds were beguiled,
To see the King of Israel
And Holy Mary mild.

With them, in cheerfulness and love
Rejoice each mother's child!

Now to the Lord sing praises,
All you within this place,
And in true loving brotherhood
Each other now embrace,
For Christmas doth in all inspire
A glad and cheerful face.

Repeat Chorus:
Oh, tidings of comfort and joy,
Comfort and joy,
Oh, tidings of comfort and joy!

Good King Wenceslas looked out
On the Feast of Stephen,
When the snow lay 'round about,
Deep and crisp and even.
Brightly shone the moon that night,
Though the frost was cruel,
When a poor man came in sight,
Gath'ring winter fuel.

"Hither, page, and stand by me!
If thou has heard telling,
Yonder peasant, who is he?
Where and what his dwelling?"
"Sire, he lives a good league hence,

Underneath the mountain,
Right against the forest fence
By Saint Agnes' fountain."

"Bring me flesh and bring me wine!
Bring me pine-logs hither!
Thou and I will see him dine
When we bear them thither."
Page and monarch, forth they went;
Forth they went together,
Through the rude wind's wild lament
And the bitter weather.

"Sire, the night grows darker now,
And the wind blows stronger.
Fails my heart, I know not how
I can go much longer!'
"Mark my footsteps, my good page.
Tread thou in them boldly.

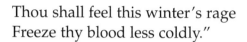

Thou shall feel this winter's rage
Freeze thy blood less coldly."

In his master's steps he trod,
Where the snow lay dinted.
Heat was in the very sod
Which the Saint had printed.
Therefore, Christian men, be sure,
Wealth or rank possessing,
Ye who now will bless the poor
Shall yourselves find blessing.

Hark! The Herald Angels Sing

Hark! The herald angels sing,
"Glory to the newborn King!
Peace on Earth and mercy mild,
God and sinners reconciled."
Joyful all ye nations, rise!
Join the triumphs of the skies.
With th'angelic host proclaim,
"Christ is born in Bethlehem!"

Chorus:
Hark! The herald angels sing,
"Glory to the newborn King!"

Christ, by highest Heav'n adored,
Christ, the everlasting Lord,
Late in time, behold Him come,
Offspring of the Virgin's womb.
Veiled in flesh the Godhead see.
Hail in th'Incarnate Deity
Pleased as Man with men to dwell—
Jesus, our Emmanuel!

Mild He lays His glory by,
Born that man no more may die,
Born to raise the sons of Earth,
Born to give them second birth.
Light and life to all He brings,
Ris'n with healing in His wings.
Hail, the Son of Righteousness!
Hail, the Heav'n-born Prince of Peace!

Repeat Chorus:
Hark! The herald angels sing,
"Glory to the newborn King!"

The Holly and the Ivy

The holly and the ivy
Now both are well grown,
Of all the trees that are in the wood
The holly bears the crown.

Chorus:
The rising of the sun,
The running of the deer,
The playing of the merry organ,
The singing in the choir.

The holly bears a blossom
As white as the lily flower,
And Mary bore sweet Jesus Christ
To be our sweet Savior.

The holly bears a berry
As red as any blood,
And Mary bore sweet Jesus Christ
To do poor sinners good.

The holly bears a prickle
As sharp as any thorn,
And Mary bore sweet Jesus Christ
On Christmas Day in the morn.

The holly bears a bark
As bitter as any gall,
And Mary bore sweet Jesus Christ
For to redeem us all.

The holly and the ivy
Now are both well grown,
Of all the trees that are in the wood
The holly bears the crown.

Repeat Chorus:
The rising of the sun,
The running of the deer,
The playing of the merry organ,
The singing in the choir.

It Came Upon a Midnight Clear

It came upon a midnight clear,
That glorious song of old,
From angels bending near the Earth
To touch their harps of gold:
"Peace on the earth!
Good will to men,
From Heaven's all-gracious King!"
The world in solemn stillness lay
To hear the angels sing.

Still through the cloven skies they come,
With seraphs' wings unfurled;
And still their heavenly music floats

O'er all the weary world.
Above its sad and lowly plains
They bend on hovering wing.
And ever o'er its Babel sounds
The blessed angels sing.

Yet with the woes of sin and strife,
The world has suffered long.
Beneath the angels' strains have rolled
Two thousand years of wrong;
And man, at war with man, hears not
The love-song which they bring.
Oh, hush the noise, ye men of strife,
And hear the angels sing!

And ye, beneath life's crushing load,
Whose shoulders are bending low,
Who toil along the climbing way
With painful steps, and slow,

Take heart! For comfort, hope, and joy
Come swiftly on the wing.
Oh, rest beside the weary road
And hear the angels sing!

For lo! The days are hast'ning on,
As prophets knew of old,
And with the ever-circling years
Comes 'round the time foretold,
When love shall reign, and men declare
The Prince of Peace their King;
And all the Earth send back the song
Which now the angels sing.

Jingle Bells

Dashing through the snow
In a one-horse open sleigh,
O'er the fields we go,
Laughing all the way.
Bells on bobtail ring,
Making spirits bright.
What fun it is to laugh and sing
A sleighing song tonight!

Chorus:
Jingle bells! Jingle bells!
Jingle all the way!
Oh, what fun it is to ride
In a one-horse open sleigh!

Jingle bells! Jingle bells!
Jingle all the way!
Oh, what fun it is to ride
In a one-horse open sleigh, hey!

A day or two ago, I though I'd take a ride,
And soon Miss Fannie Bright
Was seated by my side.
The horse was lean and lank,
But hardly worth his hay.
He veered into a drifted bank
And overturned the sleigh!

Now the ground is white.
Go for it while you're young.
Take the girls tonight
And sing this sleighing song.
Just rent a bobtail'd bay,
Two-forty for his speed.

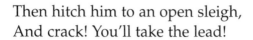

Then hitch him to an open sleigh,
And crack! You'll take the lead!

You won't mind the cold,
The robe is thick and warm.
Snow falls on the road,
Silv'ring every form,
The woods are dark and still.
The horse is trotting fast.
He'll pull the sleigh around the hill
And home again at last.

Repeat Chorus:
Jingle bells! Jingle bells!
Jingle all the way!
Oh, what fun it is to ride
In a one-horse open sleigh!

Jolly Old Saint Nicholas

Jolly old Saint Nicholas,
Lean your ear this way.
Don't you tell a single soul
What I'm going to say.
Christmas Eve is coming soon!
Now, you dear old man,
Whisper what you'll bring to me.
Tell me, if you can.

When the clock is striking twelve,
When I'm fast asleep,
Down the chimney broad and black
With your pack you'll creep.
All the stockings you will find,

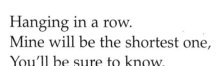

Hanging in a row.
Mine will be the shortest one,
You'll be sure to know.

Johnny wants a pair of skates,
Mary wants a sled.
Susie wants a picture book,
One she's never read.
Now I think I'll leave to you
What to give the rest.
Choose for me, dear Santa Claus,
You will know the best.

Joy to the World

Joy to the world!
The Lord is come.
Let Earth receive her King.
Let ev'ry heart prepare Him room,
And Heav'n and Nature sing,
And Heav'n and Nature sing,
And Heav'n, and Heav'n and Nature sing.

Joy to the world!
The Savior reigns;
Let men their songs employ,
While fields and floods, rock, hills, and
    plains,
Repeat the sounding joy,
Repeat the sounding joy,
Repeat, repeat the sounding joy.

No more let sins
And sorrows grow,
Nor thorns infest the ground;
He comes to make His blessings flow
Far as the curse is found,
Far as the curse is found,
Far as, far as the curse is found.

He rules the world with Truth and Grace,
And makes the nations prove
The glories of His righteousness,
And wonders of His love,
And wonders of His love,
And wonders, and wonders of His love.

Oh Christmas Tree

Oh Christmas Tree,
Oh Christmas Tree,
With lush green boughs unchanging—
Green when the summer is bright,
And when the forest's cold and white.
Oh Christmas Tree,
Oh Christmas Tree,
With lush green boughs unchanging.

Oh Christmas Tree,
Oh Christmas Tree,
Here once again to awe us,
You bear round fruits of Christmas past,
Spun out of silver, gold, and glass.

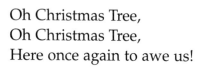

Oh Christmas Tree,
Oh Christmas Tree,
Here once again to awe us!

Oh Christmas Tree,
Oh Christmas Tree,
We gladly bid you welcome.
A pyramid of light you seem,
A galaxy of stars that gleam.
Oh Christmas Tree,
Oh Christmas Tree,
We gladly bid you welcome.

Oh Christmas Tree,
Oh Christmas Tree,
You fill the air with fragrance.
You shrink to very tiny size,

Reflected in the children's eyes.
Oh Christmas Tree,
Oh Christmas Tree,
You fill the air with fragrance.

Oh Christmas Tree,
Oh Christmas Tree,
What presents do you shelter?
Rich wrappings hide the gifts from sight,
Done up in bows and ribbons tight.
Oh Christmas Tree,
Oh Christmas Tree,
What presents do you shelter?

Oh Christmas Tree,
Oh Christmas Tree,
Your green limbs teach a lesson:

That constancy and faithful cheer
Are gifts to cherish all the year.
Oh Christmas Tree,
Oh Christmas Tree,
Your green limbs teach a lesson.

Oh Come, All Ye Faithful

Oh come, all ye faithful,
Joyful and triumphant,
Oh come ye, oh come ye to Bethlehem.
Come and behold Him,
Born the King of Angels.

Chorus:
Oh come, let us adore Him,
Oh come, let us adore Him,
Oh come, let us adore Him,
Christ the Lord!

Sing choirs of angels,
Sing in exultation.
Oh Sing, all ye citizens of Heav'n above:

"Glory to God,
Glory in the highest."

Oh True God of True God,
Light of Light eternal
Lo! He abhors not the Virgin's womb.
Son of the Father,
Begotten not created.

See how the shepherds,
Summoned to his cradle,
Leaving their flocks, draw nigh to gaze;
We too will thither
Bend our joyful footsteps.

Yea, Lord, we greet Thee,
Born this happy morning.
Jesus, to Thee all glory be giv'n,

Word of the Father,
Now in flesh appearing.

Repeat Chorus:
Oh come, let us adore Him,
Oh come, let us adore Him,
Oh come, let us adore Him,
Christ the Lord!

Oh Little Town of Bethlehem

Oh little town of Bethlehem, how still we
　see thee lie!
Above thy deep and dreamless sleep the
　silent stars go by.
Yet in thy dark streets shineth the
　everlasting light:
The hopes and fears of all the years are
　met in thee tonight.

For Christ is born of Mary, and gathered
　all above,
While mortals sleep, the angels keep their
　watch of wond'ring love.
Oh, morning stars together, proclaim the
　holy birth,

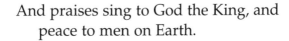
And praises sing to God the King, and
peace to men on Earth.

How silently, how silently the wondrous
gift is given!
So God imparts to human hearts the
blessings of His heaven.
No ear may hear His coming; but in this
world of sin,
Where meek souls will receive Him still,
the dear Christ enters in.

O holy Child of Bethlehem, descend to us,
we pray;
Cast out our sin and enter in—be born in
us today.
We hear the Christmas angels the great
glad tidings tell—

Oh, come to us, abide with us, Our Lord
Immanuel!

Silent Night

Silent night, holy night!
All is calm, all is bright
'Round yon Virgin Mother and Child—
Holy infant, so tender and mild.
Sleep in heavenly peace,
Sleep in heavenly peace.

Silent night, holy night!
Shepherds quake at the sight.
Glories stream from Heaven afar,
Heav'nly hosts sing, "Alleluia,
Christ the Savior is born,
Christ the Savior is born!"

Silent night, holy night!
Son of God, love's pure light,
Radiance beams from Thy holy face,
With the dawn of redeeming grace.
Jesus, Lord at Thy birth,
Jesus, Lord at Thy birth!

The Twelve Days of Christmas

On the first day of Christmas,
My true love gave to me
A partridge in a pear tree.

On the second day of Christmas,
My true love gave to me
Two turtle doves,
And a partridge in a pear tree.

On the third day of Christmas,
My true love gave to me
Three French hens,
Two turtle doves,
And a partridge in a pear tree.

On the fourth day of Christmas,
My true love gave to me
Four calling birds . . .

On the fifth day of Christmas,
My true love gave to me
Five golden rings . . .

On the sixth day of Christmas,
My true love gave to me
Six geese a-laying . . .

On the seventh day of Christmas,
My true love gave to me
Seven swans a-swimming . . .

On the eighth day of Christmas,
My true love gave to me
Eight maids a-milking . . .

On the ninth day of Christmas,
My true love gave to me
Nine ladies dancing . . .

On the tenth day of Christmas,
My true love gave to me
Ten lords a-leaping . . .

On the eleventh day of Christmas,
My true love gave to me
Eleven pipers piping . . .

On the twelfth day of Christmas,
My true love gave to me
Twelve drummers drumming,
Eleven pipers piping,
Ten lords a-leaping,
Nine ladies dancing,

Eight maids a-milking,
Seven swans a-swimming,
Six geese a-laying,
Five golden rings,
Four calling birds,
Three French hens,
Two turtle doves,
And a partridge in a pear tree.

Up on the Rooftop

Up on the rooftop, reindeer pause,
Out jumps good old Santa Claus!
Down through the chimney, with lots of
  toys—
All for the little ones' Christmas joys.

Chorus:
Ho, ho, ho! Who wouldn't go?
Ho, ho, ho! Who wouldn't go
Up on the rooftop—
Click, click, click!—
Down through the chimney
With good St. Nick.

First comes the stocking of little Nell.
Oh, dear Santa, fill it well!

Give her a dolly that laughs and cries,
One that can open and shut her eyes.

Next hangs the stocking of brother Will.
It won't take very much to fill—
Give him a hammer and lots of tacks,
Plus a red ball and a whip that cracks.

Reindeer are restless beside your sleigh,
Eager to leave and be on their way.
But on the mantel, I've left for you
Apples, an orange, and warm milk too.

Last is a stocking that's deep and strong—
I've been a good boy all year long!
Please, if you have them, and if they'll fit,
Give me a bat and catcher's mitt.

Repeat Chorus:
Ho, ho, ho! Who wouldn't go?
Ho, ho, ho! Who wouldn't go
Up on the rooftop—
Click, click, click!—
Down through the chimney
With good St. Nick.

We Three Kings of Orient Are

All:
We three kings of Orient are
Bearing gifts, we traverse afar—
Field and fountain,
Moor and mountain—
Following yonder star.

Chorus:
Oh, star of wonder, star of night,
Star of royal beauty bright,
Westward leading, still proceeding,
Guide us to thy perfect light.

King Melchior:
Born a king on Bethlehem's plain—
Gold I bring, to crown Him again—
King for ever, ceasing never,
Over us all to reign.

Chorus:
Oh, star of wonder, star of night,
Star of royal beauty bright,
Westward leading, still proceeding,
Guide us to thy perfect light.

King Caspar:
Frankincense to offer have I.
Incense owns a Deity nigh.
Prayer and praising, all men raising,
Worship Him, God most high!

Chorus:
Oh, star of wonder, star of night,
Star of royal beauty bright,
Westward leading, still proceeding,
Guide us to thy perfect light.

King Balthazar:
Myrrh is mine: its bitter perfume
Breathes a life of gathering gloom,
Sorrowing, sighing, bleeding, dying,
Sealed in the stone-cold tomb.

Chorus:
Oh, star of wonder, star of night,
Star of royal beauty bright,
Westward leading, still proceeding,
Guide us to thy perfect light.

All:
Glorious now, behold Him arise:
King and God and sacrifice!
Heav'n sings, "Ha-le-lu-ia!"
"Ha-ah-le-lu-ia!" the Earth replies.

We Wish You a Merry Christmas

We wish you a Merry Christmas,
We wish you a Merry Christmas,
We wish you a Merry Christmas
And a Happy New Year!

Chorus:
Glad tidings we bring
To you and your kin.
We wish you a merry Christmas,
And a Happy New Year.

Oh, bring us some figgy pudding,
Oh, bring us some figgy pudding,

377

Oh, bring us some figgy pudding
And a glass of good cheer!

We won't go until we get some,
We won't go until we get some,
We won't go until we get some
So bring it right here!

We'll sing you some happy carols,
We'll sing you some happy carols,
We'll sing you some happy carols
To ravish your ear!

We have quite the finest voices,
We have quite the finest voices,
We have quite the finest voices
That you'll ever hear!

We wish you a Merry Christmas,
We wish you a Merry Christmas,
We wish you a Merry Christmas
And a Happy New Year!

Repeat Chorus:
Glad tidings we bring
To you and your kin.
We wish you a merry Christmas,
And a Happy New Year.

What Child Is This?

What Child is this who, laid to rest,
On Mary's lap is sleeping;
Whom angels greet with anthems sweet,
While shepherds watch are keeping?

Chorus:
This, this is Christ the King,
Whom shepherds guard and angels sing.
Haste, haste to bring Him laud,
The Babe, the Son of Mary.

Why lies He in such mean estate,
Where ox and ass are feeding?

Good Christian, fear for sinners here,
The silent Word is pleading.

So bring Him incense, gold, and myrrh.
Come, peasants, kings, to own Him
The King of Kings salvation brings—
Let loving hearts enthrone Him!

The old year now away is fled,
The New Year now is entered.
Then let us now our sins downtread,
And joyfully all appear.

New Chorus:
Merry be the holiday,
And let us run with sport and play.
Hang sorrow, cast care away.
God send you a Happy New Year!

And now, best wishes all good friends
Unto each other they do send.
Oh, grant we may our lives amend,
And have no one's blame to fear.

Repeat New Chorus:
Merry be the holiday,
And let us run with sport and play.
Hang sorrow, cast care away.
God send you a Happy New Year!

The Star-Song, A Carol to the King

by Robert Herrick

Sung at White-Hall
[King 1] Tell us, thou clear and heavenly
    tongue,
Where is the Babe but lately sprung?
Lies He the lily-banks among?

[King 2] Or say, if this new birth of ours
Sleeps, laid within some ark of flowers,
Spangled with dew-light; thou canst clear
All doubts, and manifest the where.

[King 3] Declare to us, bright star, if we
    shall seek
Him in the morning's blushing cheek,
Or search the beds of spices through,
To find Him out?

[Star] No, this ye need not do;
But only come, and see Him rest
A princely Babe in's mother's breast.

[Chorus] He's seen, He's seen, why then a
    round,
Let's kiss the sweet and holy ground;
And all rejoice, that we have found
A King, before conception crowned.

[3 Kings] Come then come then, and let us
    bring
unto our pretty Twelfth-tide King,
Each one his several offering;

[Chorus] And when night comes, we'll
    give Him wassailing;
And that His treble honors may be seen,
We'll choose Him King, and make His
    mother Queen.

Recipes

'Twas Christmas broached the mightiest ale;
'Twas Christmas told the merriest tale;
A Christmas gambol oft could cheer
The poor man's heart through half the year.
——Sir Walter Scott

Cooking with Kids

Introduction

Christmas is for the child in all of us. For children, it builds memories that last a lifetime. It is synonymous with joy itself. A large part of our childhood memories of Christmas is the wonderful food served, gobbled up all day until we can hardly walk. For children to have a part in this food preparation allows another dimension of giving than the gifts under the tree, another way of amplifying the Christmas joy, and what a source of pride and accomplishment when everyone at the table oohs and ahs. Following the Memory are some recipes that you and your kids can make together during the holiday season, and some even all year round!

Memory

I remember putting phone books on a chair so I could sit at the "grown-up" table and help my mom decorate Christmas cookies. Santa Claus, wreaths, candy canes, reindeer, stars, trees, angels—you name a shape associated with Christmas and chances are we had a cookie cutter for it! We'd blast holiday music, sing along (usually off key but it never mattered), my dad would dip his finger in the icing, prompting raised eyebrows from my mother...and fits of giggles from my sister and me. When my mom wasn't looking, we would do the same! This is something that I loved as a child but now that I am adult, I love it even more.

Thank you to the Powers Family for several years of smiles . . . here's to many more!

Chocolate Mint Brownies
Makes 48 brownies

1 (22.5-ounce) box reduced-fat or regular
    brownie mix
¾ teaspoon peppermint extract, divided
3 tablespoons reduced-fat cream cheese
3 tablespoons margarine, melted, divided
2 cups confectioners' sugar
Few drops green food coloring
1 tablespoon cocoa
1 tablespoon water

1. Preheat the oven to 350°F. Coat a 13 x 9 x
   2-inch baking pan with nonstick cooking
   spray.
2. Prepare the brownie mix according to
   package directions, adding ¼ teaspoon of
   the peppermint extract. Pour the batter into

the prepared pan. Bake according to the package directions. Do not overbake. Remove from the oven, and cool completely to room temperature.

3. In a mixing bowl, beat together the cream cheese, 1 tablespoon margarine, the confectioners' sugar, and ½ teaspoon peppermint extract until smooth. Add a few drops of the green food coloring, mixing. Spread on the baked brownie layer.

4. In a small bowl, mix together the remaining 2 tablespoons margarine, cocoa, and water. Spread carefully over the cream cheese layer, and cool. Cut into squares.

(Tip: If you're in a hurry to cool the brownie layer, place it in the refrigerator to cool it quickly. Make sure that you don't place the hot pan next to something that will be affected by its heat.)

Chocolate Nachos

Makes 2 servings

¼ cup sugar
2 teaspoons ground cinnamon
2 large flour tortillas
2 tablespoons butter (¼ stick)
Chocolate syrup, room temperature
Whipped cream

1. Preheat the oven to 400°F.
2. In a medium bowl, combine the sugar and cinnamon.
3. Use a pair of kitchen scissors to cut the tortillas into thick strips or triangles. Place the tortilla strips on a baking sheet.
4. Place the butter in a microwave-safe glass bowl, and microwave about 20 seconds on high, until melted.

5. Use a pastry brush to brush the tortilla strips entirely with melted butter. You might not use all of the butter—just enough to thoroughly coat each strip.
6. Sprinkle the strips with cinnamon-sugar (you might not use all of it).
7. Bake for 5 to 10 minutes, or until the strips are crispy. Remove the baking sheet from the oven.
8. Using a spatula, move the strips from the baking sheet to serving plates.
9. Pour chocolate syrup over tortilla strips. Top with whipped cream.

Cinnamon Rolls
Makes 10 rolls

> 1 (10-biscuit) can refrigerated biscuits
> 4 tablespoons margarine, softened
> 2 tablespoons sugar

1 teaspoon ground cinnamon
¼ cup raisins, optional
¼ cup chopped pecans, optional

1. Preheat the oven to 425°F.
2. Flatten each biscuit with your hand or a rolling pin, and spread with margarine.
3. In a small bowl, combine the sugar and cinnamon. Sprinkle the cinnamon mixture on top of the margarine. Sprinkle with the raisins and pecans, if desired.
4. Roll up each biscuit from one side to the other.
5. On an ungreased 15 x 10 x 1-inch baking sheet, arrange each biscuit roll to form an individual circle, touching one end of the roll to the other.
6. Bake for 8 to 10 minutes or until lightly browned. Serve hot.

Double Chocolate Candy Pizza
Makes 12 to 16 slices

½ cup margarine
1 cup sugar
1 egg
1 teaspoon vanilla extract
1½ cups all-purpose flour
¼ cup cocoa
½ teaspoon baking soda
1 cup candy-coated milk chocolate
   candies, divided
¼ cup flaked coconut
1½ cups miniature marshmallows
½ cup chopped pecans, optional

1. Preheat the oven to 350°F. Coat a 12- to 14-inch pizza pan with nonstick cooking spray.

2. In a large mixing bowl, beat together the margarine and sugar until fluffy. Add the egg and vanilla, blending well.

3. In a small bowl, combine the flour, cocoa, and baking soda. Gradually add the sugar mixture, blending until well mixed.

4. Spread the dough on the prepared pan, to within 1 inch of the edge of the pan. Sprinkle the dough with the candies, coconut, marshmallows, and pecans.

5. Bake 18 to 20 minutes, or until the edges are set. Don't overbake. Cool, and cut into slices.

French Toast Kabobs with Fresh Fruit

Makes 4 to 6 servings

4 eggs
1½ cups milk

1 tablespoon vanilla

Zest of 1 orange, lemon, or lime

1 loaf unsliced quality white bread (a little stale is okay)

1 or 2 tablespoons butter or oil

½ pint strawberries, rinsed and drained, stemmed, halved

½ pint blueberries, rinsed and drained

Maple syrup (for serving)

Powdered sugar (for serving)

1. Preheat the oven to 350°F.
2. In a medium bowl, with a whisk, combine eggs and milk. Add vanilla and zest. Set the mixture aside.
3. Use a bread knife to cut the bread into 2-inch cubes.
4. Use a paper towel to spread butter or oil on a sheet pan.

5. Place one handful of cubed bread in milk-egg mixture. Working fairly quickly, skewer 1 cube of bread, followed by ½ a strawberry, followed by 1 bread cube, then 1 blueberry, 1 bread cube, ½ a strawberry, 1 bread cube, 1 blueberry, 1 bread cube, etc., until only 1 inch remains at the pointed end of the skewer.

6. Place full skewer on the buttered pan and repeat step 5 until all bread cubes are gone.

7. Make sure that the fruit does not touch the pan—only the bread should touch the tray. The fruit will cook from the heat of the oven, but if it is allowed to touch the tray, the juices from the fruit will seep out and make the bread soggy.

8. Place in the oven and bake until the bread is golden brown, about 20 to 30 minutes.

9. To serve, drizzle with maple syrup and sprinkle with powdered sugar.

A Hug and a Kiss
Makes 24 cookies

    Sugar cookie dough (recipe follows)
    24 unwrapped chocolate kisses (or a
       whole bag if you want to nibble!)
    Powdered sugar (optional)

1. Preheat the oven to 350°F.
2. Use a rolling pin to roll out the cookie dough to about ⅛-inch thick.
3. Using a 3-inch biscuit cutter (or a glass with an approximately 3-inch diameter), cut out circles of dough.
4. Place a kiss in the center of each dough circle.

5. Carefully gather the dough around each kiss, and pinch at the top to seal.

6. Transfer each one to a parchment paper-lined baking sheet. Leave plenty of room in between cookies—don't crowd them on the pan. Bake 8 to 10 minutes until the cookies are golden. Remove from the oven and cool on the pan for 5 minutes before moving to a cooling rack. Sprinkle with powdered sugar. (A tea ball or a sieve works great for this!) Enjoy!

Sugar Cookie Dough
Makes 24 cookies (2 dozen)

> 2 cups all-purpose flour
> ¼ teaspoon salt
> ½ teaspoon baking powder
> ½ cup (1 stick) unsalted butter, softened

1 cup sugar
1 egg
2 tablespoons milk
½ teaspoon vanilla extract

1. Sift together the flour, salt, and baking powder in a medium bowl.
2. Cream the butter and sugar in the mixer bowl. Add the egg, milk, and vanilla, and thoroughly mix.
3. Add the dry ingredients a little bit at a time, and mix until well blended. Unplug the mixer, clean the beaters with your fingers or a spatula, and remove the bowl.
4. Remove the dough from the bowl and place it on a sheet of plastic wrap. Press it into a big pancake that is about ¾-inch thick. Chill for at least two hours in the refrigerator.

Katie's Bear Bread

Makes 5 to 6 bears; 6 inches in length

> 1 package active dry yeast
> ⅓ cup sugar
> ¼ cup warm water (105 to 110°F on a
>   kitchen thermometer)*
> 2 eggs
> 4 tablespoons (½ stick) butter, melted
> ¼ cup milk, room temperature
> 1 tablespoon vanilla extract
> 1/2 teaspoon salt
> 1 level teaspoon fresh rosemary, minced,
>   no stems
> 2½ to 3 cups all-purpose flour
> Oil or butter
> Egg glaze (see page 407)

This temperature is important, because if the water is too hot, it kills the yeast. If the water is too cold, the yeast will not be activated.

1. In a large bowl, sprinkle the yeast and sugar into the warm water.* Gently stir until the yeast and sugar have dissolved, then allow the mixture to rest for at least 4 minutes to make sure the yeast is alive and active.
2. When the yeast has foamed up (if the yeast does not foam, you'll need to purchase new yeast), add the eggs, butter, milk, vanilla, salt, and rosemary. Stir until thoroughly mixed.
3. Stir in 2½ cups flour.
4. Place the dough onto a floured work surface and knead—adding more flour one tablespoon at a time as necessary—until

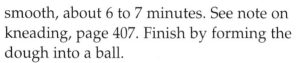

smooth, about 6 to 7 minutes. See note on kneading, page 407. Finish by forming the dough into a ball.

5. With oil or butter, grease the inside of a large bowl. Place the ball of dough in it, turning to coat the dough. Cover with plastic wrap, and leave in a warm place to rise. (A microwave where you have just heated one cup of water to boiling is a perfect place to let your bread rise.) Allow to rise for about 1½ hours.

6. With lightly floured hands, turn the dough out, and tear pieces to form each part of a bear, starting with the body. Keep the dough you are not working with covered, so that it will not dry out.

7. Preheat the oven to 350°F.

8. Shape each part of the animal by rolling the dough into a ball, then flattening it with the

palm of your hand. Place the body on a greased baking sheet. To attach the rest of the bear's body parts, use the egg glaze (see note below) as glue, and gently pinch pieces together. Repeat with the remaining dough.

9. With a pastry brush, paint the surface with the egg glaze. You can use two Cheerios, raisins, or whatever you like as eyes. Place in the oven to bake, for about 15 to 20 minutes. Cooking times will vary with the size of your bears and altitude, so watch carefully. If you see that some parts of your bears are cooking more quickly than others, gently cover those parts with pieces of aluminum foil.

10. When the bears are golden, use a spatula to remove them, and allow to cool on a wire rack for about 30 minutes.

Before You Knead, Read!

Kneading is a blast and works like this: With floured hands, fold the dough in half, from bottom to top. Use your palms to press the dough firmly from top to bottom one time. Rotate the dough ¼ turn, fold in half from top to bottom, and press with the palms of your hands. Repeat.

Using Eggs as a Glaze: Use a glaze with 1 egg yolk whisked with 1 teaspoon water to produce a rich golden color. You can also use just 1 egg white and 1 teaspoon water if you want a transparent glaze without a golden color.

Marshmallow Sushi
Makes 4 sushi rolls

> 4 dried fruit roll-ups
> 16 large marshmallows

1. Cut fruit roll-ups into flat sheets 4 to 6 inches wide and 6 to 8 inches tall, which is about the size of a sheet of nori (toasted seaweed traditionally used to make sushi).
2. Place as many marshmallows as possible along the bottom edge of the fruit roll-up. Roll the marshmallows tightly inside the fruit roll-up.
3. Cut into slices approximately ½-inch to ¾-inch thick, which is about the thickness of rolled sushi.

Munch Mix

Makes 32 (¼-cup) servings

1¼ cups reduced-fat peanut butter
1¼ cups semisweet chocolate chips
1 cup confectioners' sugar
1 (15.2-ounce) box honey nut oven-toasted
    rice and corn cereal squares

1. In a microwave-safe bowl or in a pan on the
   stovetop, melt together the peanut butter
   and chocolate chips. Mix with the cereal.
2. In a large, shallow container with a lid,
   place half the confectioners' sugar and all
   of the cereal mixture, then the remaining
   confectioners' sugar. Shake until evenly
   coated.

Peanut Butter Universe
Makes 9 snacks

1 tablespoon butter
2½ cups toasted rice cereal
2¼ cups rolled oats
¾ cup chopped dry-roasted, salted peanuts
¼ cup semisweet chocolate chips
¼ cup flaked coconut
½ cup creamy peanut butter
¾ cup firmly packed brown sugar
¾ cup light corn syrup
1 teaspoon vanilla extract

1. Place butter on a wadded-up paper towel, and coat the baking sheet.
2. In a large bowl, combine the cereal, oats, peanuts, chocolate chips, and coconut.

3. Combine peanut butter, brown sugar, corn syrup, and vanilla in a medium saucepan over low heat. Stir occasionally, until the mixture just begins to boil.

4. Pour over the cereal mixture. Stir with a spoon to mix well. When cool enough, finish mixing with your hands.

5. Spoon onto buttered baking sheet and, using the tips of your fingers, press the mixture together until it is flat, level, and pressed to the sides.

6. Allow to cool to room temperature, then cut into bars. Wrap individually in plastic wrap or store at home in an airtight container.

Popcorn Cake

Makes about 20 popcorn cakes

½ cup unpopped plain popcorn
Dash salt, optional
4 cups miniature marshmallows
½ cup margarine
⅔ cup miniature candy-coated milk
    chocolate candies

1. Pop the popcorn according to the packing directions. Add salt if desired; set aside to cool.
2. In a medium pot, melt the marshmallows and margarine over low heat, stirring constantly, until smooth. Combine the candy-coated milk chocolate candies with the popcorn.

3. Remove the marshmallow mixture from the heat, and pour over the popcorn and candies. Mix gently.
4. Spoon the mixture into a 13 x 9 x 2-inch pan or a 2-quart oblong pan coated with nonstick cooking spray. Refrigerate the mixture until it hardens, so it's easier to cut.

Reindeer Sandwiches
Makes 1 sandwich

> 1 tablespoon creamy peanut butter or enough to cover bread
> 2 slices bread
> 1 twisted pretzel
> 2 raisins
> 1 maraschino cherry, halved

1. Spread the peanut butter on one slice of bread, and top with the other slice.
2. Cut a triangular shape in the sandwich, discarding the ends and remainder of the sandwich.
3. Place a twisted pretzel between the two slices of bread on two points of the triangle to form the reindeer's antlers. Place two raisins for the eyes and a cherry half on the remaining point for the nose.

Adult Recipes

Introduction

O ne of the most important of the American (and other cultures') Christmas traditions is that of food, Christmas cookies in particular. Recipes have been passed down through generations and given as thoughtful homemade gifts (any recipe can easily be doubled for this purpose). Of course, your family has its own special Christmas recipes, and the aromas always bring back memories of family gatherings and brightly wrapped packages being passed around the Christmas tree. Here are some favorites, cookies and more nutritious foods; some may be familiar in the form given here or in a variation.

Appetizers

Artichoke Dip
Makes 12 (2-tablespoon) servings

- ½ cup fat-free sour cream
- ½ cup light mayonnaise
- 1 (.7-ounce) package cheesy Italian or Italian dressing mix
- 1 (14-ounce) can artichoke hearts, drained and finely chopped

In a medium bowl, mix all ingredients. Refrigerate until serving.

Fruit Dip
Makes 8 (¼-cup) servings

2 (8-ounce) cartons nonfat lemon yogurt
¼ cup blanched almonds, chopped and
   toasted
1 teaspoon grated orange rind
2 tablespoons orange liqueur or orange juice

1. In a small bowl, combine the ingredients
   and mix well.
2. Refrigerate at least 1 hour before serving to
   blend the flavors.

Glazed Brie
Makes 20 servings

¼ cup chopped walnuts or chopped
   pecans
¼ cup coffee liqueur
3 tablespoons light brown sugar
½ teaspoon vanilla extract

417

1 (14-ounce) round Brie cheese
Assorted crackers
Assorted sliced fruit (apples, pears, etc.)

1. Preheat the oven to 325°F.
2. In a small saucepan, sauté the walnuts until golden brown, about 3 minutes, stirring. Stir in the liqueur, brown sugar, and vanilla, cooking until the brown sugar is melted; set aside. Watch carefully, as it cooks quickly.
3. Remove the top rind of the Brie. Place the Brie in a shallow baking dish. Top with the walnut mixture. Bake for 8 to 10 minutes, or until the Brie is soft and heated through. Serve immediately with assorted crackers and fruit slices.

Guacamole
Makes 8 (3-tablespoon) servings

1 large avocado, peeled, pitted, and
  mashed
Salt and pepper to taste
1 clove garlic, minced
¼ teaspoon chili powder
1 teaspoon lemon juice
2 teaspoons minced onion
¼ cup nonfat plain yogurt

1. Put the mashed avocado in a small bowl,
   and season with salt, pepper, garlic, chili
   powder, and lemon juice. Stir in the onion.
   Cover with the yogurt to keep the mixture
   from darkening.
2. Refrigerate until serving. Just before serving,
   stir well.

*(Tip: To pit and peel an avocado, hold the avocado in one
hand. Run a sharp knife lengthwise around the avocado,*

turning only the avocado, not the knife. Twist the two halves apart. Using the edge of your knife, make a quick downward stroke into the pit, twist, and remove it. Cut each avocado half lengthwise in two, and then peel away the skin.)

Hummus

Makes 8 (¼-cup) servings

> 2 (15-ounce) cans garbanzo beans, rinsed
> and drained
> 1 teaspoon minced garlic
> 1 tablespoon tamari
> ¼ cup lemon juice
> 1 tablespoon sesame oil
> Salt and cayenne pepper to taste

Place all ingredients in a food processor or blender and purée. Serve as a dip or sauce with toasted pita bread.

Mini Taco Cups
Makes 24 servings

24 wonton wrappers
1 pound ground sirloin
1 teaspoon ground cumin
1 teaspoon chili powder
⅔ cup chipotle salsa, divided in half
1 cup shredded reduced-fat cheddar
     cheese

1. Preheat the oven to 425°F.
2. Press the wonton wrappers into mini-muffin cups coated with nonstick cooking spray.
3. Cook the meat in a skillet until browned; then drain off excess liquid. Stir in the cumin, chili powder, and ⅓ cup salsa. Spoon the beef mixture into the wonton cups.

4. Top with the remaining salsa and the cheese. Bake about 8 minutes, or until the won-tons are golden brown. Serve immediately with additional salsa, if desired.

(Tip: Make these shells ahead of time, and fill them with your favorite dip for an interesting serving presentation. Place each square in a mini-muffin pan coated with nonstick cooking spray. Bake at 350°F for 10 minutes, or until light brown. Cool and store in zipper-lock bags.)

Portabello Mushrooms Stuffed with Goat Cheese and Roasted Red Peppers
Makes 16 servings

2 ounces goat cheese, softened
4 large portabello mushroom caps

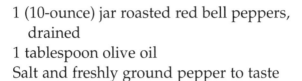

1 (10-ounce) jar roasted red bell peppers,
  drained
1 tablespoon olive oil
Salt and freshly ground pepper to taste

1. Preheat the oven to 350°F.
2. Place the mushrooms on a baking sheet that
   has been lined with foil or coated with
   nonstick cooking spray. Spread ¼ of the goat
   cheese on top of each mushroom cap. Cover
   the cheese with a layer of roasted red
   peppers. Drizzle the top of the mushrooms
   with olive oil, and season with salt and
   freshly ground pepper.
3. Roast for 15 minutes, or until the cheese
   begins to melt, cut into fourths, and serve
   immediately.

(Tip: Roasted red peppers in jars are a quick, convenient, and sometimes even cheaper substitution for roasting fresh red peppers. See the next recipe for how to roast red peppers.)

Roasted Red Bell Pepper Dip
Makes 3 cups or 12 (¼-cup) servings

1 (10-ounce) jar roasted red peppers, drained
1 tablespoon olive oil
1 (16-ounce) container reduced-fat cottage cheese
½ teaspoon minced garlic
1 tablespoon lemon juice
Dash hot pepper sauce
Salt and pepper to taste

Place all ingredients in food processor; blend until very smooth.

(Tip: To roast a red pepper: Slice the pepper in half; core and seed. Brush with olive oil. Broil until soft, about 20 minutes, turning once. Place the pepper halves in a paper bag and let steam for 10 minutes to loosen the skin. Remove the skin with a paring knife.)

Salsa with Tortilla Chips

Salsa makes 2 cups
Tortillas make 12 servings of chips

Salsa:

>   3 green onions (scallions), chopped
>   2 cloves garlic, minced
>   1 (28-ounce) can chopped tomatoes, drained
>   2 tablespoons finely chopped jalapeño pepper
>   ¼ cup chopped fresh cilantro
>   1 teaspoon dried oregano leaves
>   ¼ teaspoon ground cumin

In a small bowl, combine all ingredients. Serve with homemade tortilla chips or as a topping for chicken or fish.

Tortilla Chips:
> 12 (6- to 8-inch) whole wheat or white flour tortillas
> Water

1. Preheat the oven to 425°F.
2. Brush each tortilla with water. Cut each tortilla into eight wedges, and place on a baking sheet coated with nonstick cooking spray. Bake for 3 minutes, turn, and continue baking 3 minutes longer, or until crisp. Repeat until all the tortillas have been baked.

Shrimp, Avocado, and Artichoke
Makes 16 servings

> 1 pound peeled medium shrimp
> 1 tablespoon margarine
> Salt and pepper to taste
> 2 tablespoons lemon juice
> 2 (14-ounce) cans quartered artichoke
>   hearts, drained
> 2 avocados, peeled, pitted, and cubed
> 3 tablespoons capers, drained
> 2 bunches green onions (scallions), sliced
> ½ cup grainy mustard
> ¼ cup ketchup

1. In a small pan, sauté the shrimp in the margarine until done. Season to taste with the salt and pepper. Remove from heat and

stir in the lemon juice. Refrigerate for 15 minutes or until chilled.

2. In a bowl, combine the artichoke hearts, avocado, capers, green onion, and cooled shrimp.

3. In a small bowl, mix together the mustard and ketchup, and carefully toss with the shrimp mixture.

Refrigerate until serving.

(Tip: To speed up ripening of avocados, place in a brown paper bag overnight, or cook at medium power in the microwave for 30 seconds. Let sit for 10 minutes before using.)

Snack Mix
Makes 20 (½-cup) servings

3 tablespoons sesame oil

3 tablespoons honey
1 tablespoon low sodium soy sauce
½ teaspoon garlic powder
½ teaspoon onion powder
4 cups honey-nut toasted rice and corn
   cereal squares
6 cups mini-pretzels
1 cup soy nuts
1 cup dry roasted peanuts
1 cup candy-coated chocolate pieces
1 cup raisins, optional

1. Preheat the oven to 250°F.
2. In a small bowl, whisk together the sesame
   oil, honey, soy sauce, garlic powder, and
   onion powder.
3. In a large bowl, toss together the cereal
   squares, pretzels, soy nuts, and peanuts.

4. Drizzle the oil mixture over the cereal mixture, tossing gently to coat.

5. Scatter the mixture on a foil-lined jelly roll pan, and bake for 25 minutes, stirring often to prevent too much browning.

6. Turn off the oven and let the cereal stay in the oven for 1 hour to continue crisping.

7. When the mixture cools, toss with the chocolate candies and raisins. Store in an airtight container for up to one week.

Spinach-and-Cheese Tortilla Pizza
Makes 12 slices

2 large (10-inch) flour tortillas
2 tablespoons fat-free sour cream
1 (10-ounce) package frozen chopped spinach, thawed and squeezed dry
1 large tomato, chopped

Salt and pepper to taste
½ cup shredded reduced-fat Monterey
    Jack cheese
¼ cup thinly sliced green onions (scallions)

1. Preheat the oven to 450°F.
2. Place the tortillas on a baking sheet coated with nonstick cooking spray. Bake 3 minutes, or until golden brown. Remove from the oven, and reduce the temperature to 350°F.
3. Spread the sour cream evenly over the tortillas. Top each with the spinach, tomato, salt, and pepper to taste. Next, sprinkle evenly with the Monterey Jack cheese.
4. Bake for 5 minutes more, or until the cheese is melted. Sprinkle with the green onion.

5. Cut each tortilla into four slices, and serve immediately.

Spinach Dip
Makes 12 (¼-cup) servings

> 1 (10-ounce) package frozen chopped spinach, thawed and squeezed dry
> ½ cup light mayonnaise
> 1 cup nonfat plain yogurt
> 1 teaspoon seasoned salt
> ½ teaspoon dried dill weed leaves
> Juice of ½ lemon
> ½ cup chopped parsley
> ½ cup chopped green onion (scallion)

Blend the spinach with the remaining ingredients. Refrigerate. This dip is best when made a day ahead.

Spinach Artichoke Dip
Makes 10 servings

> ½ teaspoon minced garlic
> 1 onion, chopped
> 2 tablespoons all-purpose flour
> 1 (12-ounce) can evaporated skimmed
>   milk
> 2 (10-ounce) boxes frozen chopped
>   spinach, thawed and squeezed dry
> 4 ounces reduced-fat Monterey Jack
>   cheese, cubed
> 1 (14-ounce) can quartered artichoke
>   hearts, drained
> Salt and pepper to taste
> Dash Worcestershire sauce

In a pot coated with nonstick cooking spray, sauté the garlic and onion until very tender.

Add the flour. Gradually stir in the milk, heating until thickened. Add the spinach and cheese, stirring until the cheese is melted. Stir in the artichoke hearts. Season with the salt, pepper, and Worcestershire sauce to taste. Serve hot.

Sweet Cheese Ball
Makes 32 (2-tablespoon) servings

> 1 (8-ounce) package fat-free cream cheese, softened
> 1 (8-ounce) package reduced-fat cream cheese, softened
> 1 teaspoon seasoned salt
> 2 tablespoons finely chopped onion
> 1 cup shredded reduced-fat cheddar cheese
> 1 cup chopped dates

1 cup golden raisins
1 cup dried cranberries
½ cup chopped pecans, toasted

1. In a large bowl, mix together the cream cheeses, the seasoned salt, and the onion.
2. Stir in the remaining ingredients, mixing well. Mold into a ball, and refrigerate until serving.

For a variation, use dried cherries or other dried fruits in the cheeseball.

Sweet-and-Spicy Chicken Strips
Makes 24 servings

1 cup picante sauce
¼ cup honey
½ teaspoon ground ginger

1½ pounds skinless, boneless chicken breasts, cut into strips

1. Preheat the oven to 400°F.
2. In a medium bowl, mix the picante sauce, honey, and ginger. Toss the chicken strips with the picante sauce mixture.
3. Place in a foil-lined shallow baking pan. Bake for 40 to 50 minutes, or until glazed and done, turning and brushing often with sauce during the last 30 minutes. Serve.

Zesty Cucumber Dip
Makes 16 (2-tablespoon) servings

1 cup nonfat plain yogurt
1 (.7-ounce) package Italian dressing mix
1 tomato, seeded and chopped

½ cucumber, seeded, peeled, and chopped
    (can also substitute avocados here)
3 green onions (scallions), chopped
1 tablespoon lemon juice

1. In a medium bowl, mix together the yogurt and dressing mix until well combined. Stir in the remaining ingredients.
2. Refrigerate until ready to serve. Serve with chips.

Beverages and Cocktails

City Tavern Eggnog
Makes about 48 ounces; serves 10 to 12

7 large egg yolks
¾ cup granulated sugar
2 cups heavy cream
1 cup whole milk
¾ cup bourbon
¾ cup Jamaican rum
¼ cup brandy
Freshly grated nutmeg, for garnish

1. In the large bowl of an electric mixer, beat together the egg yolks and sugar on high speed about 5 minutes, until thick and pale yellow.

2. Gradually beat in the cream, milk, bourbon, rum, and brandy.
3. Cover and refrigerate until completely chilled.
4. Serve in cups or mugs. Garnish with the nutmeg.

Fiamma

> 1½ ounces Stoli Razberi
> ¾ ounces Cointreau
> 1 ounce white cranberry juice
> 1 raspberry

1. Shake with ice and strain into a martini glass.
2. Garnish with a raspberry.

Granny Apple Martini

> 2 ounces sour apple liqueur
> 1 ounce citrus-infused vodka
> Tiny splash of sour mix
> 4 ounces apple juice
> Slice of apple
> Maraschino cherry

1. Shake with ice and strain into a chilled martini glass.
2. Garnish with a slice of apple and a maraschino cherry.

Hot Cider
Makes 18 ounces; serves 2

> 2 cups fresh apple cider

2 sticks cinnamon
¼ cup applejack brandy or Jamaican rum

1. In a medium saucepan, bring the apple cider
   to a simmer over high heat.
2. Add the cinnamon sticks and simmer about
   5 minutes to infuse the flavor of cinnamon
   into the liquid. Remove from heat.
3. Stir in brandy or rum.
4. Serve hot in cups or mugs.

Hot Spiced Punch
Makes 34 ounces; serves 8 to 10

4 cups (1 quart) fresh apple cider
¼ cup fresh lemon juice (about 1 large
   lemon), strained
4 sticks cinnamon

1 teaspoon whole cloves (about 6)
½ teaspoon freshly grated nutmeg

1. In a medium saucepan, bring the apple cider, lemon juice, and cinnamon sticks to a simmer over medium heat. Do not boil.
2. Place the cloves in a piece of 100% cheesecloth. Tie up with kitchen twine to make a sachet and add to the cider mixture. Simmer about 10 minutes, until spices have steeped into cider.
3. Remove and discard the sachet and cinnamon sticks. Add the nutmeg.
4. Serve hot in cups or mugs.

Plum Martini

2 ounces sake
2 ounces plum wine

Shake sake and wine with ice and strain into a martini glass.

Wassail
Makes 24 ounces; serves 6

> 2 tablespoons grated orange rind (about 1 medium orange)
> 2 teaspoons grated lemon rind (about 1 medium lemon)
> 10 whole cloves
> 5 sticks cinnamon
> 1 bottle (750 ml) red burgundy wine
> ¼ cup dark brown suger
> 2 pinches freshly grated nutmeg

1. Place the orange and lemon rinds, cloves, and cinnamon sticks into a piece of 100%

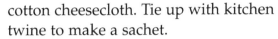
cotton cheesecloth. Tie up with kitchen twine to make a sachet.

2. Pour the wine into a saucepan.

3. Place the sugar and sachet in wine over low heat. Add the nutmeg.

4. Heat until wine is very warm. Do not let boil (boiling will burn off the alcohol content).

5. Remove and discard the sachet. Serve in a fondue pot or an ovenproof punch bowl.

Whiskey Smash / Mint Julep

3 fresh lemon wedges cut in half (for easier molding)

1 ounce simple syrup

1 sprig (approximately 6-10 leaves) of fresh mint

2 ounces bourbon

1. Muddle lemon, simple syrup, and mint well.
2. Add bourbon and shake well with ice.
3. Strain into a rocks glass over ice.
4. Garnish with mint leaves

(Leave out the lemon and it's a mint julep.)

White Chocolate Raspberry

> 1 orange slice
> Cinnamon sugar
> 1¼ ounces raspberry vodka
> ½ ounce white chocolate liqueur
> ¼ ounce white crème de cacao
> Splash of heavy cream

1. Moisten the edge of a martini glass by dragging an orange slice around the rim, then dip it in cinnamon sugar.

2. Shake ingredients with ice and strain into the martini glass.

The White Cosmo

> 2 ounces citrus-infused vodka
> 5 ounces white cranberry juice
> ½ ounce fresh lime juice
> ½ teaspoon powdered sugar
> Lime twist

1. Shake all ingredients except lime twist with ice and strain into a martini glass.
2. Garnish with a lime twist.

White Russian

2 ounces vodka
1 ounce coffee liqueur
Milk or cream

Pour coffee liqueur and vodka in a rocks glass over ice and fill with milk or cream.

Breads, Salads, and Soups

Breads

Butterscotch Banana Bread

Makes 16 slices

    1¾ cups all-purpose flour

    2 teaspoons baking powder

    ½ teaspoon baking soda

    ½ teaspoon ground cinnamon

    ½ teaspoon ground nutmeg

    ¾ cup sugar

    1 egg

    2 egg whites

    1 cup mashed banana (2 large bananas)

    ¼ cup canola oil

    ¼ cup skim milk

½ cup butterscotch chips

1. Preheat the oven to 350°F. Coat a 9 x 5 x 3-inch loaf pan with nonstick cooking spray.
2. In a large bowl, combine the flour, baking powder, baking soda, cinnamon, and nutmeg; set aside.
3. In a large mixing bowl, combine the sugar, egg, egg whites, mashed banana, and oil, blending well. Add the flour mixture alternately with the milk to the banana mixture, mixing only until combined. Stir in the butterscotch chips.
4. Pour into the prepared pan. Bake for 50 minutes to 1 hour, or until a toothpick inserted in the center comes out clean. Cool in the pan.

Chocolate Gingerbread

5½ ounces bittersweet chocolate

1⅓ sticks (¾ cup plus 1 tablespoon) sweet
butter, at room temperature

¾ cup sugar

3 large eggs, separated

½ cup plus 1 tablespoon ground almonds

¾ cup plus 1½ tablespoons self-rising flour

1 tablespoon unsweetened cocoa

3 pieces preserved ginger, chopped, and 2
tablespoons syrup from jar

1. Chop the chocolate and melt very gently in
a heatproof bowl set over a pan of steaming
water. Stir until smooth, remove from heat,
and let cool. Using an electric mixer or
wooden spoon, beat the butter until creamy,
then gradually beat in the sugar. Beat until

light and fluffy, then beat in the egg yolks one at a time, beating well after each addition. Beat in the cooled chocolate, then sift the almonds, flour, and cocoa into the bowl. Add the chopped ginger and syrup, and fold in using a large metal spoon.

2. Whisk the egg whites until stiff peaks form, then fold into the mixture in 3 batches. Spoon the mixture into the prepared pan and smooth the surface. Bake in a preheated oven at 375°F for about 40 minutes or until a skewer inserted into the center of the cake comes out clean. Leave for 5 minutes, then turn out onto a wire rack and let cool completely. The chocolate topping recipe follows.

Chocolate Topping:
    1½ ounce bittersweet chocolate
    1 tablespoon sweet butter

1 piece of preserved ginger, sliced, and 1 tablespoon syrup from the jar, to finish
One loaf pan, 8½ x 4½ x 3 inches, greased and lined with baking parchment

1. Chop the chocolate and melt it with the butter and ginger syrup in a heatproof bowl set over a pan of steaming water. Stir until smooth, then spoon over the top of the gingerbread. When almost set, decorate with finely sliced, diced, or grated preserved ginger.
2. Store in airtight container and eat within 1 week—it improves in taste after several days. If undecorated, it can be frozen for up to 1 month.

Cinnamon Crescents
Makes 8 crescents

¼ cup light brown sugar

¼ cup chopped pecans
1 teaspoon ground cinnamon
2 cups biscuit baking mix
1 tablespoon sugar
½ cup cold water
3 tablespoons margarine, softened

1. Preheat oven to 425°F.
2. In a small bowl, combine the brown sugar, pecans, and cinnamon; set aside.
3. In a separate, large bowl, mix the baking mix, sugar, and water until a soft dough forms; beat vigorously for 30 seconds. Roll the mixture into a ball with hands dusted with baking mix so the dough will not stick. Knead 1 minute. Pat or roll the dough into a 10- to 12-inch circle. Spread with the margarine and sprinkle the brown sugar

mixture, and cut into eight wedges. Roll up, beginning with wide edges, to point.

4. Place the crescents on an ungreased baking sheet; shape into a semicircle. Bake for 10 minutes, or until golden brown. Cool slightly on the baking sheet; drizzle with the glaze (see recipe below).

Glaze:

> ½ cup confectioners' sugar
> 1 tablespoon margarine, softened
> ¼ teaspoon vanilla extract
> 1 tablespoon water

In a small bowl, mix the confectioner's sugar, margarine, vanilla, and water with a fork, adding more water as needed, until blended and smooth.

Cranberry Bread
Makes one 8-inch loaf

> 4½ ounces (1 stick plus 1 tablespoon)
>   unsalted butter, at room temperature
> ¾ cup granulated sugar
> 4 large eggs
> 2⅓ cups sifted cake flour
> 1 tablespoon baking powder
> 1 teaspoon salt
> ¾ cup whole milk
> 2 cups fresh cranberries
> ½ cup chopped pecans
> 2 teaspoons grated orange zest

1. Preheat the oven to 350°F. Grease an 8½ x 4½ x 2½-inch loaf pan with butter.
2. In the bowl of an electric mixer fitted with the paddle attachment on medium speed,

beat together the butter and sugar until light and fluffy, 2 to 3 minutes.

3. Add the eggs one at a time, and beat until combined.

4. In a medium-sized mixing bowl, add the flour, baking powder, and salt; stir to combine. Fold the dry ingredients into the butter mixture in thirds, alternating with the milk.

5. In a medium-sized mixing bowl, combine the cranberries, pecans, and orange zest. With a rubber spatula, gently fold into the batter.

6. Pour the batter into the prepared pan. Bake about 45 minutes, or until golden brown and a toothpick inserted near the center comes out clean.

7. Remove the pan from oven, and let cool for 10 minutes. To remove the bread, flip the pan on its side and gently pull out the bread.

Cranberry Orange Bread
Makes 16 slices

2 cups all-purpose flour
1½ teaspoons baking powder
½ teaspoon baking soda
1 cup sugar
¼ cup canola oil
¾ cup orange juice
1 egg, beaten
1 tablespoon grated orange rind
½ teaspoon almond extract
1½ cups cranberries, coarsely chopped

1. Preheat the oven to 350°F. Coat a 9 x 5 x 3-inch loaf pan with nonstick cooking spray.
2. In a large bowl, combine the flour, baking powder, baking soda, and sugar.

3. In a separate small bowl, combine the oil, orange juice, egg, orange rind, and almond extract.

4. Add the orange juice mixture to the dry ingredients, stirring just until the dry ingredients are moistened. Fold in the cranberries.

5. Pour the batter into the prepared pan. Bake for 45 to 50 minutes, or until a toothpick inserted in the center comes out clean. Cool in the pan.

(Tip: Coat only the bottoms of loaf pans for fruit breads. The ungreased sides allow the batter to cling while rising during baking, helping to form a gently rounded top.)

Cranberry Orange Scones
Makes 10 scones

2 cups all-purpose flour

¼ cup sugar

2 teaspoons baking powder

½ teaspoon baking soda

1 teaspoon grated orange rind

3 tablespoons chilled margarine, cut into
   small pieces

1 cup nonfat plain yogurt

⅓ cup dried cranberries

1. Preheat the oven to 400°F.

2. In a large bowl, combine the flour, sugar,
   baking powder, baking soda, and orange rind;
   cut in the margarine with a pastry blender
   until the mixture resembles coarse meal. Add
   the yogurt to the dry ingredients, stirring just
   until the ingredients are mixed. Stir in the
   cranberries. The dough will be sticky.

3. Turn the dough onto a floured surface and
   knead with floured hands several times, or

until rolling consistency. Roll dough into a circle about 8 inches in diameter, and cut into rounds with a 2-inch biscuit cutter or glass.
4. Place on a baking sheet, and bake for 15 minutes, or until golden brown.

Gingerbread

Makes 2 dozen mini houses/1 regular-sized house

   1 cup vegetable shortening
   1 cup sugar
   1 cup dark molasses or corn syrup (dark gives dark, chocolate-colored dough; corn syrup gives light dough . . . or use half molasses and half corn syrup for a medium-colored dough)
   1 teaspoon baking soda
   ½ teaspoon salt

1 teaspoon ginger
1 teaspoon nutmeg
1 teaspoon cinnamon
4–4½ cups flour

1. Preheat the oven to 375°F.
2. Melt the first 3 ingredients in microwave. Stir in the next 5 ingredients. Then stir in the flour, 1 cup at a time. (You may have to enlist the help of an electric mixer on the last cup as the dough gets quite thick and hard to stir.) Split the dough into manageable balls, wrapping excess in plastic wrap.
3. Working with half a batch at a time on a lightly floured work surface with lightly floured hands, knead dough until smooth. Place a piece of parchment paper on a cookie sheet, and with lightly floured rolling pin, roll dough to ³⁄₁₆-inch or ⅛-inch thickness.

4. Cut pieces of dough the size you need for however you plan to use it once baked. Remove scraps and reserve for re-rolling.
5. Bake until golden brown and not over-soft when you touch it lightly. (6–10 minutes)
6. When the gingerbread is no longer soft, carefully slide the whole piece of parchment off the cookie sheet and let it cool completely (about 20 minutes).

Pumpkin-Raisin Bread
Makes two 8-inch loaves

> 2 cups pumpkin purée
> 1 cup vegetable oil
> ⅔ cup water
> 4 large eggs
> 3⅓ cups sifted all-purpose flour
> 3 cups granulated sugar

2 teaspoons baking soda
1½ teaspoons salt
1 teaspoon ground nutmeg
1 teaspoon ground cinnamon
½ cup raisins

1. Preheat the oven to 350°F. Grease two 8½ x 4½ x 2½-inch loaf pans with butter.
2. In a medium-size mixing bowl, add the pumpkin purée, oil, water, and eggs; stir to combine.
3. In a large mixing bowl, add the flour, sugar, baking soda, salt, nutmeg, and cinnamon; stir to combine. Fold the egg mixture into the dry ingredients.
4. With a rubber spatula or wooden spoon, gently fold the raisins into the batter.
5. Divide the batter between the prepared pans. Bake about 1 hour, or until the top

springs back when touched or pulls away from the sides of the pan and a toothpick inserted near the center comes out clean.

Cool in the pans on a wire rack for 10 minutes. To remove, flip the pans on their sides and gently pull out the bread. Let cool to room temperature on a wire rack. Slice when completely cool.

Surprise Corn Bread
Makes 12 to 16 servings

> 2 (8-ounce) packages corn muffin mix
> 2 eggs
> ⅔ cup skim milk
> 1 cup picante sauce
> 1 cup reduced-fat shredded cheddar cheese

1. Preheat the oven to 400°F. Coat a 9 x 9 x 2-inch square pan with nonstick cooking spray.
2. In a bowl, mix together the corn muffin mix, eggs, and milk, stirring well.
3. Spread half the batter into the prepared pan, and top with the picante sauce and cheese. Carefully spread the remaining batter on top.
4. Bake for 20 minutes, or until golden brown. Cut into squares, and serve warm.

Yam Biscuits
Makes 20 to 24 biscuits

   1 (15-ounce) can sweet potatoes (yams), drained and mashed
   4 cups biscuit baking mix
   ½ teaspoon ground cinnamon
   ¾ cup skim milk
   3 tablespoons margarine, softened

1. Preheat the oven to 450°F.
2. In a mixing bowl, mix the mashed yams with the baking mix and cinnamon. Add the milk and margarine to the mixture, stirring until blended.
3. Roll on a floured surface to 1-inch thickness. Cut with a 2-inch cutter or glass, and place on an ungreased baking sheet.
4. Bake for 10 to 12 minutes, or until golden brown. Serve hot.

Salads

Apple and Walnut Salad
Makes 4 servings

> 4 large apples, peeled, cored, and thinly sliced
> ¼ cup fresh lemon juice (about 1 large lemon), strained

½ cup chopped walnuts
¼ cup mayonnaise
2 tablespoons heavy cream
¼ teaspoon Worcestershire sauce
⅛ teaspoon curry powder
Salt and freshly ground white pepper
Fresh parsley, chopped, for garnish

1. In a medium mixing bowl, toss the apple slices with the lemon juice.
2. In a small mixing bowl, combine the walnuts, mayonnaise, cream, Worcestershire sauce, and curry.
3. Pour the mayonnaise over the apples and toss gently to coat. Season with salt and pepper to taste.
4. Cover and refrigerate for 1 hour, until well chilled.
5. Just before serving, garnish with the parsley.

Mixed Green Salad with Cranberries and Sunflower Seeds

Makes 8 servings

6 cups mixed greens
½ cup dried cranberries
¼ shredded carrot
½ cup sliced green onion (scallion)
¼ cup raspberry wine vinegar
2 tablespoons red wine vinegar
2 tablespoons olive oil
2 tablespoons honey
2 tablespoons sunflower seeds

1. Place the greens in a large bowl. Add the cranberries and carrot.
2. In a small bowl, combine the green onion, raspberry wine vinegar, red wine vinegar, olive oil, and honey, mixing well. Just before serving,

pour over the greens mixture, and toss.
Sprinkle with the sunflower seeds, and serve.

Soups

Broccoli Soup
Makes 6 to 8 servings

4 cups fresh broccoli florets (or two 10-
ounce packages frozen chopped broccoli)

¼ cup water

1 onion, chopped

⅔ cup all-purpose flour

1½ cups skim milk

2 (14½-ounce) cans vegetable broth or fat-
free chicken broth

1 cup shredded reduced-fat Monterey Jack
cheese

Salt and pepper to taste
⅛ teaspoon dried thyme leaves

1. Cook the broccoli in a microwave dish in the water, covered, for 8 to 10 minutes, or until tender. Drain and set aside.
2. In a large pot coated with nonstick cooking spray, sauté the onion over medium heat until softened, about 3 to 5 minutes.
3. In a small bowl, mix together the flour and milk.
4. Stir the flour and milk mixture into the onion. Gradually add the vegetable broth and the broccoli. Stir to combine.
5. Cook over medium heat until the mixture comes to a boil, stirring constantly, for about 5 minutes, or until thickened.
6. Transfer the soup to a food processor or blender, purée the soup, and return to the

pot over low heat. Add the cheese, salt, pepper, and thyme, cooking until heated through and the cheese is melted. Serve immediately.

Creamy Potato Soup
Makes 8 servings

1 tablespoon margarine
1 cup chopped onion
½ teaspoon minced garlic
3 tablespoons all-purpose flour
2 (16-ounce) cans fat-free chicken broth
4 cups peeled diced potatoes (about 3 large potatoes)
Salt and pepper to taste
1 cup liquid nondairy creamer
Chopped parsley or sliced green onions (scallions), for garnish

1. Melt the margarine in a large pot over medium heat, and sauté the onion and garlic in the margarine until tender, about 5 minutes.
2. Lower the heat and add the flour, stirring until smooth. Gradually add the broth, stirring constantly. Add the potato.
3. Bring to a boil; cover, reduce the heat, and simmer for 20 minutes, stirring occasionally, or until the potato chunks are tender.
4. Transfer the mixture to a blender or food processor, and blend until smooth, in batches if necessary. Return to the pot. Add salt and pepper, stir in the nondairy creamer, and heat thoroughly. Garnish with the parsley or green onions, and serve.

Chicken Cherry Jubilee
Makes 10 to 12 servings

> 3 pounds skinless, boneless chicken
> breasts and thighs
> Salt and pepper to taste
> 2 onions, thinly sliced
> 1 cup water
> 1 (12-ounce) bottle chili sauce
> ½ cup light brown sugar
> 1 cup sherry
> 1 (16-ounce) can pitted dark cherries,
> drained

1. Preheat the broiler.

2. Season the chicken with the salt and pepper. Place in a 3-quart oblong pan, and cover with the sliced onion. Broil until the chicken is brown, 5 to 7 minutes.

3. Meanwhile, in a medium saucepan, combine the water, chili sauce, brown sugar, sherry, and cherries over low heat, until melted together.

4. When the chicken is brown, remove and discard the onion and transfer the chicken to a baking dish. Lower the oven temperature to 325°F. Pour the sauce over the chicken.

5. Bake, covered, for 1½ hours, or until the chicken is very tender. Serve.

Chicken Primavera

Makes 6 to 8 servings

1 (12-ounce) package linguine

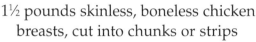

1½ pounds skinless, boneless chicken
   breasts, cut into chunks or strips
¼ cup olive oil
1 teaspoon minced garlic
½ pound fresh mushrooms, sliced
1 onion, chopped
1 red bell pepper, seeded and chopped
½ teaspoon dried oregano leaves
½ teaspoon dried basil leaves
½ teaspoon thyme leaves
Salt and pepper to taste
1 cup frozen peas
¼ cup grated Parmesan cheese

1. Cook the linguine according to the package
   directions, omitting any oil and salt; drain.
2. In a large skillet, cook the chicken pieces in
   the olive oil and garlic over medium-high

heat until lightly brown and done, about 7 minutes. Watch carefully, tossing to keep from sticking. Add the mushrooms, onion, red pepper, oregano, basil, thyme, salt, and pepper, sautéing until tender.
3. Add the peas, tossing until heated. Add the pasta to the vegetable mixture, combining well.
4. Add the Parmesan cheese, and serve.

Cornish Hens with Wild Rice Stuffing
Makes 16 servings

> 8 Cornish game hens (about 1½ pounds each)
> 1 tablespoon paprika
> 1 tablespoon garlic powder
> Salt and pepper to taste

2 onions, chopped
2 green bell peppers, seeded and chopped
4 celery stalks, chopped
1 tablespoon minced garlic
1 bunch green onions (scallions), chopped
3 (6-ounce) packages long-grain and wild
    rice mix
1 cup peach preserves
3 tablespoons honey
2 tablespoons light brown sugar
½ cup golden raisins
4 baking apples, cored and sliced

1. Preheat the oven to 350°F.
2. Clean and rinse the Cornish game hens. Lay
   the hens in a large casserole dish, and pat
   dry. Season with the paprika, garlic powder,
   salt, and pepper; set aside.

3. In a large pot coated with nonstick cooking spray, sauté the onion, green peppers, celery, garlic, and green onions until tender, about 7 minutes. Add all of the long grain and wild-rice mix and water according to the package directions, omitting any oil and salt. Cook until the rice is done and the liquid is absorbed, about 35 to 40 minutes.

4. Stuff each of the Cornish game hens with equal amounts of the wild rice mixture.

5. In another saucepan, heat the peach preserves, honey, and brown sugar over medium-low heat until the mixture is bubbly, about 4 minutes. Pour over the stuffed hens. Sprinkle with the raisins and sliced apples.

6. Bake for 1½ to 2 hours, or until the hens are done. You might have to cover them with foil during the last 30 minutes if the hens get too brown.

7. To serve, cut each hen in half, and serve with the dressing.

Cranberry Chicken with Wild Rice
Makes 4 to 6 servings

　　1 (16-ounce) can wholeberry cranberry sauce
　　2 tablespoons orange liqueur or orange juice
　　2 tablespoons lemon juice
　　½ teaspoon dry mustard
　　1½ pounds skinless, boneless chicken breasts
　　1 (6-ounce) package long grain and wild rice mix
　　2 tablespoons grated orange rind
　　¼ cup sliced green onion (scallion)

1. Preheat the oven to 350°F.
2. In a medium saucepan over medium heat or in a microwave-safe pan, combine the cranberry sauce, orange liqueur, lemon juice, and mustard, cooking until hot.
3. Place the chicken in a baking dish, and pour the cranberry sauce mixture over the chicken. Bake uncovered for 45 minutes, or until the chicken is done.
4. Meanwhile, cook the wild rice according to the package directions, omitting any oil and salt. When the rice is done, stir in the orange rind and green onion.
5. To serve, place the rice on a plate and top with the chicken and cranberry sauce.

(Tip: Include toasted pecans and dried cranberries in the rice for a dish full of texture and flavor.)

Honey-Glazed Turkey Breast
Makes 10 to 12 servings

1 (5-pound) turkey breast
Salt and pepper to taste
⅓ cup honey
3 tablespoons Dijon mustard
1½ teaspoons dried rosemary leaves

1. Preheat the oven to 325°F.
2. Remove the skin from the turkey breast and discard; place the breast in a roaster pan. Season with the salt and pepper.
3. In a small bowl, mix together the honey, Dijon mustard, and rosemary. Pour half the glaze over the turkey breast, and bake, uncovered, for about 2 hours, or until the meat thermometer registers 170° to 175°F in the thickest part of the breast. You may want

to add a little water to the bottom of the pan, if needed.

4. During the final 15 minutes of the baking, brush the remaining glaze over the turkey breast. Serve.

Honey Pecan Chicken
Makes 6 servings

> 1 cup Wheat Chex cereal crumbs
> ⅓ cup finely chopped pecans
> 2 tablespoons honey
> 2 tablespoons low-sodium soy sauce
> 6 skinless, boneless chicken breasts
> Salt and pepper to taste

1. Preheat the oven to 425°F.
2. Cover a baking sheet with foil, and spray with nonstick cooking spray.

3. On a plate or on waxed paper, combine the cereal crumbs and pecans.
4. In a bowl, mix together the honey and the soy sauce.
5. Season the chicken with salt and pepper. Dip both sides of the chicken breast into the honey mixture; then roll in the pecan mixture to coat.
6. Arrange the chicken on the pan. Bake for 12 to 15 minutes on each side, or until the chicken is done. Serve.

(Tip: If you're in a pinch and don't have Wheat Chex, use bread crumbs or another wheat cereal.)

Meatballs for a Crowd
Makes 14 to 16 servings

4 pounds ground sirloin
1 tablespoon onion powder
1 tablespoon dried oregano leaves
1 tablespoon dried basil
½ teaspoon pepper
1 tablespoon minced garlic
2 tablespoons Worcestershire sauce
2 tablespoons low-sodium soy sauce
1 cup Italian bread crumbs
3 egg whites
Tomato sauce (recipe follows)

1. Preheat the broiler.
2. In a large bowl, mix together the meat, onion powder, oregano, basil, pepper, garlic, Worcestershire sauce, soy sauce, bread

crumbs, and egg whites until well combined. Shape the mixture into meatballs, using about ¼ cup of the mixture for each.

3. Place the meatballs on a baking sheet coated with nonstick cooking spray. Broil about 6 to 8 minutes on each side.

4. Transfer the meatballs to the pot of tomato sauce (see recipe below), and continue cooking for 30 minutes. Serve with pasta.

(Tip: To keep your hands from getting sticky when shaping meatballs or other sticky foods, moisten them with cool water.)

Tomato Sauce:

   1 cup finely chopped onion
   2 (28-ounce) cans chopped tomatoes, with juice
   2 (6-ounce) cans tomato paste

2 cups water
1 tablespoon minced garlic
1 tablespoon dried oregano leaves
1 tablespoon dried basil
¼ teaspoon pepper

1. While the meatballs are broiling, place the onion in a large pot coated with nonstick cooking spray.
2. Over medium-high heat, sauté the onion until tender, about 5 minutes.
3. Add the remaining ingredients. Bring to a boil, lower the heat, and simmer for 30 minutes.
4. Add the meatballs to the sauce.

Old-Fashioned Lasagna
Makes 8 servings

½ pound lasagna noodles

1 teaspoon minced garlic
1 onion, chopped
1½ pounds ground sirloin
Salt and pepper to taste
2 teaspoons dried basil leaves
1 tablespoon chopped parsley
1 teaspoon dried oregano leaves
½ cup finely chopped carrots
2 (6-ounce) cans tomato paste
1½ cups hot water
1 large egg white
1 (15-ounce) container reduced-fat ricotta
    cheese
1 cup shredded part-skim mozzarella cheese

1. Preheat the oven to 350°F.
2. Cook the noodles according to the package
   directions, omitting any oil and salt. Drain
   and set aside.

3. In a large skillet coated with nonstick cooking spray, sauté the garlic and onion over medium-high heat until tender. Add the ground meat, salt, pepper, basil, parsley, oregano, and carrots, cooking until the meat is done, about 7 minutes; drain excess liquid. Add the tomato paste and hot water; simmer for 5 minutes, and then set aside.

4. In a small bowl, blend the egg white and ricotta cheese.

5. In a 13 x 9 x 2-inch baking dish coated with nonstick cooking spray, put a thin layer of the meat sauce, half the noodles, all of the ricotta cheese mixture, and half the mozzarella cheese. Repeat with half the remaining meat sauce, all of the remaining noodles, then the remainder of the meat sauce, and top with the remainder of the mozzarella.

6. Bake for 30 minutes, or until bubbly and well heated. Let sit for 10 minutes before serving.

(Tip: When layering lasagna, always spread a little sauce on the bottom so the pasta doesn't stick. End with sauce on top, as exposed noodles will turn dry and hard.)

Penne with Spinach, Sun-Dried Tomatoes, and Goat Cheese

Makes 4 to 6 servings

    ½ cup sun-dried tomatoes (not oil-packed)
    ⅔ cup boiling water
    12 ounces penne or other tubular pasta
    2 tablespoons olive oil
    1 tablespoon minced garlic
    6 cups stemmed fresh spinach, washed
    1 tablespoon dried basil leaves

2 tablespoons balsamic vinegar
Salt and pepper to taste
½ cup crumbled goat cheese

1. In a small bowl, combine the sun-dried tomatoes and boiling water; set aside to soften, about 10 minutes.
2. Coarsely chop the sun-dried tomatoes, and reserve the soaking liquid.
3. Meanwhile, prepare the pasta according to the package directions, omitting any oil and salt. Drain, and set aside.
4. In a large skillet coated with nonstick cooking spray, heat the oil and add the garlic, sun-dried tomatoes with soaking liquid, spinach, basil, vinegar, salt, and pepper, cooking until the spinach is just wilted, about 5 minutes.

5. Stir in the goat cheese and pasta, heating until the cheese begins to melt. Serve immediately.

(Tip: Any short pasta, such as ziti, rigatoni, or mostaccioli, is a substitute for penne.)

Quick Beef Stew
Makes 6 servings

> 2 pounds lean boneless top round steak, trimmed of fat and cut into 1-inch cubes
> ⅓ cup all-purpose flour
> 2 cups sliced carrots (1-inch slices)
> 1¾ pounds red potatoes, peeled and cubed
> 1 large onion, sliced
> ½ pound fresh mushrooms, quartered
> ½ teaspoon minced garlic
> ¼ cup chopped parsley

½ teaspoon dried thyme leaves
Salt and pepper to taste
1 (14½-ounce) can beef broth
1 cup light beer

1. Combine the meat and flour in a plastic bag; close the bag, and shake.
2. Coat a large pot with nonstick cooking spray, and cook the meat over high heat until browned, about 8 minutes, stirring often. Add the remaining ingredients.
3. Cover, and cook about 1 hour, or until the meat is tender and the vegetables are done.

Quick Vegetarian Chili
Makes 8 servings

2 cups salsa
1 (28-ounce) can diced tomatoes, with juice

1 (15-ounce) can pinto beans, drained and rinsed

1 (15-ounce) can red kidney beans, drained and rinsed

1 (19-ounce) can garbanzo beans, drained and rinsed

1 green bell pepper, seeded and chopped

½ teaspoon minced garlic

1 onion, chopped

2 medium zucchinis, halved lengthwise and thinly sliced

2 tablespoons chili powder

½ teaspoon ground cumin

1 teaspoon dried oregano leaves

½ teaspoon sugar

1. In a large pot, combine all the ingredients. Heat to boiling.

2. Reduce the heat and simmer, covered, for 40 minutes, stirring occasionally.

Speedy Chili
Makes 6 to 8 servings

> 2 pounds ground sirloin
> 1 teaspoon minced garlic
> 1 tablespoon chili powder
> 1 teaspoon ground cumin
> 1 (16-ounce) jar chipotle chunky salsa
> 1 (16-ounce) package frozen whole-kernel corn
> 2 (14½-ounce) cans seasoned beef broth with onion
> 1 (15-ounce) can red kidney beans, rinsed and drained, optional

1. In a large pot, brown the meat and garlic over medium high heat until done. Drain any excess liquid.
2. Add the remaining ingredients. Bring the mixture to a boil, reduce the heat, and cook for 15 minutes.

Stuffed Peppers
Makes 6 servings

> 6 medium green bell peppers, seeded (can use red, yellow, or orange if desired)
> 1 pound ground sirloin
> 1 cup chopped fresh mushrooms
> ¾ cup chopped onion
> 1 cup tomato sauce
> 1 tablespoon minced garlic
> 1 teaspoon dried basil leaves
> 1 teaspoon dried oregano leaves

1 tablespoon Worcestershire sauce
Salt and pepper to taste
2 cups cooked rice
½ cup (2 ounces) shredded part-skim
   mozzarella cheese

1. Preheat the oven to 350°F.
2. Cut the tops off the green peppers, and remove the cores. Trim the stems from the tops, and discard. Chop the remaining tops; set aside.
3. Arrange the pepper shells in a steamer over boiling water, cover, and steam for 5 to 10 minutes, or until tender. Drain the shells, and set aside.
4. In a large skillet coated with nonstick cooking spray, combine the meat, mushrooms, onion, and reserved chopped green pepper. Cook over medium heat until

the meat is brown, about 7 minutes; drain off any excess grease. Add the tomato sauce, garlic, basil, oregano, Worcestershire sauce, salt, and pepper. Bring to a boil; reduce the heat and simmer 5 minutes. Mix in the rice.

5. Spoon the mixture into the pepper shells; then place the peppers upright in an 8-inch square baking dish. Sprinkle with the mozzarella. Bake for 15 minutes, or until the cheese is melted and the peppers are thoroughly heated. Serve.

Vegetable Lasagna
Makes 8 servings

> 1 onion, chopped
> 1 teaspoon minced garlic
> 1 green bell pepper, seeded and chopped
> 1 (6-ounce) can tomato paste

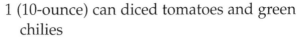

1 (10-ounce) can diced tomatoes and green chilies
1 (10-ounce) can chopped tomatoes
1 (11.5-ounce) can tomato juice
1 teaspoon dried basil
1 teaspoon dried oregano
1 teaspoon dried thyme
1½ tablespoons red wine vinegar
1 bay leaf
½ pound fresh mushrooms, sliced
½ cup shredded peeled carrots
1 bunch broccoli cut into florets
½ pound lasagna noodles
Cheese mixture (recipe follows)
1½ cups shredded part-skim mozzarella cheese

1. Preheat the oven to 350°F.

2. Coat a large skillet with nonstick cooking spray, and add the onion, garlic, and green pepper; sauté over medium-high heat for 5 to 7 minutes, or until tender. Add the tomato paste, diced tomatoes, and green chilies, chopped tomatoes, and tomato juice, bringing to a boil. Add the basil, oregano, thyme, vinegar, bay leaf, mushroom slices, carrot, and broccoli, lower the heat, and simmer 20 to 30 minutes, or until the vegetables are tender and the sauce has thickened. Discard the bay leaf.

3. Cook the lasagna noodles according to the package directions, omitting any oil and salt; drain.

4. In a 13 x 9 x 2-inch baking dish, spoon a layer of vegetable sauce along the bottom. Layer one-third each of the lasagna noodles, cheese mixture (see recipe that follows), vegetable sauce, and mozzarella cheese.

Repeat the layers. Bake, covered, for 30 minutes. Let stand 10 minutes before cutting.

Cheese Mixture:
>   2 cups fat-free cottage cheese
>   1 egg white
>   2 tablespoons chopped parsley
>   ¼ cup Parmesan cheese

In a food processor, combine all ingredients, blending well.

Sides

Almond Asparagus
Makes 6 servings

>   1½ pounds fresh asparagus spears
>   1 tablespoon margarine

2 tablespoons lemon juice
¼ cup slivered almonds, toasted
Salt and pepper to taste

1. Trim off the tough ends of the asparagus.
2. Coat a large skillet with nonstick cooking spray; add the margarine.
3. When the margarine is melted, add the asparagus stems, and sauté at medium heat for 3 to 5 minutes.
4. Add the lemon juice, cover, and simmer until crisp-tender.
5. Add the almond slivers, and season with the salt and pepper, tossing gently. Serve.

Broccoli Casserole

Makes 6 to 8 servings

> 2 (10-ounce) packages frozen chopped
> broccoli, thawed and drained
> 1 egg
> 2 egg whites, slightly beaten
> 3 tablespoons all-purpose flour
> 1 (12-ounce) carton reduced-fat cottage cheese
> 6 ounces reduced-fat pasteurized
> processed cheese spread, cut into pieces

1. Preheat the oven to 350°F.
2. In a large bowl, mix the broccoli, egg, egg whites, flour, cottage cheese, and cheese spread; pour into a 2-quart baking dish coated with nonstick cooking spray.
3. Bake, uncovered, for 1 hour, or until bubbly. Serve.

Candied Sweet Potatoes
Makes 6 to 8 servings

> 6 medium sweet potatoes (about 3 pounds)
>   peeled and cut into julienne strips
> 1¼ cup water
> 1 cup light brown sugar
> 1 large orange, peeled and chopped
> 1 large lemon, peeled and chopped
> 2 tablespoons unsalted butter
> ¼ teaspoon salt

1. Preheat the oven to 350°F.
2. Arrange the sweet potatoes in a large baking dish.
3. In a medium mixing bowl, combine the remaining ingredients. Pour over the sweet potatoes.
4. Cover with aluminum foil and bake for 30 minutes.

5. Uncover and bake, basting frequently, about 30 minutes more, until the potatoes are tender and golden brown.

Corn Bread Dressing
Makes 8 servings

> 2 (8½-ounce) boxes corn muffin mix
> 1 egg
> ⅓ cup skim milk
> 4 ounces bulk light sausage, optional
> 2 onions, chopped
> 1 green bell pepper, seeded and chopped
> 1 teaspoon minced garlic
> 1 cup chopped celery
> 1 (10¾-ounce) can 98% fat-free cream of mushroom soup
> 1 (16-ounce) can fat-free vegetable (or chicken) broth

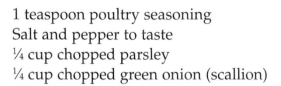

1 teaspoon poultry seasoning
Salt and pepper to taste
¼ cup chopped parsley
¼ cup chopped green onion (scallion)

1. Preheat the oven to 350°F.
2. Prepare the corn muffin mix with the egg and milk, and bake in a 13 x 9 x 2-inch pan according to the package directions. Crumble and set aside.
3. In a large skillet coated with nonstick cooking spray, sauté the sausage, onion, green pepper, garlic, and celery until tender. Add the cream of mushroom soup, broth, poultry seasoning, salt, pepper, and crumbled corn bread. Stir in the parsley and green onion.

4. Transfer to a 2-quart casserole, and bake for 30 minutes, or until lightly browned and heated. Serve.

Cranberry Mold
Makes 10 servings

> 1 (16-ounce) package fresh cranberries
> 1 whole orange
> ½ cup chopped pecans
> 1 cup crushed pineapple, in its own juices, drained
> 1 (3-ounce) package raspberry gelatin
> 1 cup boiling water

1. Combine the cranberries, orange, and pecans in a food processor, and mix until chopped finely. Add the crushed pineapple.

2. Dissolve the gelatin in the boiling water, stirring until dissolved. Combine with the cranberry mixture, mixing well. Pour into a 5-cup mold. Refrigerate until firm.

(Tip: Purchase cranberries when they're in season and freeze in airtight plastic bags for up to a year.)

Cranberry Relish
Makes 2 cups; serves 8

> 3 cups fresh cranberries (about 12 ounces)
> ½ cup granulated sugar
> ½ cup water
> 2 tablespoons grated orange rind

1. In a stainless steel or enameled saucepan, combine the cranberries, sugar, water, and orange rind.

2. Bring to a simmer over medium-low heat.
3. Cook, stirring occasionally, about 5 minutes, until the cranberries burst.
4. Remove from the heat and let cool. Store in a tightly sealed plastic or glass container and refrigerate for up to 8 weeks.

Green Bean Casserole
Makes 8 servings

1 (16-ounce) package frozen French-cut green beans
1 onion, chopped
1 tablespoon margarine
2 tablespoons all-purpose flour
Salt and pepper to taste
½ cup skim milk

½ cup nonfat plain yogurt or fat-free sour cream

1 cup shredded reduced-fat sharp cheddar cheese

1. Cook the green beans according to the package directions; drain well.
2. Preheat the broiler.
3. In a small pot, sauté the onion in the margarine until tender.
4. Blend in the flour, salt, and pepper. Gradually add the milk, stirring and cooking over medium heat until thickened and bubbly. Stir in the yogurt and green beans; heat thoroughly, about two minutes.
5. Transfer to 1½-quart casserole. Sprinkle with the cheese, and broil in the oven until the cheese melts. Serve.

Garlic Smashed Potatoes
Makes 8 servings

> 3 pounds red potatoes, peeled and
>   quartered
> 10 garlic cloves, peeled
> 2 tablespoons margarine
> 1 cup skim milk
> ⅓ cup plain nonfat yogurt
> ½ cup sliced green onion (scallion)
> Salt and pepper to taste

1. Preheat the oven to 350°F.
2. On a baking sheet coated with nonstick cooking spray, spread the potatoes and garlic.
3. Bake for 45 minutes, or until the potatoes are tender.
4. In a large mixing bowl, mix together the potato mixture, margarine, milk, and yogurt

until creamy. Fold in the green onion, and add the salt and pepper to taste. Serve.

Molasses Baked Beans
Overnight preparation recommended
Makes 8 servings

> 1 pound dried navy beans
> 9 slices lean bacon, chopped
> ¼ cup packed dark brown sugar
> ½ cup molasses
> 1½ teaspoons dry mustard
> ½ cup chicken stock, optional
> Salt and freshly ground black pepper

1. Pre-soak the beans. Drain.
2. Preheat the oven to 300°F.
3. In a large saucepan, cover the pre-soaked beans with water and bring to a boil over

high heat. Reduce the heat to medium and cook, covered, for 30 minutes.

4. Drain the beans. Stir in the bacon, sugar, molasses, and mustard.

5. Transfer the bean mixture to a medium bean pot or casserole dish and bake, covered, about 7 hours, until tender.

6. Check the consistency several times during baking. If the beans become overly dry, add the chicken stock.

7. Season with salt and pepper to taste.

Orange Glazed Carrots
Makes 8 to 10 servings

1 tablespoon margarine
¼ cup fat-free canned vegetable (or chicken) broth

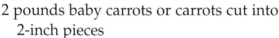

2 pounds baby carrots or carrots cut into
   2-inch pieces
1 cup orange marmalade
Salt and pepper to taste
2 tablespoons chopped parsley

1. In a large saucepan, bring the margarine and broth to a boil.
2. Add the carrots, and cook, covered, over medium heat for 10 to 20 minutes, or until crisp-tender.
3. Uncover, and stir in the marmalade.
4. Cook, stirring over low heat until the liquid has reduced to a glaze, 3 to 5 minutes. Season with the salt and pepper.
5. Sprinkle with parsley before serving.

Sautéed Cherry Tomatoes with Basil
Makes 6 servings

> 1 pound cherry or grape tomatoes
> 1 garlic clove, minced
> 1 tablespoon dried basil leaves
> 2 tablespoons chopped parsley
> ½ teaspoon dried thyme leaves
> 1 teaspoon sugar
> Salt and fresh ground pepper to taste

1. Wash the tomatoes, and dry them well.
2. In a small bowl, combine the garlic, basil, parsley, and thyme.
3. Heat a skillet coated with nonstick cooking spray over medium heat, and add the tomatoes. Sprinkle with the sugar, salt, and pepper, and toss briefly until well heated.

4. Stir in the garlic mixture, and sauté for 1 minute, or until the sugar melts and the mixture is heated thoroughly. Serve immediately.

Squash Casserole
Makes 6 to 8 servings

> 2 pounds fresh squash, thinly sliced
> 2 green bell peppers, seeded and chopped
> 1 large onion, chopped
> 2 tablespoons canola oil
> 1 (15-ounce) can cream-style corn
> 1 tablespoon sugar
> ¼ cup cornmeal
> Salt and pepper to taste

1. Preheat the oven to 350°F.

2. Steam the fresh squash until very tender on top of the stove for about 10 minutes in ¼ cup water or in the microwave; drain. Mash or purée the squash in a food processor.

3. In a large skillet, sauté the green pepper and onion in the oil until tender.

4. Combine the puréed squash, onion mixture, corn, sugar, and cornmeal. Add the salt and pepper.

5. Place the mixture in a 2-quart casserole dish coated with nonstick cooking spray. Bake for 30 minutes, or until bubbly and thoroughly heated. Serve.

Squash Rockefeller
Makes 12 stuffed squash

    6 yellow medium squash

2 (10-ounce) packages frozen chopped
　spinach
1 bunch green onions (scallions), chopped
½ cup finely chopped parsley
3 stalks celery, chopped
2 cloves garlic, minced
¼ cup margarine
½ cup Italian bread crumbs
Hot pepper sauce to taste
Salt and pepper to taste

1. Preheat the oven to 350°F.
2. Cut the squash in half lengthwise. Steam in
   ½-inch water, covered, on the stove or in the
   microwave, until almost tender. Cool
   slightly, and scoop out the pulp, being
   careful not to break the shell; discard the
   pulp.

3. Cook the spinach according to the package directions; drain well.

4. In a skillet coated with nonstick cooking spray, sauté the green onions, parsley, celery, and garlic in the margarine until tender. Combine with the spinach, bread crumbs, hot pepper sauce, and salt and pepper, mixing well.

5. Stuff the squash shells with the mixture. Bake for 20 minutes, or until well-heated. Serve.

Sweet Potato Casserole with Praline Topping
Makes 8 to 10 servings

> 3 cups cooked mashed sweet potatoes (yams)
> ½ cup sugar
> 1 egg
> 1 egg white

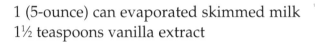

1 (5-ounce) can evaporated skimmed milk
1½ teaspoons vanilla extract

1. Preheat the oven to 350°F.
2. In a mixing bowl, blend all the ingredients.
3. Place in a 2-quart casserole dish coated with nonstick cooking spray, and cover with praline topping (see recipe below).
4. Bake for 45 minutes until topping is browned and casserole is thoroughly heated. Serve.

Praline Topping:

1 cup light brown sugar
½ cup all-purpose flour
½ teaspoon ground cinnamon
6 tablespoons margarine, melted
1 teaspoon vanilla extract
½ cup chopped pecans, optional

1. In a medium bowl, mix together the brown sugar, flour, and cinnamon.
2. Add the margarine, vanilla, and pecans, stirring until crumbly.
3. In a medium bowl, mix together the brown sugar, flour, and cinnamon.
4. Add the margarine, vanilla, and pecans, stirring until crumbly.

Sweet Potato Pizza

Makes 6 to 8 servings

4 to 5 cups thinly sliced fresh sweet
  potatoes (yams), peeled
¼ cup light brown sugar
1 teaspoon ground cinnamon
¼ teaspoon ground nutmeg

1. Preheat the oven to 400°F. Coat a 12-inch pizza pan with nonstick cooking spray.
2. Arrange the sweet potato slices to cover the pizza pan, overlapping the slices. Spray the slices with nonstick cooking spray. Bake 15 minutes or until tender.
3. In a small bowl, mix together the brown sugar, cinnamon, and nutmeg, and sprinkle evenly over the potato slices. Return to the oven, and continue baking until the potato slices are crispy, 5 to 10 minutes more. Slice, and serve immediately.

Sweet Potatoes and Apples
Makes 8 servings

6 medium sweet potatoes (about 3 pounds)

4 medium Granny Smith apples, peeled, cored, and sliced
1 cup packed light brown sugar
4 tablespoons unsalted butter
1 teaspoon ground mace
Salt and freshly ground black pepper

1. Preheat the oven to 325°F.
2. In a Dutch oven, cook the sweet potatoes in enough boiling water to cover for 15 to 20 minutes, until just fork-tender. Do not overcook. Drain.
3. Peel and cut the potatoes into ¼-inch-thick slices.
4. Place half of the potato sliced in the bottom of a buttered large baking dish. Top with half of the apple slices. Sprinkle with half of the sugar, butter, and mace. Season to taste with salt and pepper.

5. Repeat with alternate layers of the remaining potato slices, apple slices, sugar, butter, and mace.
6. Bake about 1 hour, until the top is brown and the liquid has evaporated.

Yam Corn Bread Stuffing
Makes 10 servings

  2 cups chopped, peeled, sweet potatoes (yams)
  1 cup chopped onion
  1 cup sliced celery
  2 tablespoons margarine
  ¼ cup chopped parsley
  1 teaspoon ground ginger
  5 cups crumbled cooked corn bread
  ¼ cup chopped pecans, toasted
  Vegetable (or chicken) broth, as needed

1. Preheat the oven to 375°F.
2. In a large skillet, cook the sweet potatoes, onion, and celery in the margarine over medium-high heat for 7 to 10 minutes, or until just tender.
3. Spoon the mixture into a large mixing bowl. Stir in the parsley and ginger. Add the corn bread and pecans, and toss gently to coat. Add enough broth to moisten.
4. Place the stuffing in a 2-quart oblong casserole. Bake, uncovered, for 45 minutes, or until heated through. Serve.

Yam Veggie Wraps
Makes 6 wraps

> 1 sweet potato (yam), peeled and shredded (about 1 cup)
> ½ cup chopped red onion

1 cup canned black beans, rinsed and
  drained
2 green onions (scallions), sliced
¼ cup chopped roasted peanuts
2 tablespoons light Italian or Caesar
  dressing
1 teaspoon honey
6 (6- to 8-inch) flour tortillas, warmed to
  soften

1. In a skillet coated with nonstick cooking
   spray, sauté the shredded yam over
   medium-high heat for about 5 minutes, or
   until crisp-tender. Transfer to a bowl.
2. In the same skillet coated with nonstick
   cooking spray, sauté the red onion until tender.
3. Add the sautéed onion, black beans, green
   onions, and peanuts to the shredded yams,
   mixing well.

4. In a small bowl, mix together the dressing and honey, and toss with the yam mixture to coat.
5. Fill the tortillas, and wrap. Serve.

Zucchini with White Beans and Mint
Makes 4 servings

2 tablespoons extra-virgin olive oil, fruity-flavored if possible
½ teaspoon minced garlic
3 or 4 small zucchinis, cut into long (¼ x ¼-inch) strips
1 cup cooked cannellini beans
½ tablespoon chopped fresh mint leaves
Salt and fresh ground black pepper
Parmesan cheese

1. In a large sauté pan set over medium-high heat, heat the oil until it ripples. Add the garlic and cook for 2 minutes. Add the zucchinis and a few drops of water. Cook, tossing gently, until just tender, about 4 minutes. Add the beans and heat through.

2. Remove the pan from the heat. Stir in the mint and salt and pepper to taste. Serve hot, or let cool to room temperature, cover, and refrigerate for up to 2 days. Reheat before serving, and shave Parmesan cheese on top if desired.

Cookies & Bars

Butterballs

Makes about 36 cookies

> 8 tablespoons (1 stick) sweet butter, softened
> 3 tablespoons honey
> 1 cup unbleached all-purpose flour
> ½ teaspoon salt
> 1 tablespoon vanilla extract
> 1 cup shelled pecans, chopped moderately fine
> ¾ cup confectioners' sugar

1. Preheat oven to 300°F. Grease one or two cookie sheets.

2. Cream butter. Beat in honey; gradually mix in flour and salt, then vanilla. Add pecans. Wrap dough in plastic wrap and chill for 1 hour.

3. Form balls by hand, the size of quarters. Place 2 inches apart on the prepared cookie sheets. Bake for 35 to 40 minutes.

4. Remove from oven; as soon as cool enough to touch, roll in confectioners' sugar. Allow to cool and roll again in sugar.

Butterscotch Bars with Meringue Topping
Makes about 1 dozen bars

Butterscotch Cookie Layer:
   Vegetable oil spray or vegetable oil, for greasing
   ¼ cup (½ stick) unsalted butter

529

1 cup packed dark brown sugar
½ cup all-purpose flour
1 teaspoon ground cinnamon
½ teaspoon salt
1 egg
1 teaspoon vanilla extract

Meringue Topping:
1 egg white
⅛ teaspoon cream of tartar
1 tablespoon corn syrup
½ cup superfine sugar
1 cup chopped walnuts

1. Preheat the oven to 350°F. Invert an 8-inch square baking pan. Mold a sheet of foil over the bottom of the pan, smoothing it evenly around the corners. Remove the foil and turn the pan right side up. Press the foil into

the pan, smoothing it into the sides and corners. Grease the foil.

2. In a medium saucepan over medium heat, simmer the butter and brown sugar for about 3–5 minutes, until the sugar dissolves. Remove from the heat and cool. Sift the flour, cinnamon, and salt into a medium bowl.

3. Beat the egg and vanilla extract into the cooled butter mixture until well blended. Stir in the flour mixture until just blended. Spread over the bottom of the pan, smoothing the surface evenly.

4. Meringue Topping: In a medium bowl, beat the egg white until foamy. Add the cream of tartar and continue beating until soft peaks form. Gradually beat in the corn syrup, then the sugar and continue beating until the whites are stiff and glossy. Fold in half the

nuts and carefully spread the topping over the butterscotch layer. Sprinkle the top with the remaining nuts.

5. Bake for about 30 minutes, until the topping is puffed (the meringue may crack) and golden. Remove to a wire rack and cool completely. Using the foil as a guide, remove to a board and peel off the foil. Cut into 1½-inch fingers. Store in airtight containers in single layers.

Chewy Caramel Nut Squares
Makes about 3 dozen squares

Pastry Crust:

    3 cups all-purpose flour

    ½ cup cornstarch

    ½ teaspoon salt

    1½ cups (3 sticks) unsalted butter, softened

⅔ cup sugar
Grated zest of 1 lemon

Caramel Nut Topping:
    10 tablespoons (1¼ sticks) unsalted butter
    ½ cup packed dark brown sugar
    ½ cup honey
    1½ tablespoons whipping cream
    1 cup salted cashews, lightly toasted and
        coarsely chopped
    1 cup whole blanched almonds, toasted
        and coarsely chopped
    1 cup pine nuts, toasted

1. Invert 13 x 9-inch baking pan. Mold foil over
   the bottom, smoothing it evenly around the
   corners. Remove the foil and turn the pan
   right side up. Press the foil into the pan,

smoothing it into the sides and corners. Grease the foil.

2. Preheat the oven to 350°F. Sift the flour, cornstarch, and salt into a medium bowl. In a large bowl, using an electric mixer, beat the butter, sugar, and lemon zest for 1–2 minutes, until light and fluffy. On low speed, beat in the flour mixture, until blended and a soft dough forms.

3. Press the dough evenly onto the bottom and 1 inch up the sides of the pan, pressing into the corners. Prick the bottom with a fork and bake for about 30 minutes, until the pastry is very lightly browned, turning the pan halfway through cooking and pricking with a fork if the pastry puffs up. Remove the pan to a wire rack.

4. In a medium saucepan over medium heat, bring to a boil the butter, sugar, honey, and

cream, stirring until the sugar dissolves. Boil, without stirring, for about 1 minute, until the mixture thickens slightly. Remove from the heat and stir in the cashews, almonds, and pine nuts until well mixed.

5. Pour the nut mixture over the crust, spreading evenly. Bake for about 20 minutes, until sticky and bubbling. Remove to a wire rack to cool completely. Using the foil as a guide, remove to a board. Peel off the foil and cut into 1½-inch squares. Store in airtight containers in single layers.

Christmas Cut-out Cookies

Makes about 6 dozen (depending on the size of the cutters)

2 cups all-purpose flour
2 teaspoons baking powder

½ teaspoon salt
½ cup (1 stick) unsalted butter, softened
1 cup superfine sugar
1 egg, lightly beaten
Grated zest of 1 lemon
1 tablespoon lemon juice
1 tablespoon vanilla extract
½ teaspoon lemon extract

1. Sift the flour, baking powder, and salt into a medium bowl. In a large bowl, using an electric mixer, beat the butter for about 30 seconds, until creamy. Add the sugar and continue beating for 1-2 minutes, until light and fluffy. Beat in the egg, lemon zest and juice, and vanilla and lemon extracts until well blended and a soft dough forms.
2. Form the dough into a ball and flatten to a disc shape. Wrap tightly and refrigerate for

several hours or overnight, until the dough is firm enough to handle.

3. Preheat the oven to 350°F. On a lightly floured surface, using a floured rolling pin, roll out one third of the dough ⅛-inch thick. Keep the remaining dough refrigerated. Using floured cookie cutters, cut out as many shapes as possible and, if necessary, use a thin-bladed metal spatula to transfer the shapes to 2 large, ungreased baking sheets, placing them 1 inch apart.

4. Bake for about 8 minutes, until the cookies are just colored around the edges. Using a pancake turner, transfer the cookies to wire racks to cool completely. Repeat rolling, cutting, and baking with the remaining dough.

Icing

> 3 cups confectioners' sugar
> 2–3 tablespoons milk
> 1 tablespoon lemon juice
> Red and green food coloring (optional)

1. Sift the confectioners' sugar into a medium bowl. Stir in 2 tablespoons of milk and lemon juice, adding a little more milk if the icing is too thick. Spoon about one-third of the icing into a small bowl and another third into another small bowl. Add a few drops of red coloring to one bowl and green to the other, mixing until you achieve the desired shades.

2. Spoon the 3 colors into 3 paper cones. Pipe designs onto each shape. Alternatively, you can spread icing with a knife. Allow to set for about 2 hours, then store in airtight

containers with waxed paper between the layers.

Cinnamon Chocolate Stars
Makes 30 cookies

1½ sticks (¾ cup) plus 1 tablespoon sweet
   butter at room temperature
7 tablespoons sugar
1½ cups all-purpose flour
A good pinch of salt
1 teaspoon ground cinnamon
5 tablespoons rice flour or cornstarch
2 ounces bittersweet chocolate, to finish
One star-shaped cookie cutter

1. Using a wooden spoon or electric mixer,
   beat the butter until creamy. Gradually beat
   in the sugar. When the mixture is pale and

fluffy, sift the flour, salt, cinnamon, and rice flour into the bowl and mix.

2. When the mixture comes together, turn it onto a lightly floured surface and knead lightly and briefly to make a smooth, but not sticky dough. In hot weather, or if the dough feels sticky, wrap it and chill until firm. Roll out the dough to about ¼-inch thick and cut out shapes with the cutter. Gently knead together the trimmings, then re-roll and cut more stars.

3. Arrange the stars slightly apart on greased baking trays. Prick with a fork and chill for about 15 minutes.

4. Bake the cookies in a preheated oven at 350°F for about 12 to 15 minutes or until firm and barely colored.

5. Let cool on the baking trays for a couple of minutes until firm enough to transfer to a wire cooling rack.

6. When they are completely cold, gently melt the chocolate in a small heatproof bowl set over a pan of steaming water. Stir until smooth, then remove the bowl from the heat. Dip the points of the stars into the melted chocolate, then leave to set on waxed paper, non-stick parchment paper, or a wire rack.

7. When the cookies are firm, store in an airtight container and eat within 3 days. Undecorated cookies can be frozen for up to 1 month.

Coconut Macaroons

Makes about 2 dozen cookies

3 cups sweetened, shredded coconut
1 cup unsalted macadamia nuts, chopped
⅔ cup sweetened condensed milk
1 teaspoon vanilla extract
2 egg whites
Pinch of salt

1. Preheat the oven to 350°F. Place the shredded coconut onto a large baking sheet and the macadamia nuts onto another baking sheet. Toast for 7-10 minutes, until lightly golden, stirring and shaking each sheet frequently. Pour the coconut onto a plate and the nuts onto another plate to cool completely.

2. Line 2 large baking sheets with nonstick baking parchment paper, and very lightly grease with oil. In a large bowl, stir together the condensed milk, vanilla extract, shredded coconut, and macadamia nuts until well blended.

3. In a medium bowl, using an electric mixer on medium speed, beat the egg whites until foamy. Add the salt and increase the mixer speed to high. Continue beating until the whites are stiff but not dry. Fold the whites into the coconut mixture. Drop rounded tablespoonfuls onto the baking sheets, and shape each one into a cone. Bake for 10-12 minutes, until golden around the edges. Remove the baking sheets to wire racks to cool completely, then gently peel off the paper.

Cookie Jar Gingersnaps
Makes about 4 dozen cookies

> 2 cups all-purpose flour
> 1 tablespoon ground ginger
> 2 teaspoons baking soda
> 1½ teaspoons ground cinnamon
> ½ teaspoon ground cloves
> ½ teaspoon salt
> ¾ cup white vegetable shortening
> 1 cup sugar
> 1 egg, lightly beaten
> ¼ cup molasses
> Sugar, for rolling

1. Preheat the oven to 350°F. Sift the flour, ginger, baking soda, cinnamon, ground cloves, and salt into a medium bowl.

2. In a large bowl, using an electric mixer, beat the shortening for 1 minute, until soft. Gradually add the sugar and continue beating until the mixture is light and fluffy. Beat in the egg and molasses, then stir in the flour mixture until thoroughly blended.

3. Pour the sugar into a medium bowl. Using a heaped teaspoon, scoop out the mixture. Using your palms, roll into ¾-inch balls and roll in the sugar. Place 2 inches apart on ungreased baking sheets.

4. Bake for about 10 minutes, until the cookies are slightly rounded and the tops are lightly browned and crackled. Remove the baking sheets to wire racks to cool. Remove the cookies to wire racks to cool completely. Store in an airtight container.

Death by Chocolate
Makes about 2 dozen large cookies

9 ounces bittersweet or semisweet chocolate, chopped

¾ cup (1½ sticks) unsalted butter; cut into pieces

3 eggs

¾ cup superfine sugar

2 teaspoons vanilla extract

½ cup all-purpose flour

6 tablespoons cocoa powder, sifted

1½ teaspoons baking powder

¼ teaspoon salt

9 ounces semisweet chocolate, chopped into ¼-inch pieces (about 1½ cups) or 1½ cups semisweet chocolate chips

6 ounces chocolate, chopped into ¼-inch pieces

6 ounces white chocolate, chopped into ¼-inch pieces

1½ cups pecans or walnuts, toasted and chopped

1. Preheat oven to 325°F. Lightly grease two large baking sheets. In a medium saucepan over low heat, melt the chocolate and butter, stirring frequently until smooth. Set aside to cool slightly.

2. In a large bowl, using an electric mixer, beat eggs and sugars for 2–3 minutes on low speed, until thick and pale. Gradually beat in the melted chocolate and vanilla extract until well blended. In a small bowl, stir together the flour, cocoa powder, baking powder, and salt until blended, then gently

stir into chocolate mixture. Stir in the chocolate pieces and nuts.

3. Drop heaping tablespoonfuls of the mixture at least 4 inches apart onto the baking sheets. Wet the bottom of a drinking glass and flatten each dough round slightly, to make each about 3 inches round; you will fit only 4–6 cookies on each sheet. Bake for 10 minutes, until the tops are cracked and shiny. Do not overbake or the cookies will break when removed from the baking sheet.

4. Remove the baking sheets to wire racks to cool slightly and set. Using a metal pancake turner or thin-bladed metal spatula, carefully remove each cookie to wire racks to cool completely. Repeat with the remaining cooking dough. Store in an airtight container.

Fruit 'n' Nut Oatmeal Cookies
Makes about 3 dozen cookies

3 cups raisins
1 cup dried cranberries or cherries
1 cup boiling water
¾ cup (1½ sticks) unsalted butter, softened
1½ cups packed light brown sugar
2 eggs, lightly beaten
1½ teaspoons vanilla extract
2½ cups all-purpose flour
½ teaspoon baking powder
1½ teaspoons baking soda
½ teaspoon salt
2 teaspoons ground cinnamon
1 teaspoon ground ginger
½ teaspoon ground allspice
2 cups old-fashioned (rolled) oats

2 cups chopped walnuts or pecans, lightly toasted

1½ cups pitted prunes, chopped

1 cup chopped pitted dates

1. In a small bowl, combine the dried fruit. Pour over the boiling water and allow to stand, covered, for ¼ hour, stirring occasionally. Drain, reserving ⅓ cup of the soaking liquid, and set aside.

2. Preheat the oven to 400°F. Lightly grease two large baking sheets. In a large bowl, using an electric mixer, beat the butter until creamy. Add the sugar and continue beating for about 2 minutes, until light and fluffy. Slowly beat in the eggs and vanilla extract.

3. Sift the flour, baking powder, baking soda, salt, cinnamon, ginger, and allspice into a large bowl. Add the butter mixture

alternately with the reserved soaking liquid, mixing well until blended. Stir in the oats, walnuts or pecans, prunes, dates, and soaked raisins and cranberries or cherries.

4. Drop heaping tablespoonfuls of the mixture onto the baking sheets at least 3 inches apart. Flatten slightly with the back of a moistened spoon. Bake for 6–8 minutes, until golden and set. Remove the baking sheets to wire racks to cool slightly. Using a metal pancake turner, transfer the cookies to wire racks to cool completely. Repeat with the remaining cookie dough. Store the cookies in an airtight container.

Gingery Chocolate Cookies
Makes about 3 dozen cookies

    2–3-inch piece of fresh gingerroot, peeled

2½ cups all-purpose flour

2 tablespoons unsweetened cocoa powder (preferably Dutch-processed)

½ teaspoon ground ginger

½ teaspoon salt

¼ teaspoon finely ground black pepper

1 cup (2 sticks) unsalted butter, softened

1 cup packed dark brown sugar

2 egg yolks

2 teaspoons vanilla extract

12 ounces bittersweet or semisweet chocolate, chopped

Chopped candied ginger, to decorate

1. Grate the piece of gingerroot against the small round holes of a box grater and set aside. Sift the flour, cocoa powder, ground ginger, salt, and pepper into a medium bowl.

2. In a large bowl, using an electric mixer, beat the butter for 30 seconds, until creamy. Add the brown sugar and continue beating for 1-2 minutes, until light and flufffy. Beat in the egg yolks and vanilla extract until the mixture is smooth and well blended. Sift the flour mixture until blended.

3. Scrape the dough onto a piece of plastic wrap and, using the wrap as a guide, shape it into a 2½-inch log. Wrap tightly and refrigerate for 3–4 hours, or freeze until hard.

4. Preheat the oven to 350°F. Line 2 large baking sheets with nonstick cookie parchment. Unwrap the dough and, using a sharp knife, cut the log into ¼-inch slices and place 1 inch apart on the baking sheets.

5. Bake for about 12 minutes, until lightly browned, rotating the baking sheets from the top to the bottom shelf and from front to

back halfway through the cooking time. Remove the baking sheets to wire racks to cool for about 1 minute. Using a metal pancake turner, transfer each cookie to wire racks to cool completely.

6. Put the chocolate in a bowl over a pan of just simmering water. Stir until melted. Set aside to cool, stirring occasionally. When it reaches a spreading consistency, use a small spoon to swirl a little chocolate on each cookie. Sprinkle with a little candied ginger and allow the cookies to set. Store in airtight containers with waxed paper between the layers.

Holiday Cookies
Makes 48 cookies

½ cup margarine

1 cup sugar
1 egg
1 teaspoon vanilla extract
2 cups all-purpose flour
½ teaspoon baking powder
¼ cup cocoa
1 (7-ounce) jar marshmallow crème
½ cup chopped white chocolate chips
½ cup dried cranberries
½ cup chopped pecans

1. Preheat the oven to 350°F.
2. In a large mixing bowl, cream the margarine and sugar. Add the egg and vanilla, mixing well.
3. In a medium bowl, combine the flour, baking powder, and cocoa; add to the margarine mixture. Add the marshmallow

crème, stirring until combined. Stir in the white chocolate chips, cranberries, and pecans just until blended. The batter will be thick.

4. Drop by spoonfuls onto a baking sheet coated with nonstick cooking spray. Bake for 10 to 12 minutes, or until lightly browned. Remove to wire rack, and cool.

Lacy Oatmeal Wafers
Makes about 2 dozen cookies

    1½ cups quick-cooking rolled oats
    1 cup packed light brown sugar
    ½ cup superfine sugar
    2 tablespoons all-purpose flour
    ¼ teaspoon salt
    ⅔ cup (1 stick) plus 2⅔ tablespoons
       unsalted butter, melted

1 egg, lightly beaten
1 teaspoon vanilla extract
½ cup mini chocolate chips (optional)

1. Preheat oven to 350°F.
2. In a large bowl, stir together the oats, sugars, flour, and salt. Make a well in the center and add the melted butter, egg, and vanilla. Stir until well blended and a soft batter-like dough forms. Stir in the chocolate chips, if using.
3. Drop teaspoonfuls of the mixture 2½ inches apart onto ungreased baking sheets. Bake for 3–5 minutes, until the edges are lightly brown and the centers are bubbling; the cookies will spread to large discs. Remove the baking sheets to wire racks to cool slightly.

4. When the edges of the cookies are firm
   enough to lift, use a thin-bladed metal
   spatula to remove to wire racks to cool.
   Store in airtight containers with waxed
   paper between each layer of cookies.

Molasses Cookies
Makes 24 large flat cookies

> 12 tablespoons (1½ sticks) sweet butter
> 1 cup granulated sugar
> ¼ cup molasses
> 1 egg
> 1¾ cups unbleached all-purpose flour
> ½ teaspoon ground cloves
> ½ teaspoon ground ginger
> 1 teaspoon ground cinnamon
> ½ teaspoon salt
> ½ teaspoon baking soda

1. Preheat oven to 350°F.
2. Melt butter, add sugar and molasses, and mix thoroughly. Lightly beat egg and add to butter mixture; blend well.
3. Sift flour with spices, salt, and baking soda, and add to first mixture; mix. Batter will be wet.
4. Lay a sheet of foil on a cookie sheet. Drop tablespoons of cookie batter on foil, leaving 3 inches between the cookies. These will spread during the baking.
5. Bake until cookies start to darken, 8 to 10 minutes. Remove from oven while still soft. Let cool on foil.

Moravian Spice Squares

Makes about 2 ½ dozen cookies

¼ cup (½ stick) unsalted butter
¼ cup packed dark brown sugar
2 tablespoons molasses
1¼ cups all-purpose flour
Grated zest of 1 lemon
1 teaspoon ground ginger
1 teaspoon ground cinnamon
¼ teaspoon ground cloves
½ teaspoon baking soda
Sugar, for sprinkling

1. In a medium saucepan over medium heat, heat the butter, brown sugar, and molasses until melted and smooth, stirring often. Remove from the heat and stir in the flour,

lemon zest, ginger, cinnamon, cloves, and baking soda until blended.

2. Scrape the dough onto a piece of waxed paper or plastic wrap and, using the paper or wrap as a guide, shape into a flat disc. Wrap tightly and refrigerate for several hours or overnight. The dough can be made up to 5 days ahead.

3. Preheat the oven to 350°F. Lightly grease 2 large baking sheets. On a lightly floured surface, using a floured rolling pin, roll one half of the dough into a 10 x 10-inch square. Using a sharp knife or pastry wheel, cut the dough into 1¼-inch squares and place about 1 inch apart on the baking sheet.

4. With a fork, gently prick the cookie squares to prevent the pastry puffing, and sprinkle with a little sugar. Bake for 7 minutes, until

just set. Using a pancake turner, transfer to wire racks to cool completely. Repeat with the remaining dough. Store in airtight containers.

New Wave Peanut Butter Cookies
Makes 18 cookies

1 cup freshly shelled peanuts
1 cup all-purpose flour
½ teaspoon baking soda
¼ teaspoon salt
½ cup chunky peanut butter
½ cup (1 stick) unsalted butter, softened
½ cup packed light brown sugar
2 tablespoons sugar
1 egg, lightly beaten
1 teaspoon vanilla extract

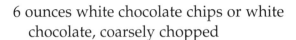

6 ounces white chocolate chips or white
chocolate, coarsely chopped

1. Put the peanuts in a medium skillet or
frying pan, and toast over medium-low heat
for about 5 minutes, until golden and
fragrant, stirring frequently. Pour the nuts
onto a plate and leave to cool.
2. Preheat the oven to 375°F. Lightly grease
two large baking sheets.
3. Sift the flour, baking soda, and salt into a
medium bowl.
4. In a large bowl, using an electric mixer, beat
the peanut butter, butter, and sugars
together for 2–3 minutes, until light and
fluffy. Gradually add the egg and continue
beating for 2 minutes more. Beat in the
vanilla extract. Stir in the flour mixture

until blended, then the chocolate and peanuts.

5. Drop heaping tablespoonfuls of the mixture at least 2 inches apart onto the baking sheets. Flatten slightly with the back of a moistened spoon. Bake for 10 minutes until golden brown. Do not overbake.

6. Remove the baking sheets to wire racks to cool for 5 minutes. Transfer each cookie to wire racks to cool completely. Store in an airtight container.

Peanut Butter Cookie-Cups

Makes about 2 dozen cookies

Peanut-Butter Cookie:

    1 cup all-purpose flour
    1 teaspoon baking powder
    ¼ teaspoon salt

½ cup (1 stick) unsalted butter, softened
½ cup packed light brown sugar
¼ cup sugar
1 cup smooth peanut butter
1 egg
1 teaspoon vanilla extract

Chocolate Filling:
12 ounces semisweet or bittersweet
    chocolate, chopped
6 tablespoons (¾ stick) unsalted butter,
    softened

1. Sift the flour, baking powder, and salt into a small bowl.
2. In a large mixing bowl, using an electric mixer, beat the butter for 1 minute, until creamy. Add the sugars and continue beating until the mixture is light and fluffy.

Add the peanut butter in 3 batches, beating well after each addition, until the mixture is well blended. Beat in the eggs and vanilla extract. Stir in the flour mixture until just blended. Refrigerate the dough for about 1 hour, until chilled.

3. Preheat the oven to 375°F. Using a tablespoon, scoop out the mixture, and using slightly moistened hands, roll between your palms to form 1-inch balls. Place the balls 1½ inches apart on 2 large, ungreased baking sheets. Using a finger or the handle of a wooden spoon, press down into the center of each ball to make a deep hole. Bake for 10–12 minutes, until just set and golden, rotating the baking sheets from top to the bottom shelf and from front to back halfway through the cooking time.

4. Remove the baking sheets to wire racks to cool for 2–3 minutes, until the cookies are firm enough to move. Using a metal pancake turner, transfer to a wire rack to cool. Repeat with the remaining mixture.

5. When the cookies are completely cooled, put the chocolate into a medium bowl. Set the bowl over a saucepan of just simmering water and heat until the chocolate is melted and smooth, stirring frequently. Remove from the heat and cool slightly. Gently beat in the butter until the mixture just thickens. Spoon into a decorating bag fitted with a medium star tip. Pipe a small amount of chocolate ganache into the center of each cookie and allow to set until firm. Store in airtight containers with waxed paper between the layers.

Pecan Squares
Makes 36 squares

Crust:

⅔ cup confectioners' sugar

2 cups unbleached all-purpose flour

½ pound (2 sticks) sweet butter, softened

1. Preheat oven to 350°F. Grease a 9 x 12-inch baking pan.
2. Sift sugar and flour together. Cut in butter, using two knives or a pastry blender, until fine crumbs form. Pat crust into the prepared baking pan. Bake for 20 minutes; remove from oven.

Topping:

⅔ cup (approximately 11 tablespoons) melted sweet butter

½ cup honey
3 tablespoons heavy cream
½ cup brown sugar
3½ cups shelled pecans, coarsely chopped

1. Mix melted butter, honey, cream, and brown sugar together. Stir in pecans, coating them thoroughly. Spread over crust.
2. Return to oven and bake for 25 minutes more. Cool completely before cutting into squares.

Peppermint Cookie Canes
Makes about 2 dozen cookies

2½ cups all-purpose flour
¼ teaspoon salt
1 cup (2 sticks) unsalted butter, softened
1 cup confectioners' sugar, sifted

1 egg, lightly beaten
½ teaspoon vanilla extract
½ teaspoon peppermint extract
¼ teaspoon red food coloring, optional
¼ cup crushed peppermint candy

1. Sift the flour and salt into a medium bowl.
   In a large bowl, using an electric mixer, beat
   the butter for about 30 seconds, until
   creamy. Gradually add the sugar and beat
   for 1–2 minutes, until light and fluffy. Beat in
   the egg and the vanilla and peppermint
   extracts, until blended. With the mixer on
   low speed, gradually beat in the flour
   mixture.

2. Remove half the dough and wrap tightly in
   a piece of plastic wrap. Add the red food
   coloring and crushed peppermint candy to

the remaining dough and beat until thoroughly mixed. Wrap tightly in plastic wrap and refrigerate both doughs for about 1 hour, until firm.

3. Preheat the oven to 350°F. Line 2 large baking sheets with foil or nonstick baking parchment. To form cookies, use a teaspoon to scoop a piece of plain dough, then roll into a rope shape 4–6 inches long. Repeat with the red-colored dough, then twist the ropes together and bend the top end to make a cane shape. Repeat with the remaining doughs and set the canes about 2 inches apart on the baking sheets.

4. Bake the canes for 8–10 minutes, until firm; do not allow them to brown or the color effect will not show sufficiently. Remove the baking sheets to wire racks to cool slightly for a few minutes. Transfer the canes to wire

racks to cool completely. Store in airtight containers.

Raspberry Jam Sandwiches
Makes about 18 cookies

1¼ cups blanched almonds
1½ cups all-purpose flour
¾ cup (1½ sticks) salted butter, softened
½ cup superfine sugar
1 egg, separated
Grated zest of 1 lemon
1 teaspoon vanilla extract
½ teaspoon salt
½ cup slivered almonds
1 cup raspberry jam
1 tablespoon lemon juice

1. Put the blanched almonds and ¼ cup of the flour in the bowl of a food processor. Using the metal blade, process until very finely ground.

2. In a large bowl, using an electric mixer, beat the butter for about 30 seconds, until creamy. Add the sugar and continue beating for 1–2 minutes, until light and fluffy. Beat in the egg yolk, lemon zest, and vanilla extract until well blended. On low speed, beat in the almond mixture, the remaining flour, and salt until well blended.

3. Scrape the dough onto a sheet of waxed paper or cling film and, using the paper or film as a guide, form into a flat disc. Refrigerate for 2 hours or overnight, until firm enough to handle. The dough can be made up to 2 days ahead.

4. Preheat the oven to 350°F. Line 2 baking sheets with nonstick baking parchment. On a lightly floured surface, using a floured rolling pin, roll half the dough into a square about 12 x 12 inches. Keep the remaining dough refrigerated. Cut the square crosswise into 6 strips to make 24 2-inch squares. Using a floured ¾-inch round cutter, cut out the centers from half the rectangles. Alternatively, use a square fluted cutter and cut out as many squares from the dough as possible.

5. Using a pancake turner, transfer the squares to the baking sheets ½ inch apart. In a small bowl, whisk the egg white until frothy. Brush the top of the cookie rings only, then sprinkle each ring with a few slivered almonds. Bake for 8–10 minutes, until just golden. Remove the baking sheets to a wire

rack to cool slightly, then transfer the cookies to wire racks to cool completely. Repeat with remaining dough and trimmings.

6. In a small saucepan over low heat, heat the jam and lemon juice until melted. Spoon over the squares, then top with a cookie ring, pressing gently. Allow to set, then store in airtight containers with waxed paper between the layers.

Rich Rolled Sugar Cookies
Makes 2½ to 3½ dozen 2½- to 3½-inch cookies

Beat on medium speed until very fluffy and well-blended:

> ½ pound (2 sticks) unsalted butter, softened
> ⅔ cup sugar

575

Add and beat until well combined:
1 large egg
¼ teaspoon baking powder
⅛ teaspoon salt
1½ teaspoons vanilla

Stir in until well-blended and smooth:
2⅓ cups all-purpose flour

1. Divide the dough in half. Place each half between 2 large sheets of wax or parchment paper. Roll out to a scant ¼ inch thick, checking the underside of the dough and smoothing any creases. Keeping the paper in place, layer the rolled dough on a baking sheet and refrigerate until cold and slightly firm but not hard, 20 to 30 minutes. Position a rack in the upper third of the

oven. Preheat the oven to 375°F. Grease cookie sheets.

2. Working with 1 portion of dough at a time (leave the other refrigerated), gently peel away and replace 1 sheet of the paper. (This will make it easier to lift the cookies from the paper later.) Peel away and discard the second sheet. Cut out the cookies using 2- or 3-inch cutters. With a spatula, transfer them to the cookie sheets, spacing about 1 inch apart. Roll the dough scraps and continue cutting out cookies until all the dough is used; briefly refrigerate the dough if it becomes too soft to handle. If desired, very lightly sprinkle the cookies with colored sprinkles or colored sugar.

3. Bake, 1 sheet at a time, just until the cookies are lightly colored on top and slightly darker at the edges, 5 to 7 minutes; rotate

the sheet halfway through baking for even browning. Remove the sheet to a rack and let stand until the cookies firm slightly. Transfer the cookies to racks to cool. If desired, decorate with icing.

Scottish Shortbread
Makes 16 large wedges or 32 thin wedges

¼ cup confectioners' sugar
¼ cup superfine sugar
¼ teaspoon salt
10 tablespoons (1¼ sticks) unsalted butter, softened
1½ cups all-purpose flour

1. Preheat the oven to 275°F. Lightly brush with softened butter two 8-inch tart or cake pans with removable bottoms.

2. Sift the confectioners' sugar into a large bowl. Add the superfine sugar and salt, and mix well. Add the butter and, using an electric mixer, beat the butter and sugars for 1–2 minutes, until light and fluffy. Stir in the flour in 2–3 batches until well blended. On a lightly floured surface, knead the dough very lightly to ensure an even bleeding.

3. Divide the dough evenly between the pans and pat onto the bottoms in even layers. Using a kitchen fork, press ¾-inch radiating lines around the edge of the dough. Prick the surface lightly with a fork (this helps keep an even surface as well as creating the traditional pattern). If you like, score each shortbread dough round into 8 or 16 wedges for easier cutting later.

4. Bake for about 40 minutes, until pale golden (do not brown—shortbread should be very

pale), rotating the pans halfway through cooking. Reduce the oven temperature if the shortbread begins to color too quickly. Remove the pans to a wire rack to cool for 10 minutes.

5. Carefully remove the side of each pan and place the pan bottoms onto a heatproof surface. Cut each shortbread circle into 8 wide or 16 thin wedges, following the scored marks, if used. This must be done while the shortbread is warm and soft, or it will break. Return the shortbread wedges on their bases to wire racks to cool completely.

Shortbread Hearts
Makes 20 cookies

> ¾ pound (3 sticks) sweet butter, softened
> 1 cup confectioners' sugar
> 3 cups unbleached all-purpose flour, sifted

½ teaspoon salt
½ teaspoon vanilla extract
¼ cup granulated sugar

1. Cream butter and confectioners' sugar together until light.
2. Sift flour and salt together and add to creamed mixture. Add vanilla and blend thoroughly.
3. Gather dough into a ball, wrap in wax paper, and chill for 4 to 6 hours.
4. Roll out chilled dough to ⅝-inch thickness. Using a 3-inch long heart-shaped cookie cutter, cut out cookies. Sprinkle tops with granulated sugar. Place cut-out cookies on ungreased cookie sheets and refrigerate for 45 minutes before baking.

5. Preheat oven to 325°F. Bake for 20 minutes, or until just starting to color lightly; cookies should not brown at all. Cool on a rack.

Spiral Spice Cookies
Makes about 1 dozen cookies

1½ cups all-purpose flour
½ teaspoon baking soda
1 teaspoon ground cinnamon
½ teaspoon freshly grated nutmeg
½ teaspoon ground ginger
½ teaspoon ground cardamom
¼ teaspoon finely ground black pepper
⅛ teaspoon salt
⅓ cup white vegetable shortening
⅓ cup sugar
⅓ cup molasses
1 egg

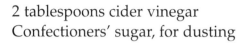

2 tablespoons cider vinegar
Confectioners' sugar, for dusting

1. Sift the flour, baking soda, cinnamon, nutmeg, ginger, cardamom, black pepper, and salt into a medium bowl.
2. In a large bowl, using an electric mixer, beat the shortening and sugar for 1–2 minutes, until light and fluffy. Beat in the molasses, egg, and vinegar until blended. On low speed, beat in the flour-spice mixture until a soft dough forms.
3. Preheat the oven to 350°F. Lightly grease two large baking sheets. Spoon the dough into a large pastry bag fitted with a ¼-inch plain tip. Pipe the dough into 3-inch circles, beginning at the center point and working to the outer edge, 2 inches apart on the baking sheets.

4. Bake for about 10 minutes, until just set and beginning to brown at the edge. Remove the baking sheets to wire racks. Using a pancake turner, transfer the cookies to wire racks to cool completely. Lightly dust with confectioners' sugar. Store in airtight containers.

Spritz Cookies
Makes about 4½ dozen cookies

    1 cup (2 sticks) unsalted butter, softened
    ½ cup superfine sugar
    1 egg, lightly beaten
    1½ teaspoons vanilla or 1 teaspoon
       almond extract
    2–2½ cups all-purpose flour, sifted
    Sugar sprinkles or other cookie
       decorations, to decorate

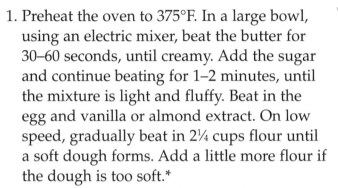

1. Preheat the oven to 375°F. In a large bowl, using an electric mixer, beat the butter for 30–60 seconds, until creamy. Add the sugar and continue beating for 1–2 minutes, until the mixture is light and fluffy. Beat in the egg and vanilla or almond extract. On low speed, gradually beat in 2¼ cups flour until a soft dough forms. Add a little more flour if the dough is too soft.*

2. Pack the cookie dough into a cookie press fitted with the design plate of your choice. Press out cookies onto 2 cold, ungreased baking sheets. Depending on the shape, sprinkle each cookie with a few sprinkles, or other cookie decorations, or press a candied cherry into the center of each cookie. Bake for about 8 minutes, until set and just golden.

3. Remove the baking sheets to wire racks to cool slightly. Using a thin-bladed metal

spatula, transfer the cookies to wire racks to cool completely. Clean and chill the baking sheets and repeat with the remaining cookie dough. Store the cookies in airtight containers.

Cookie press cookies can be difficult to form unless the dough is the right temperature. If the dough or weather is too warm, the dough won't hold its shape and may have to be chilled for about 1/2 hour before pressing. If the dough is chilled too long or is too firm, it will be difficult to press through the design plate.

To stiffen the dough, add a little more flour. If too stiff, add a little milk. Form a log shape slightly smaller than the diameter of the cookie press and insert into the prepared press. Every cookie press has its own directions, which you should read thoroughly. You may want to practice with a few turns.

Toffee Bars

Makes about 30 bars

> ½ pound (2 sticks) sweet butter
> 1 cup light brown sugar
> 1 egg yolk
> 2 cups unbleached all-purpose flour
> 1 teaspoon vanilla extract
> 12 ounces semisweet chocolate chips
> 1 cup shelled walnuts or pecans, coarsely chopped

1. Preheat the oven to 350°F. Grease a 9 x 12-inch baking pan.
2. Cream butter and sugar. Add egg yolk; beat well.
3. Sift in flour, mixing well, then stir in vanilla. Spread batter in the prepared pan. Bake for 25 minutes.

4. Cover cake layer with chocolate chips and return to oven for 3 to 4 minutes.

5. Remove pan from oven and spread melted chocolate evenly. Sprinkle with nuts. Cool completely in pan before cutting.

Cakes, Pies, & Puddings

Apple Pie
Makes 8 servings

Pastry for Two-Crust Pie

Filling:
⅓ to ⅔ cup sugar
¼ cup all-purpose flour
½ teaspoon ground cinnamon
½ teaspoon ground nutmeg

Dash of salt

8 cups thinly sliced peeled tart apples (8 medium apples)

2 tablespoons butter or stick margarine, if desired

1. Heat oven to 425°F. Make pastry.
2. Mix sugar, flour, cinnamon, nutmeg, and salt in large bowl. Stir in apples. Turn into pastry-lined pie plate. Cut butter into small pieces; sprinkle over apples. Cover with top pastry that has slits cut in it (or vent); seal and flute. Cover edge with 2- to 3-inch strip of aluminum foil to prevent excessive browning; remove foil during last 15 minutes of baking.
3. Bake 40 to 50 minutes or until crust is golden brown and juice begins to bubble

through slits in crust. Cool on wire rack at least 2 hours.

Chestnut Cake
Makes 8+ portions

2 cups granulated sugar
4 eggs
1 cup vegetable oil
1 cup dry white wine
2 ½ cups unbleached all-purpose flour
½ teaspoon salt
2 ¼ teaspoons baking powder
1 teaspoon vanilla extract
Chocolate icing, warmed
¾ cup sweetened chestnut purée*
Whole chestnuts preserved in syrup
    (optional, as garnish)*
*available at specialty food shops.

1. Preheat oven to 350°F. Grease and flour two 9-inch round layer cake pans.
2. Beat sugar and eggs together, using an electric mixer, for 30 seconds on medium speed. Add oil, wine, flour, salt, baking powder, and vanilla; beat for 1 minute.
3. Pour batter into the prepared pans. Set on the middle rack of the oven and bake for 30 minutes, or until cake has pulled away from sides of pan and a knife inserted in the center comes out clean.
4. Let cakes cool in pans for 5 minutes. Turn them out on rack and let cool for at least 2 hours before frosting.
5. Arrange 1 cake layer on a serving plate. Spread with warm chocolate icing. Set second layer on top of first and spread with chestnut purée. Cover sides of cake with remaining icing. Decorate top with well-

drained whole preserved chestnuts if desired. Chill cake for 45 minutes before serving.

Cinnamony Baked Apples
Makes 6 portions

2 cups water
2¼ cups brown sugar
1½ tablespoons ground cinnamon
1½ tablespoons fresh lemon juice
6 medium-large tart baking apples, washed (do not peel)
¾ cup raisins
½ cup shelled pecans, chopped
1 tablespoon grated lemon zest
3 tablespoons Calvados or applejack liqueur
3 tablespoons sweet butter

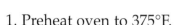

1. Preheat oven to 375°F.
2. Mix water, ¾ cup of the brown sugar, ½ tablespoon of the cinnamon and the lemon juice in a saucepan. Bring to a boil and cook for 3 minutes. Remove syrup from heat and reserve.
3. Remove the apple cores, but do not cut all the way through the bottoms.
4. In a bowl, mix remaining 1½ cups brown sugar, the raisins, pecans, lemon zest, and remaining 1 tablespoon cinnamon. Fill each apple to within ¼ inch of the top. Pour 1 teaspoon of applejack over the filling in each apple and top with ½ tablespoon butter.
5. Transfer apples to a baking dish 9 x 13 inches and pour syrup over apples. Pour remaining tablespoon of the applejack into the syrup.

6. Bake apples for 40 minutes, or until tender, basting them occasionally with syrup in pan.

7. When apples are done, transfer them with a slotted spoon to a serving dish. Pour syrup from pan into a small saucepan, bring to a boil, and cook until slightly reduced, about 5 minutes. Cool slightly, pour a tablespoon of syrup over each apple, and serve remaining syrup on the side.

Cranberry Cake
Makes 16 servings

½ cup margarine
1 cup sugar
1 egg
2 egg whites
½ teaspoon almond extract
2 cups all-purpose flour

1 tablespoon baking powder
1 cup nonfat plain yogurt
1 cup wholeberry cranberry sauce
½ cup sliced almonds
1 cup confectioners' sugar
2 tablespoons skim milk
½ teaspoon vanilla extract

1. Preheat the oven to 350°F. Coat a 13 x 9 x 2-inch baking pan with nonstick cooking spray.
2. In a large mixing bowl, cream the margarine and sugar until light and fluffy. Add the egg and egg whites, beating after each addition. Add the almond extract.
3. In a small bowl, combine the flour and baking powder. Add to the sugar mixture alternately with the yogurt, beginning and ending with the flour mixture.

4. Pour the batter into the prepared pan. Spoon the cranberry sauce evenly over the batter. Sprinkle with the almonds. Bake for 35 minutes, or until the cake slightly pulls away from the sides of the pan.

5. In a small bowl, combine the confectioners' sugar, milk, and vanilla, stirring until smooth. Drizzle the glaze over the hot cake. Cool before serving.

Cranberry Cheesecake
Makes 8 to 10 servings

½ cup graham cracker crumbs
1 tablespoon margarine, melted
1 (8-ounce) package reduced-fat cream cheese, softened
1 (8-ounce) container part-skim ricotta cheese

½ cup sugar
½ teaspoon almond extract
3 egg whites
Cranberry topping (recipe follows)

1. Preheat the oven to 350°F. Coat a 9-inch pie plate with nonstick cooking spray.
2. In a small bowl, combine the graham crackers and margarine. Pat the mixture into the bottom of the pie plate.
3. In a large mixing bowl, combine the cream cheese and ricotta until well blended. Add the sugar and almond extract, mixing well.
4. In another mixing bowl, beat the egg whites until soft peaks form. Fold the egg whites gradually into the cheese mixture until well combined.
5. Pour half of the batter into the pie plate. Spread with ¾ cup of the cranberry topping

(recipe follows), and cover with the remaining cheesecake batter. Bake for 40 to 45 minutes, or until set. Remove from the oven, and cool on a rack. When cool, spread with the remaining cranberry topping. Refrigerate until chilled, about 2 hours.

Cranberry Topping:
> 1 (16-ounce) can wholeberry cranberry sauce
> ¼ cup sugar
> 1 tablespoon cornstarch
> ¼ cup water

1. In a medium saucepan, cook the cranberry sauce and sugar over medium-low heat until the mixture is smooth, about 3 minutes.
2. In a small bowl, combine the cornstarch and water; add to the saucepan.

3. Cook over medium heat, stirring constantly, until the mixture thickens.

4. Refrigerate until lukewarm, 15 to 20 minutes, stirring in the refrigerator every 10 minutes.

5. Remove ¾ cup cranberry topping for the inside of the cheesecake. Refrigerate the remaining topping until well chilled.

Glazed Chestnuts
Makes 18 pieces

18 fresh chestnuts (about ½ pound)
2 cups granulated sugar
1¼ cups water
1 cup honey
1 teaspoon cream of tartar
¼ cup light rum
One-pound box confectioners' sugar

1. Bring a medium-size saucepan of water to a boil. Prepare an ice bath in a large stainless steel bowl.

2. Using a paring knife, slice an X in the skin of each chestnut. Add 5 chestnuts at a time to the pot of boiling water, and cook for one minute. Using a slotted spoon, remove the nuts from the pot, and set them atop a dry kitchen towel. Carefully remove the skins with a paring knife while they're still hot. Let them cool.

3. In a medium-sized saucepan with a wooden spoon, stir together the sugar, 1 cup of the water, the honey, and the cream of tartar. Wash down the sides of the pot with cool water and a pastry brush, making certain no sugar crystals remain. Bring the mixture to a boil; then remove the pot from the stove.

4. Add the chestnuts to the syrup, return the pan to medium heat, and cook until the mixture reaches a temperature of 260°F on a candy thermometer, 5 to 10 minutes. Set the pot in the ice bath, and allow to cool to room temperature.

5. Transfer the mixture to a plastic container. With a wooden spoon, stir in the rum. Cover and refrigerate the chestnuts in the syrup for 2 days in order to allow them to absorb the syrup.

6. Strain the chestnuts and set them atop a wire rack to dry at room temperature for half an hour.

7. Meanwhile, in a small plastic bowl, stir together the confectioners' sugar and the remaining ¼ cup of water until a paste the consistency of yogurt is formed. Pour the glaze over the chestnuts, to coat each evenly

601

and completely. Serve immediately, or store covered in the refrigerator for up to 3–4 days.

Orange Cranberry Cake
Makes 16 servings

½ cup margarine
1 cup sugar
1 egg
1 tablespoon grated orange rind
2¼ cups all-purpose flour
1 teaspoon baking soda
½ cup orange juice
½ cup skim milk
1½ cups chopped fresh or dried cranberries
⅔ cup chopped dates
½ cup confectioners' sugar
1½ tablespoons orange juice

1. Preheat the oven to 350°F. Coat a 10-inch Bundt pan with nonstick cooking spray.
2. In a large mixing bowl, cream the margarine and sugar until light and fluffy. Add the egg and orange rind, beating well.
3. In a medium bowl, combine the flour and baking soda, and add to the creamed mixture alternately with the orange juice and milk. Stir in the cranberries and dates.
4. Pour into the prepared pan, and bake for 40 minutes or until a toothpick inserted comes out clean.
5. Cool 10 minutes. Invert the cake onto a serving plate.
6. Meanwhile, in a small saucepan, combine the confectioners' sugar and orange juice over low heat or in the microwave oven until smooth. Pour the orange glaze over the hot cake. Cool before serving.

Plum Cake

Makes one 10-inch cake; serves 10 to 12

Sweet Dough:

> 2 cups all-purpose flour
> 4 tablespoons (½ stick) unsalted butter, at
>   room temperature
> 2 tablespoons honey
> ¼ teaspoon salt
> ¼ cup whole milk, at room temperature
> 1 large egg
> 2 large egg yolks
> ½ tablespoon active dry yeast

Topping:

> 7 large plums
> 1 cup (8 ounces) sour cream
> 3 tablespoons honey
> 1 lemon, zest grated

1½ cups slivered almonds
¼ cup light brown sugar
Pinch of ground cardamom
1 teaspoon ground cinnamon
2 tablespoons unsalted butter, melted
Cream, or whipped cream, for serving
(optional)

1. Prepare the sweet dough: In the bowl of an electric mixer fitted with the dough hook attachment, place the flour, butter, honey, and salt.
2. In a small mixing bowl, whisk together the milk, egg, yolks, and yeast, and add these wet ingredients to the electric mixer bowl. Mix on low speed for 4 minutes. Increase the speed to medium, and mix for another 4 minutes, or until the dough pulls away from and slaps against the sides of the bowl.

3. Cover the dough with plastic wrap and allow it to rise in a warm place until doubled in volume, about 1 hour.

4. Preheat the oven to 375°F. Grease a 10-inch round cake pan with butter, and coat lightly with flour.

5. Prepare the topping: Slice the plums in half and remove the stones. Slice each half into thirds. Set the plums aside.

6. In a medium-sized mixing bowl, whisk together the sour cream, honey, and lemon zest.

7. Once the dough has doubled in volume, punch it down and set it inside the prepared cake pan. Spread the sour cream mixture atop the dough. Sprinkle the almonds atop the sour cream, and arrange the sliced plums nicely atop.

8. In a small bowl, stir together the brown sugar, cardamom, and cinnamon. Brush the sliced plums with the melted butter, and dust the top of the cake with the sugar mixture. Allow the dough to relax for 30 minutes.

9. Bake in the preheated oven for 40 minutes, or until the plums have caramelized and a toothpick inserted comes out clean. Let the cake cool in the pan for 20 minutes, then turn out onto a serving plate. The cake can be served either warm or at room temperature. Serve with cream or whipped cream, if desired.

Plum Pudding
Makes one 2-quart casserole dish; serves 12

    1 cup dried pineapple
    1 cup dark raisins

½ cup golden raisins

½ cup currants

½ cup dried cherries

½ cup freshly grated unsweetened coconut, toasted

¼ cup almonds, toasted

½ cup chopped candied fruit (orange, lemon, etc.)

¼ cup finely chopped candied ginger

1 lemon, zest grated

1 lime, zest grated

1½ cups Appleton gold rum

2 cups water

2 cups chopped suet (¼-inch pieces, available at local butcher's market), or substitute lard

2 cups all-purpose flour

4 cups finely crumbled day-old bread, or substitute any egg bread

1½ teaspoons salt
1 teaspoon ground nutmeg
1 tablespoon ground allspice
1 tablespoon ground cinnamon
Pinch of ground cloves
6 large eggs
1 cup light brown sugar
½ cup plus 2 tablespoons dark beer

1. In a large bowl, toss together the dried pineapple, dark raisins, golden raisins, currants, dried cherries, coconut, almonds, candied fruit, candied ginger, and citrus zests. Add 1 cup of the rum and the water, stir to mix, and soak overnight.

2. On a large work surface, cut the suet into the flour, running the mixture through your fingertips until a coarse meal is formed. In a large bowl, combine the flour-suet mixture

with the finely crumbled bread, salt, nutmeg, allspice, cinnamon, and cloves. Stir to mix well. Add the presoaked dried fruit mixture, including any liquid in the bowl, and toss until thoroughly combined.

3. In another medium-sized bowl, whisk together the eggs, brown sugar, the remaining ½ cup of rum, and the beer. Add the liquid ingredients to the dry, and mix until a smooth dough is formed. If the mixture seems too dry, add more ale until the dough is smooth.

4. Grease a 2-quart casserole dish or decorative mold with plenty of butter, and lightly dust it with flour.

5. Place the batter in the prepared casserole dish or mold, packing it well. Cover it with foil. Place the dish in a large saucepan filled with enough water to come halfway up the

sides of the dish. Cover the entire pan with foil, and bring the water in the pan to a simmer. Keep the water at a simmer, and steam the pudding for 4 hours, checking the water level regularly and refilling as necessary. The pudding is done when firm and a toothpick inserted near the center comes out clean.

6. Allow the pudding to cool in the casserole dish or mold at room temperature for about 1 hour. Unmold and serve.

Sweetened Whipped Cream

Well-chilled cream will whip the best, so keep it refrigerated until ready to use. When the cream begins to thicken as you beat it, reduce the speed so you can watch carefully and beat just until soft peaks form.

For 1 cup whipped cream: Beat ½ cup whipping (heavy) cream and 1 tablespoon granulated or powdered sugar in chilled small bowl with electric mixer on high speed until soft peaks form.

For 1½ cups whipped cream: Beat ¾ cup whipping (heavy) cream and 2 tablespoons granulated or powdered sugar in chilled small bowl with electric mixer until soft peaks form.

Sweet Potato Bread Pudding with Praline Sauce
Makes 10 to 12 servings

> 1 (16-ounce) loaf French bread, cut into squares
> 1 (15-ounce) can sweet potatoes (yams), drained and mashed

1 (12-ounce) can evaporated skimmed milk

1½ cups skim milk

2 eggs

2 egg whites

2 tablespoons molasses

1 teaspoon cinnamon

½ teaspoon nutmeg

2 teaspoons vanilla extract

Praline sauce (recipe follows)

1. Preheat the oven to 350°F.
2. Place the French bread squares in a 2-quart oblong casserole dish coated with nonstick cooking spray.
3. In a mixing bowl, beat the sweet potatoes, evaporated milk, milk, eggs, egg whites, molasses, cinnamon, nutmeg, and vanilla. Pour evenly over the bread, and press with

your hands to submerge the bread in the liquid mixture.

4. Bake 35 to 45 minutes, or until the pudding is set. Top each serving with the praline sauce (recipe follows), and serve immediately.

Praline Sauce:

    2 cups sugar
    3 tablespoons margarine
    ½ teaspoon baking soda
    1 cup buttermilk

1. In a very large pot (mixture foams up while cooking), cook all ingredients over medium heat, stirring frequently, until the sugar is dissolved. The mixture will foam; stir to beat down the foaming. The color will begin to caramelize.

2. Cook until a slight brown color, about 20 to 30 minutes.

Sweet Potato Pecan Crumble Pie
Makes 8 to 10 servings

¼ plus ⅓ cup light brown sugar
½ cup chopped pecans, divided
1 unbaked (9-inch) pie shell
1 (15-ounce) can sweet potatoes (yams), drained
⅓ cup sugar
2 eggs
1½ teaspoons ground cinnamon, divided
¼ teaspoon ground allspice
1 (12-ounce) can evaporated skimmed milk
2 teaspoons vanilla extract, divided
½ cup all-purpose flour
3 tablespoons margarine

1. Preheat the oven to 425°F.
2. In a small bowl, mix together ¼ cup brown sugar and ¼ cup pecans. Sprinkle on the bottom of the pie shell.
3. In a mixing bowl, mix together the sweet potatoes, sugar, eggs, 1 teaspoon cinnamon, allspice, milk, and 1 teaspoon vanilla until creamy. Pour into the pie shell, and bake for 15 minutes. Reduce the oven temperature to 350°F, and continue baking for another 25 minutes.
4. Meanwhile, in a small bowl, mix together the remaining ⅓ cup brown sugar, remaining 1 teaspoon vanilla, flour, and the margarine with a fork until crumbly. Stir in the remaining ¼ cup pecans.
5. Sprinkle over the pie, and continue baking for another 20 minutes, or until done. Cool for 15 minutes, and serve.

Yule Log
Makes 1 jelly roll; serves 8 to 10

Chocolate Filling:

>   9 ounces semisweet chocolate
>   1 cup whole milk
>   4 large egg yolks
>   1 pound (2 sticks) unsalted butter
>   1 cup sifted confectioners' sugar

Chocolate Sponge Cake:

>   4 large eggs
>   ½ cup granulated sugar
>   ¾ cup sifted all-purpose flour
>   ¼ cup unsweetened Dutch cocoa powder
>   Candies and chocolates, for garnish
>   (optional)

1. Prepare the chocolate filling: Place water in the bottom of a double boiler so that the top of the water is ½-inch below the upper pan. Place the chocolate in the upper pan. Then place the double boiler over low heat. Stir the chocolate constantly until it is melted. The water in the bottom of the double boiler should not come to a boil while the chocolate is melting. Transfer to a bowl and set aside.

2. Wash and dry the upper pan of the double boiler. Add the milk and yolks, stir to combine, and heat just until warm.

3. Add the melted chocolate to the milk and yolk mixture, stirring until combined. Transfer to a bowl. Cover with plastic wrap and refrigerate for 30 minutes.

4. In the bowl of an electric mixer fitted with the paddle attachment on medium to high

speed, beat the butter and confectioners' sugar until light and fluffy, scraping down the sides of the bowl often.

5. Add the cooled chocolate-milk mixture to the electric mixer bowl and mix until combined. Refrigerate.

6. Prepare the chocolate sponge cake: Preheat the oven to 400°F. Grease a 15 x 10 x 1-inch jelly-roll pan with butter, and line the bottom with parchment paper.

7. In the bowl of an electric mixer fitted with the whip attachment on high speed, beat the eggs and sugar for 5 minutes, or until pale yellow and thick. With a rubber spatula, gently fold in the flour and cocoa.

8. Pour the batter into the prepared pan. Bake for 12 to 15 minutes, or until golden and the cake springs back when lightly

touched and pulls away from the sides of the pan.

9. While the cake is still warm, immediately turn it out onto a towel sprinkled with confectioners' sugar.

10. Carefully peel back the parchment paper. With the towel under the cake, gently roll up the long side of the cake into a jelly-roll shape so that the towel is both rolled up inside and covers the outside of the cake. Let the cake cool completely.

11. To assemble the cake, unroll the cake. Spread with a third of the chocolate filling, reserving the rest for coating the outside. Roll the cake back up into a log shape, with the seam side down. To make the roll look like a log, cut a ½-inch diagonal piece from each end of the roll. Form "branches" by placing these wedge-shaped pieces of the

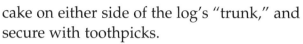

cake on either side of the log's "trunk," and secure with toothpicks.

12. Spread the remaining chocolate filling evenly on the outside of the log and around each of the branches to secure them in place. To give the log a realistic look, carefully score the frosting with the tines of a fork, so that it resembles the irregular texture of bark. Dust the "bark" with cocoa powder and them some confectioners' sugar to create "snow." If desired, decorate with candies and chocolates. Refrigerate until ready to serve. To serve, cut the roll into slices and serve on dessert plates.

Christmas Tips and Crafts

Perhaps the best yuletide decoration is being wreathed in smiles.

—*Unknown*

Holiday Tips

1. The number one hint to keep in mind is take it easy. Do not overextend yourself and try to enjoy the holiday season.

2. Make a list of expectations for the holiday season and hopefully you'll be pleasantly surprised.

3. Think about who you want to buy presents for. Make a list and start thinking about the type of gifts you want to get early. Sometimes the smallest things, like cards, can mean the most to show others you care.

4. If you are a baker, choose a few favorite recipes (See the "Recipes" section of this book) and invite friends

and family to help you out in the kitchen. If you don't bake, buy some festive foods at the bakery or grocery store, but make a list first of what you want before you head outside.

5. Have a look at the holiday decorations that are in their usual box and determine whether or not they belong in the trash can or on/around your home. If you need some new ones, go get some or better yet, make them with friends and family.

6. Be realistic about your budget and see how far your dollar can stretch. Sometimes being creative is more special to people because it shows how much you care (See the section on creative gift ideas).

7. Are you a host or hostess with the mostest? Think about whether or not you want to take on entertaining and if you do, plan in advance; you'll be glad you did. A potluck is a good way to get everyone involved so you don't have to do all the cooking.

8. Thinking about getting away for the holidays? Plan in advance because holiday ticket prices tend to be expensive. Also keep in mind that many restaurants and businesses are closed on Christmas Eve and stay closed on Christmas Day.

9. Worried about family members fighting and ruining the holidays? Try to talk in advance of spending time together. Meditate, go for a walk,

exercise, or do yoga to rid yourself of stress. Remember, you cannot solve everything for everyone.

10. Go out and have a ball! To get yourself in the holiday spirit, try playing music if you are inside baking or cleaning. Build a snowman or a sandman and decorate him/her however you want!

11. Be a kid again and make a snow angel, go to a play or concert. Above all else, just relax (the holidays can be stressful) and have fun.

And now for some more expansive Christmas advice and solutions!

How To Wrap a Gift

1. Have a clean, clear space ready, like a table, not a bed.

2. Have handy scissors, tape, pens, and ribbons; empty a wastebasket and stand up rolls of paper in it. Wrap a rubber band around each roll to keep it from unfurling.

3. Unroll enough paper to wrap around the box with at least a 2-inch overlap. There should be enough paper at each end to cover the ends completely when you fold over them. Position the gift box in the middle of the paper, face down, first removing all price tags. Keep the paper taut and the creases firm.

629

4. Fold the long sides of the paper over the box and seal them with tape. Then fold paper over the ends of the package. Seal each end with tape. Add either stick-on bows or full-length ribbon. You may get creative at this stage if not earlier. Why not design your own Christmas wrapping paper or substitute customized themes like blueprint paper or Sunday comics? Use paint, markers, and rubber stamps to make homemade wrapping paper on brown or white construction paper. It's also a good way to recycle brown grocery bags! "Designed" bags from retail stores can be cut to the size of your gift, with advertising removed. Aluminum foil is a further option.

5. To wrap a bottle, cut out a large square of wrapping paper twice the length of the bottle. Choose reversible paper, since both inside and outside will show. Center the bottle on the paper, draw up the corners, and add a bow around the neck of the bottle. Jauntily pull out the corners of the paper for a more festive package.

6. To wrap a cylinder, cut two circles of paper to cover the top and bottom ends of your gift. Wrap the rest, folding paper over the top and bottom, and then use the circles to cover the folds at each end. Double-sided tape is a handy addition also.

Additional Tips:

Using yarn instead of ribbon on gifts is a less expensive alternative. Although yarn does not curl in the way that some ribbon does, it is an attractive substitution and often is available in more colors, including multicolored varieties, than ribbon is.

Fresh holly or other greens, especially pine, tied into the ribbon (or yarn) on a gift adds a festive touch. Best of all, this is generally free, because you can simply cut it from a tree in the yard, or a neighbor's yard once permission is obtained. Remember that holly berries are poisonous and may not be the best option for gifts or for decoration if there are children or pets in the house. You can also tie a Christmas ornament to the package as an additional "gift."

Assemble a Gift Basket

One idea for a truly customized Christmas gift, a real labor of love, is a gift basket. The only limitation, of course, is the size of the gifts, in that most baskets can be held and lifted easily.

Your basket can contain holiday foods, like cookies (See "Recipes," this book), plum pudding, or fruitcake, or foods you know are your recipient's favorites. For sports fans, you can line your basket with the sports section of your newspaper and add a baseball hat or glove, a hockey puck, or other customized paraphernalia; books or catalogues, a sports video or CD, hobby cards, peanuts and crackerjacks from the popular song, and advance tickets to relevant public events or subscriptions to sports periodicals.

For your music lover, you can line your basket with music scores—those you don't need; don't buy new ones—or reviews or event ads from your newspaper. Then add sheet music—roll it up and tie it with a ribbon—a music box or cassette, CD, or music-themed movie, books or periodicals (or subscriptions to the latter), and again tickets to concerts or other events. Decorate with plastic music notes and other insignia available at music stores or in catalogues.

Remember, your basket can also be assorted, a potpourri of imaginative spontaneity.

And where can you find just the right basket? At your local discount store, supermarket (sometimes), florist, crafts outlet, department store, or flea market. The size should be appropriate to the amount and size of gifts you've selected, unless you buy the basket first. In that case, be sure the contents fit, and fill any gaps with decorations (see below) if necessary.

Let your imagination fly as you decorate. Use ribbon, crepe paper or tissue paper, tinsel or other garland (see the section on decorating your Christmas tree), or sew significant objects onto the handle or paint the entire basket in one or many colors. Paint or paste the recipients' name on the basket or handle. The possibilities are infinite.

Additional Tips:

Red- or green-colored or patterned cellophane makes a gift basket even more Christmasy.

Hassle-free Christmas Shopping

Think Christmas all year round. Carry with you at all times, for those spontaneous shopping sprees or bargain sales you stumble upon, a list of recipients and gifts you'd like to buy for them. Write down gift ideas when they occur to you. Then grab them when you come upon bargains.

Begin shopping at the after-Christmas sales, when prices are low. It's a good time also to buy your next year's wrapping paper, ribbon, and decorations. Brave the crowds. If you prefer home shopping, order via television advertisements or on-line sources.

Start a holiday fund at your local bank or in your piggy bank, if your budget is limited.

If your list is long, divide it by twelve and shop for designated groups each month.

Remember, gift certificates are wild cards that few will not welcome. Custom-select stores appropriate to individuals' interests. You may also give money, but personalize it with Christmas decorations or other small but thoughtful additions—a key chain or money clip, for example.

Hide your gifts but make notes where they are, and keep a list of what you've purchased for whom, to avoid forgetfulness or scrambled thoughts during the Christmas rush.

How to Choose Gifts For Just About Anyone

"Easy" people are not a problem. You know what to get for them. But for the others, the person who has everything, or is impossible to shop for, buy a gift certificate. That way you can be reasonably sure that your gift won't be discarded as useless or inappropriate.

1. Here is another option: tickets to a sporting event, movie, play, or concert, whatever might strike the recipient's fancy.
2. Home-made gifts are always welcome. Bake Christmas cookies or

gingerbread men; knit or sew seasonable objects; create appropriate art work; there are infinite possibilities (See the "Recipes" and "Crafts" sections of this book).

3. Make a charitable donation to a favorite cause.

4. A magazine subscription is a further option.

5. If at all possible, invest in a gift that will last rather than a less expensive equivalent, if your gift is nonperishable.

6. Picture frames or photo albums are a gift idea that will rarely be unwelcome.

7. For the young couple with a new baby who never get to go out, volunteer to babysit for free for one night or several; similarly for friends who have young children.

8. Other nonmaterial offerings might include, from responsible children, for example, a night without doing dishes, a trip to the grocery store, or other forms of taking over mundane activities, a great gift idea. I have a friend whose daughter gave her a coupon book full of that sort of gift, a memorable Christmas for her and a real token of filial love.

How to Choose and Decorate a Christmas Tree

Choose, Purchase, Position, and Care For

Choose a place in your home for your tree that is away from a heat source and high-traffic areas, so no one will bump into it, overturn it, or trip over light cords. The area should be cool and out of direct sunlight. Be sure there is a nearby outlet so you can plug in Christmas lights. Measure the height and width of this area carefully. Measure your tree stand also, to determine the maximum width of the tree trunk you can buy. Be aware also of the dimensions of your tree-top ornament.

When you go to select your tree, bring along a tape measure, gloves to protect your hands, a blanket to protect your car from tree sap and needles, and a saw to fresh-cut the tree as soon as you have it home. Have a bucket of water ready to provide the tree with water. Choose a tree stand, if you need one, that will hold plenty of water so you will have to refill it less often. Have the trunk trimmed to your desired length and request a disposable bag to use after the holidays the size of your tree. Place your tree in water as soon as possible after you arrive home.

As far as your actual choice of tree is concerned, those with shorter needles are easier to decorate; stems are stronger and there is more room on branches for decorations.

Fraser and Noble Fir are two relevant varieties. Look for a symmetrical shape, a pleasing aroma, needles that won't drop off or dry out easily, a healthy green color, and strong, springy branches.

Decorate!

Drape your tree with decorations from the top down, beginning with the lights (test these to see if they work before placing them on the tree). Go next to the garland. Place your larger ornaments closer to the bottom, lighter weight ones toward the top for optimum aesthetic balance. Use handmade, homemade, as well as commercially provided tree ornaments. Here is another area where Christmas creativity delights to flourish.

Choose a single theme or Christmas in general, whatever your family favors, or go spontaneous and hang whatever seizes your spirit. Homemade cranberry or popcorn garlands are popular additions, or instead of garlands, you can opt for wide ribbons. You can, in addition, spray-paint pine cones or add seashells to your tree décor. Bake Christmas cookies or gingerbread men (see recipes in this book) for further adornments. Your own jewelry can also enhance the tree, but be careful that it doesn't get lost!

Preserve Your Christmas Tree

A preservative can help keep your Christmas tree moist and prevent needles from shedding. Follow the directions for this preservative to help make your tree more fireproof.

2 cups corn syrup

2 ounces of liquid chlorine bleach

2 pinches of Epsom salt

½ teaspoon of Borax

1 teaspoon of chelated iron (purchase from a garden shop or plant store)

Hot water

The first step is to make sure you buy a fresh tree. When looking for a tree, make sure the needles are still green and that they do not pull off too easily.

Mix the ingredients in a 2-gallon bucket filled with hot water to within one inch of the top. Stir thoroughly, dissolving ingredients.

Make a fresh, level cut 1 inch above the base of the tree trunk. Immediately stand the trunk of the tree in the solution and leave for 24 hours. Keep the remaining solution.

Place your tree in a tree stand that contains a well for watering. Once the tree is set up, fill the well with the solution, using a plastic cup to dip from the bucket. Make sure to replenish the solution every day.

Anecdote

My mom and I have a special "present wrapping" tradition where we spend the night before Christmas Eve in the living room with all our unwrapped gifts, scissors, cellophane tape, and 2-3 bottles of our favorite champagne. This is a fabulous decorating tip as you can imagine the craftiness of our ribbons and bows.—K. C. & Patti DuFay

Add Poinsettias to Your Christmas Décor!

Here are some pointers on how to keep these plants around as long as possible.

1. Place the plant in bright light, but not direct sun.
2. Keep soil slightly moist, not waterlogged.
3. Feed with a liquid houseplant fertilizer; read label for directions on how often to feed.
4. When the flowers fade, keep the leaves healthy by watering and feed as you would during the flowering season.

5. The flowerless plant still needs bright light.

6. Prune back during the growing season to control its size and shape so it won't get thin and ungainly.

7. To stimulate flowering for next year, start in October to keep the plant in total darkness from 5 P.M. to 7 A.M. every day for 4 weeks.

8. Maintain a night temperature of 60 to 67°F.

9. Mist leaves daily if atmosphere is too dry.

10. When your plant begins to flower, place it in bright light and begin the procedure over again.

Needless to say, poinsettias make great Christmas decorations!

Additional, Miscellaneous Tips:

1. Putting on Christmas music can really help get you in the mood when decorating.

2. Use food to decorate. The kitchen in particular is a place in which items such as nuts or the brightly colored fruits and vegetables of the winter season can be particularly effective, whether in a basket on a table or arranged on the counter.

3. Try to cover (with afghans or slipcovers) furniture that does not fit with the Christmas season, anything in pastel colors in particular.

4. Try "wrapping" your front door with wrapping paper and ribbon to give guests a sense of anticipation about

what they will find within. You can also do this, with the ribbon especially, with the cushions on your furniture, although if guests will be sitting, this may get in the way. Covering windows may block light from entering the room. Wrapping lampshades, however, can illuminate the fanciful designs on the paper and adds a festive touch (make sure, however, that the paper does not come too close to the light bulb). Wrapping hanging pictures is another idea.

5. Wire garland and wire wreaths can be easier to hang (they will be more likely to stay where you put them and in the shape that you mold them). Wire wreaths also do not lose their shape in the way some do while in storage, which makes them last longer.

6. Fresh greens can bring an unmistakable Christmas feeling to the house. Make sure to cut about twice as much in length as you think you'll need and cut at a 45-degree angle to preserve freshness. You can also try smashing the end (or making it wider in some way) to enhance water absorption. Remember that some plants, holly in particular, have poisonous parts (the holly berries), so although they are pretty, they should be kept away from children and pets.

7. At a loss for what to do with all of those holiday greeting cards you receive? Add a festive element to your room or home by displaying them in the slats of mini-blinds or hang them from clothespins along a wire that spans the length of a hallway.

8. Nothing can conjure up Christmas as well as the smell of Christmas cookies fresh from the oven. If possible, pull a pan out of the oven just as guests are supposed to arrive or keep a plate out in the kitchen. This can also serve as an appetizer, making mouths water and stomachs growl (see the "Recipes" section of this book).

Christmas Crafts Projects

1. Create your own reindeer—It requires green construction paper, brown paint, black paint, and red paint. Oh, and one small child. You paint the sole (including toes) of one chubby bare foot with brown paint and make a footprint on the paper. Turn the paper so the toe prints are pointing up. That makes the reindeer head. Then you use two handprints for antlers (the thumbs touch the reindeer "head"). Dip a thumb into red paint to make the red nose, and dip a different finger into black paint to make eyes. Voilà!

2. An alternative route is to glue two wooden clothespins together with one

round part on top of the other and add eyes, antlers, bells, and a piece of string to hang it from your Christmas tree.

3. As an alternative to popcorn or cranberry garland, paper garland can be constructed simply by using colored construction paper, cutting strips about an inch wide and either taping, gluing, or stapling the ends together to form a ring. Repeat and attach new rings to create a garland. Wrap the garland around any large mirror and place berries/bows on it to add color.

4. Staircase—Best to wrap this with a wire garland as it is easier to drape and wrap around the railings. However, it is dangerous to wrap it all the way around because it makes it difficult to hold on to the banister when people

walk up and down the stairs. Adding red or white bows will brighten any foyer or hallway.

5. Pine cones—Add glue and glitter and place on a mantle or table, or affix a colored pipe cleaner and hang from your Christmas tree. Note: An outside alternative is to roll pine cones in peanut butter and then in birdseed—attach a string and hang on trees for treats for the birds.

6. Paper Santa plate—Make a cotton ball beard and paper eyes (markers/crayons work too). Glue on wiggle eyes if you have some (Santa is always watching!). Make Santa's nose a red circle and add a construction paper hat with a cotton ball brim and ball on the tip of hat.

7. Snowflakes—Grab some colored paper, fold it and cut out snowflakes. Hang them from the ceiling to create a winter wonderland or paste them on your windows to give the illusion of snow falling!

8. Beaded Wreath and Beaded Candy Cane:
   - Materials Needed: Beads, Pipe cleaners or florist's wire, and paper curling ribbon.
   - For the wreath, string beads on a pipe cleaner, wire, or a long twist tie. Twist the ends of the wire together. Tie a ribbon on the top and it's ready to hang!
   - For the candy cane, use red and white beads, string on a white or red pipe

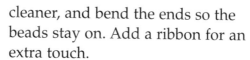

cleaner, and bend the ends so the beads stay on. Add a ribbon for an extra touch.

9. Christmas Place Mats—A wonderful craft for your children to enjoy and one that will keep them busy while inspiring creativity. All they need is an active imagination!

- Materials Needed: Scrap material (adult should sew together to the size of a place mat), permanent magic markers, fabric paint, paint brushes, fabric glue, fabric to cut out, scissors, templates of Christmas shapes (cookie cutters to trace), glitter, sequins, feathers, ribbon—whatever you have that could work, use it.

- Use sturdy scrap material sewn double, preferably a solid color. Provide children with the materials above and let them go to work.

Crafty Present Ideas (including a Gingerbread House!)

Gather your family and friends to create works of art together!

1. Calendar of Photos—Make a personalized calendar with pictures of you and your family for grandparents or other relatives. Buy a blank calendar or make blank calendar pages on your computer and print them out. Then place pictures of your choice in the blocks. (Note: Local copy stores usually offer this service at a low price.)

2. Handprints—A second idea, good for grandparent gifts, are handprints. You start with nice white paper. You press the child's hand onto a stamp pad and then make a hand print on the paper. (There are stamp pads now that wash off very easily—they are supposedly whatever the police department uses.) It works best if you start at the palm and kind of roll toward the fingers. Then you take a nice black felt-tip marker and write the child's name at the base of the handprint. In the lower right hand corner, you write "Christmas XXXX (year)" or "winter XXXX (year)," or whatever.

3. Recycle old Christmas Cards—Use the front of the card as a tag for presents. Cut the card front off and make sure the back is blank. Punch a hole in the top

left-hand corner and write To and From on the blank side! For an extra touch, tie bright-colored ribbon or yarn through the hole in order to tie it onto the ribbon on the package.

4. A Friendship Book—Gather up pictures from the time you and a friend first met until the present (favorite memories, trips, and special inside jokes). Put them in order and write a story beginning with how you met, first impressions, where you first got to know each other, how your relationship grew, and what you love about your friend. Paste one or two pictures per page, with text captions below, and create a story of your friendship.

5. Paint Christmas Tree Ornaments—Pick up some ceramic Christmas tree

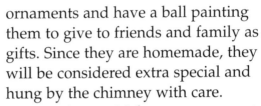

ornaments and have a ball painting them to give to friends and family as gifts. Since they are homemade, they will be considered extra special and hung by the chimney with care.

6. Shining Stars—Make star ornaments using construction paper and put a photo of your child, pet, or someone special inside. Punch a hole through the top and affix string or yarn and let it hang from your tree for all to see.

7. Build Your Own Gingerbread House.

To bake gingerbread, see page 460.

Putting Your Gingerbread House Together

Icing bags and tips work best for applying icing for construction. You will need:

- Icing bags (there are convenient disposable ones)*
- Round decorating tip (#3 or #4) and possibly a star tip (#19) or leaf tip (#67)*
- Some couplers (these are two plastic pieces that hold the decorating tip in the bag)*

*All of the above are available at cake decorating stores. Someone at the cake store can show you how they go together and an instructional cake decorating book will give basic tips.

Construction Steps

House Walls

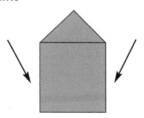

Step 1: Put icing on these edges.

- Take one house end, and pipe a line of icing along both side edges.
- Resting the pieces on a surface, take one rectangular piece, and match the end to the house side at a right angle. The pieces should set upright.
- Take a second rectangular piece and match it to the other side of the house end at a right angle. Now you should have a house end, with two sides.
- Take the opposite house end, and put icing on the two ends. Fit this piece in between the two house sides to complete the four walls of your house.
- Apply icing to sides.
- Slip the end piece with iced ends in between the two walls.

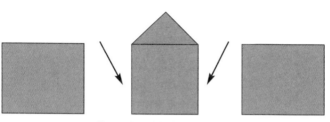

Steps 2 and 3: Attach sides.

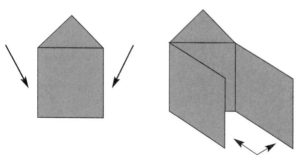

Step 4: Apply icing to sides.
Slip the end piece with iced ends in between the two walls.

Roof

- Pipe a line of icing on the four angled roof edges of the house.
- Pipe a line of icing on the two top edges of the sides of the house.
- Take the two rectangle pieces for the roof, and pipe icing along one of the long edges. Place the two roof pieces on the house, resting one piece against the iced edge of the other piece in the

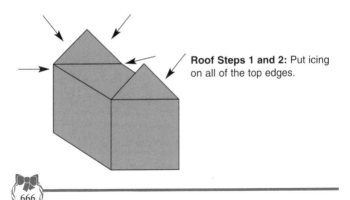

Roof Steps 1 and 2: Put icing on all of the top edges.

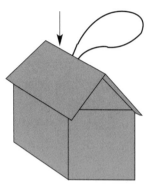

Roof Step 3: Put icing at the seam of the roof pieces and put on the house.

middle to form a bond. The roof pieces should overhang the sides of the house slightly.

- Put icing at the seam of the roof pieces and put on the house.

Hint: If you want to turn the house into a Christmas ornament, this would be the time to insert a string or light ribbon into the house at the middle of the roof.

To reinforce the house, you may want to pipe an additional line of icing at all edges.

Let dry completely (at least 2 hours) before handling or decorating.

Decorating Your House

This is the fun part! Find little candies to create your one-of-a-kind house.

You can also use icing to create outlines for doors, windows, and "evergreen boughs."

Here is a simple idea, but let your imagination run wild!

1. Cut 2 small rectangles from gum to represent doors. Affix them to the

front and back of the house using icing as glue.

2. Use rectangular candies (like Pez) to represent windows on the sides of the house.

3. Apply miniature M&Ms to the house randomly. (Tweezers come in handy for this.)

4. Apply icing to the roof to make it sticky, then crumble shredded wheat over it to represent a thatched roof.

5. Tint some icing green. Using a pastry bag, pipe some icing along the roof line to represent evergreen trim. You can use your round tip, or use a number 67 leaf decorating tip to do this. While the icing is still wet, take some little pieces of multi-colored gumdrops and stick into the icing to represent lights, or use Red Hots to represent holly.

6. Place the house on a piece of wax paper or parchment paper so that it will be easy to pick up later. Pipe a side border of white icing along the base of the house (using your round tip, or a star tip) to give it a finished look. Let dry completely until the icing hardens.

7. When the icing is dry, you should be able to pick up the house and the base trim will stay attached to the house.

Other Decorating Ideas

If you decide to make a neighborhood, be sure to use some larger items like ice cream cones for trees, or large green gumdrops for shrubbery.

1. Red and black licorice bites, ropes, and twists: Use your imagination!
2. Pretzel sticks, large and small: good for fences, log piles.
3. Candy pebbles: great for chimneys or accent on house front or back.
4. Hershey's chocolate bars: break them into sections for shutters, walkways, etc.
5. Chocolate chips: use for accent anywhere.
6. Round swirled red-and-white peppermint candies: use as accent around the house border, stack for a fence post.
7. Ice-cream cone tips: cover in frosting for trees, use as turrets on the house.
8. Crackers: use as walkways or shutters.
9. Round cookies: use as whimsical accent, or as wheels if you have a cart, or as a round window accent.

10. Flat almonds or other nuts: good roof material.
11. Gum: cut into pieces for shingles or roofing material.
12. Shredded Wheat: good for hay in a barnyard scene or roof material.
13. Wafer cookies: build a porch, steps or walkway, shutters.
14. Silver dragees (in the cake decorating aisle of your store, they are little silver balls): use for accent anywhere.
15. Wafer candies (flat, round, old-fashioned candies, wrapped in a wax paper wrapper): Use your imagination!
16. Marshmallows: good for snow piles, snowmen, etc.
17. Gumdrops, M&Ms, Red Hots, Chiclets, little candy fruits: use for accent anywhere.

Where Do You Go from Here?

Now that you've enjoyed baking your gingerbread house, you might want to tackle a bigger project. For more in-depth instructions and photos, visit Ginger B. Lane's web site, www.gingerbreadlane.com

Santa Claus and Christmas Traditions Around the World

Christmas waves a magic wand over this world, and behold, everything is softer and more beautiful.

— Norman Vincent Peale

Santa Claus

In many cultures around the world, the Santa Claus figure is of the utmost importance. He is not always known by that name, and he has many different aspects depending on the culture represented. Some of this variation is within the United States itself. In Louisiana, for example, it is said that Santa rows in on the bayous rather than flying overhead in his sleigh.

The American version of Santa Claus comes from the Dutch. Many of the original European immigrants to the New World, particularly those who settled around New York, were Dutch. They brought their traditions, including the celebration of Saint Nicholas, with them. In fact, Saint Nicholas came over as the prow of a ship,

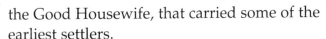

the Good Housewife, that carried some of the earliest settlers.

The story of Saint Nicholas himself begins almost 2,000 years ago, in A.D. 270, when he was born in northern Turkey. His wealthy parents died when he was a young child, leaving him to be raised by guardians and creating his connection to children and the poor. Nicholas became the bishop of Myra (an ancient city in Asia Minor) and was known for his work with the poor. The celebration of the day of Nicholas's death, December 6, became the precursor of our Christmas.

The tradition of giving gifts in honor of Saint Nicholas, however, did not begin until many centuries after his death. The gift giving that most of us associate irrevocably with Christmas may have begun in France in the 1100s and then spread to the rest of Europe.

Because Saint Nicholas was the patron saint of children and was closely allied to the poor, the tradition began with the giving of gifts to poor children on the Eve of Saint Nicholas, December 5.

Saint Nicholas, the model for the modern "Santa Claus," is the patron saint of children, among other groups. In fact the name "Santa Claus" derives from the Dutch "Sinter Klaas," which is itself a variation of the Dutch pronunciation of "Saint Nicholas." Washington Irving, author of such famous American tales as *The Legend of Sleepy Hollow* and *Rip Van Winkle*, wrote his *History of New York from the Beginning of the World to the End of the Dutch Dynasty* under the name Diedrich Knickerbocker. This humorous work contains many references to the Dutch celebration of Christmas and to their version of Santa Claus.

This Sinter Klaas was often portrayed wearing the red bishop's robes that Nicholas would have worn and carrying the miter he had as bishop of Myra. "Knickerbocker," however, used a different "Saint Nicholas" portrayal, envisioning his Santa Claus in Flemish clothing, than most Americans would now recognize.

Santa Claus as we know him, and as he is increasingly portrayed in many European countries, was the invention of Thomas Nast, a political cartoonist and illustrator who worked in the mid-1800s. His drawing of Santa Claus began in 1862, when the images were used as propaganda for the North during the Civil War. Nast often depicted Santa as "the jolly old elf," complete with the red cheeks, the belly that shakes like a bowl full of jelly, and the famous pipe. Nast, however, often drew his

Santa as rather short, shorter than we are used to in contemporary times, perhaps reflecting the idea that Santa was originally thought of as an elf, although now he is generally portrayed as human-sized. Nast's illustrations were also generally done in black and white—until one fateful day.

In 1886, Nast's publisher asked him to produce a color illustration of his Santa Claus for a book. Before he could do so, Nast had to decide what color his Santa Claus should wear. Nast selected the crimson suit with which we are now so familiar and paired it with a white ermine collar and cuffs, and thus the Santa Claus that we know today was born.

Santa's suit varies depending on his incarnation and the culture in which that particular Santa character developed. In some cultures, he still wears green, a dark forest green that reflects the fact that Christmas developed as a combination of the Christian celebration of Christ's birth and the winter festivals of the pagans, which generally celebrated the importance of nature to those cultures. It is also from this combination of cultures that we get our tradition of having a Christmas tree in the house.

Santa Claus and Other Christmas Figures Around the World

Among Santa Claus's many different names and different looks around the world, in some cultures he is an elf and in others it is an angel who brings gifts to children on Christmas. Some countries or cultures have evil Christmas characters who can tell which children have been naughty. Although most of these characters are no longer thought to be real, they have become part of the cultural traditions.

Belief in Santa Claus originated with worship of Saint Nicholas and Christmas itself celebrates the birth of Christ. Christmas as a holiday is generally associated with the Christian tradition.

Thus, in many countries it is not celebrated at all. Some countries that do not have large Christian populations, however, also celebrate Christmas and thus often have a Santa Claus figure.

Because the United States is a country settled by immigrants from other countries, many of the American Christmas traditions come from, or have evolved from, those of other cultures. Many of those activities have aspects in common, such as specific church services or other religious traditions (these are often similar across countries based on the dominant religion—Protestantism or Catholicism—in a country). Some traditions, though, are unique to certain countries.

The following paragraphs describe the traditions of many different countries, some of which are Santa-centered and others of which emphasize other aspects of the holiday festivities and observances.

Australia

Christmas in Australia happens on the same day as that in the United States, but it is very different! Because Australia is in the Southern Hemisphere, and the seasons are the opposite of those in the Northern Hemisphere, Christmas occurs in the middle of the summer. Santa still wears the traditional red and white fur suit.

One of the most popular Australian traditions is Carols by Candlelight. This tradition began on Christmas Eve in 1937 in Melbourne, when a radio DJ noticed a woman singing along to the radio by candlelight. This inspired him to organize a gathering of people to sing Christmas carols by candlelight. The first year,

10,000 people responded to the invitation, at first extended only to those from Melbourne, and gathered at Alexandra Gardens. The tradition since has spread throughout the country (it is broadcast over television), and now it is held at the Arts Centre of the Sidney Myer Music Bowl. Now, people purchase tickets to attend the concert given by professional musicians.

Brazil

In Brazil, Papai Noel, or Father Christmas, brings gifts to all the children. He is said to live in Greenland, not at the North Pole, as American tradition says. Brazil is in the Southern Hemisphere, meaning that the seasons are the reverse of those in North America: the South American Christmas is on December 25, but it occurs in the middle of summer! Thus the Brazilian Santa Claus does not wear the heavy red suit with white ermine cuffs that has become his typical costume in the United States. Instead, Papai Noel wears a suit made of silk, a much lighter fabric, for his journey to Brazil. (See also "Mexico.")

Egypt

Most Egyptians are not Christian, and those who are mostly belong to the Coptic Church (this is a Christian religion that developed originally in Egypt). The Coptic Church, like the Russian Orthodox Church, celebrates Christmas on January 7, which is around the day of the Epiphany.

One of the most important traditions associated with the Coptic celebration of Christmas involves food. The members of this church fast for the forty-five days leading up to January 7, eating no meat or dairy products during that time. After attending church late that night, they go home and eat "fatta," a dish made of meat and rice.

England

Santa Claus is generally known as "Father Christmas" in England. Early images of Father Christmas portray him with garlands of leaves, connecting him to the pagan traditions. When Christianity first arrived in England, the people already living there had their own religion. The Christians, however, wanted to convert these people to Christianity, and so they made the pagan traditions part of their own religion. By relating figures in the native religion to those in Christianity, those spreading the new religion were able to win converts and thus assimilate the old culture into the new.

Father Christmas was a popular character in children's plays and eventually became the embodiment of Saint Nicholas in England, particularly after the Reformation in the 1500s. The Protestants did not believe in saints, and particularly disliked those strongly associated with Catholicism, so they had to find a new Christmas figure to represent the being much of the world called Saint Nicholas. They chose Father Christmas.

Finland

In Finland, Santa Claus is called "Joulupukki." It is reported that Santa Claus actually lives in Finland, not in the North Pole, in a town called Korvantunuri, which is north of the Artic Circle. Joulupukki, his elves, and his reindeer are the only ones who know the exact way to get to this town.

Joulupukki's elves are the ones who make the list of naughty and nice children, and they write down anything that Joulupukki should know. As Christmas approaches, they also go around towns and cities—and are not seen, of course—to watch how children are behaving.

Because Finland is his home country (or so the people of Finland say), Joulupukki has time to give the gifts directly to the children; he does not merely leave them for children to find in the morning.

France

Père Noël, or "Father Christmas," as Santa is known in France, is much like the American Santa Claus. The French believe, however, that Santa's reindeer are just as important as Santa himself. The night before Christmas, they leave hay and carrots out in their shoes. Santa takes this reindeer food and leaves gifts in return.

In France, as in some other European countries, Santa visits twice for some families. He comes once on the Eve of Saint Nicholas, December 5, and once on Christmas Eve, December 24.

Germany

After the Reformation, a time during which the Catholic Church fell out of favor in many countries and the Protestant church was established, the Germans no longer had a celebration of Saint Nicholas. Martin Luther, the leader of the Reformation movement, thus invented the character of das Christkindl or das Christkind. The original Christkind was a secular equivalent to the Baby Jesus, but over the years it evolved into an adult angel, often portrayed as a woman dressed in white fur. Christkindl distributed toys that she carried with her on a reindeer.

In more recent years, however, the Weinachtsmann, the German Santa Claus, which evolved in part from the Christkindl, has displaced celebration of the Christkindl. Because Germany has many regions with many different customs, there are many more specific versions of Santa Claus or Saint Nicholas, each with a different name. Some other names are Ruprecht, Pelznickel, and Aschenmann. Ruprecht, for example, is often portrayed with bright red hair, although his long beard is white. He is associated with thunder and has a stone hammer, connecting him to the Norse god Thor.

Some of the names given to German versions of the Weinachtsmann have come to be considered separate beings, generally assistants to the Weinachtsmann.

Holland

In Holland the Dutch Santa Claus, or Sinter Klaas, arrives on a boat every year on December 6, Saint Nicholas Day, and all the church bells ring for him. He brings his assistant, Black Peter, or "Zwarte Piet" in Dutch, with him. Sinter Klaas travels to Amsterdam, on a white horse, to meet the queen at the palace. Some Dutch traditions state that Sinter Klaas comes from Madrid, Spain, and that he chooses a new harbor to arrive in every year. That way, more children get to see him.

Sinter Klaas carries a big book where Black Peter has recorded the names of naughty and nice children. The nice children receive gifts from Sinter Klaas, and the bad ones are taken away to be punished by Black Peter, who sometimes chases them with a stick.

Like the French, Dutch children leave out shoes that they fill with hay and carrots for Sinter Klaas's horse, and they may also receive presents on both Saint Nicholas's Eve and Christmas Eve, although these presents are brought by Santa Claus (also called Christmas Man), who is considered a different person than Sinter Klaas.

One of the most popular traditions in this country involves the disguising or hiding of gifts. At Sinter Klaas parties, held on December 5, often at schools, children must find their gifts based on clues or riddles supplied to them. The person giving the gift is a secret, often chosen at random, kind of like the American "secret Santa." Sometimes a small gift will be wrapped in a much larger package simply to fool the recipient. In other cases, one gift may be wrapped with many layers of paper. Each layer has a different person's name on it, so the gift is passed around and gradually unwrapped until it finally reaches the intended receiver, who removes the last layer of paper.

Iceland

In ancient Iceland, a troll called Grýla (pronounced "Greela") heard naughty children and captured them to bring them back to her cave. She and her husband then boiled the children and fed them to their thirteen sons. The legend of Grýla dates as far back as the 1100s, so it may have come over with the Norwegians who settled Iceland.

Grýla's sons, whose stories date back at least to the 1500s, are known as the "Yulemen," or jólasveinar, in Icelandic, and stories about their exploits, eating children as their parents did, among other things, terrified children for centuries. Finally, because the stories scared children so much, they were outlawed in 1746 by the Danes, who ruled Iceland at the time. By this time, the Yulemen had become more pranksters and thieves than eaters of children. By earlier this century, the brothers had evolved into Santa Claus figures who leave little presents in the children's shoes. Each of the thirteen visits on a different night of Christmas, beginning on December 12, when the first (there is a very specific order) comes down from the mountains. They then leave, one by one, beginning on Christmas day and ending on January 6. They do not wear red, as Santa Claus does, because Grýla does not approve of red clothes.

Italy

In Italy, Befana gives gifts to good children. Unlike most other versions of Santa Claus, Befana is a woman, and she delivers presents on the night of January 5, the eve of the Epiphany, which marks the day that the Wise Men found Jesus in the manger.

There are two versions of the Befana story. In one, the Wise Men invited her to go with them on their quest to find the newly born Savior. She declined but then changed her mind. She left her house with gifts but was unable to locate the Wise Men and thus could not give her gifts to the Christ child.

In the second version, Befana was the mother of one of the male children that King Herod ordered killed. She was unable to accept the loss of her child, so she packed up all of his belongings and set out in search of him. When she happened upon the manger where Jesus was, she believed that she had found her child and thus gave him all of the belongings she had carried with her. Out of gratitude, the Christ child gave her all of the children of the world to be hers for one night per year for the rest of eternity.

On the morning of January 6, children all over Italy wake up to find their stockings filled with sweet curly candy if they have been good or a piece of coal if they have been bad. A plate of broccoli and spiced sausage and a glass of wine are left out for Befana.

The Italians also have Babbo Natale, a Father Christmas figure. The children leave their shoes out on the eve of the Epiphany and wake up to find them filled with treats. As is true of many Catholic countries, Christmas itself is a time to celebrate the birth of Christ and so it is not a day of loud celebration or gift giving. That all happens on the day of the Epiphany, January 6, which marks the day the Wise Men arrived in Bethlehem and gave gifts to the newly born Savior.

Japan

A very small percentage of the Japanese population are Christian, but still, most of the people celebrate during the Christmas season. Most Japanese, those who are not Christian, celebrate more the custom of gift giving and the togetherness that the season brings than the birth of Christ or good works of Saint Nicholas.

Because Santa Claus is a part of the more secular side of Christmas, associated more with the gifts of Christmas than with the birth of Christ, the Japanese have their own version. Their Santa Claus figure is Hoteiosho, or Hoteiosha, sometimes called a priest, who brings gifts and leaves them for the children.

He often said to have eyes in the back of his head. Children are very careful to be on their best behavior when Hoteiosho is around because he can see everything they do!

Mexico

In Mexico, Christmas celebrations are much more religious than they are in its neighbor to the north, the United States. Children there do not tell Santa Claus what they want during the Christmas season. Instead, they speak directly to "el Niño Dios" (the Holy Child) or to the "Reyes Magos" (Wise Men), depending on whether the gifts are for Christmas or for Three Kings Day.

Christmas celebration begins on December 16, which is the start of "Las Posadas" (The Inns), nine days of children's processions and parties. The processions are reenactments of Joseph and Mary's quest for lodging in Bethlehem on the night that Jesus was born. The children stop at two houses, or inns, and are turned away. At the third, they are told that there is space not in the inn but in the manger.

Other traditions include the "Pastorelas," which are plays about the shepherds' journey to worship the Christ child, and the use of "El Nacimiento" (the Nativity) in decoration. The Pastorelas are also performed in other countries, particularly those colonized by the Spanish, such as the Philippines. They are performed in Brazil (colonized by the Portuguese) with a few variations: There are shepherdesses instead of shepherds, and a gypsy woman tries to kidnap the Baby Jesus.

The poinsettia, a traditional flower in the American Christmas (and the flower for the month of December), comes from Mexico. It is named for Dr. Joel R. Poinsett, the American minister to Mexico in the early 1800s. When Poinsett returned to the United States, he brought cuttings of the flowers and was able to cultivate them.

Norway

Christmas was taken very seriously in Norway for many years. There were several mythical creatures, including Lussi, a witch, and the julebukk, a half-human half-goat, that enforced preparation for Christmas and punished those who were not ready for the holiday celebration. These characters have become a part of the Christmas tradition, although most Norwegians no longer believe in them.

In Norway, Santa Claus is known as "Julenisse," and he is one of a larger group of elf-like beings called "nisser." The nisser, of which there are two portrayals, were generally considered protectors. The older type of nisse is the elfin nisse. The newer type of nisse, which evolved in the 1800s, is the one that has become the Norwegian version of Santa Claus. He is a tall, thin character who wears a long gray coat and has a long beard. Both types of nisse wore red stocking caps. In the same way that American children leave out cookies for Santa, Norwegians leave out porridge, which is expected by the Julenisse.

Many people in Norway still follow the tradition of the "seven kinds," which requires that seven kinds of cookies or sweet breads be on the table at Christmas dinner. The seven types of cookies can vary but often include smultringer (doughnuts), hjortetakk (cruellers), sirupsnipper (diamond shaped and ginger flavored), sandkaker (almond cookies), berliner kranser, krumkake (made with an iron), goro (a rectangular cookie also made with an iron), and fattigmann (twisted, fried

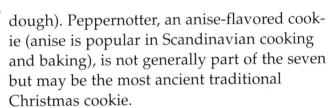

dough). Peppernotter, an anise-flavored cookie (anise is popular in Scandinavian cooking and baking), is not generally part of the seven but may be the most ancient traditional Christmas cookie.

Christmas preparation was extremely important for all Scandinavians. In Norway, there were believed to be several creatures that would fly by on certain nights to ensure that the proper steps were being taken. If preparation was not satisfactory, those responsible would be punished.

Philippines

There are more than 7,000 islands in the Philippines, so traditions vary. Some common elements include the "parol" (paper lantern) and the "belen" (nativity scene) used in decoration. The "misa de gallo" is the dawn mass (the term literally translates as "mass of the rooster," because church bells wake everyone at four A.M., about the time a rooster would). This mass is said every morning from December 16 until Christmas. Christmas is called "Pasko" in the Philippines, and "Merry Christmas" is "Maligayang Pasko." Just before the midnight mass, Filipino children receive their gifts, not from Santa Claus, but from Lolo and Lola, which mean "Grandfather" and "Grandmother." After the midnight mass on Christmas Eve, the family goes home to celebrate "noche buena" ("good night"; many terms in Filipino culture, particularly those having to do with religion, come from Spanish because the Philippine Islands were colonized by the Spanish [see "Mexico"], who brought Catholicism with them), which is a family meal. Noche buena lasts until morning.

Filipino children have a Christmas tradition similar to American children's trick or treating at Halloween. After the noche buena, the children go around to relatives' houses, where they receive small gifts, often toys. Groups of children called "Cumbancheros" go around to houses singing and playing instruments, much like our caroling tradition, except that people give them coins instead of cider, egg nog, or hot chocolate.

Christmas celebration in the Philippines officially lasts until the first Sunday in January, which is the day of the Epiphany, or Three Kings Day.

Poland

In Poland, Christmas Eve was traditionally a time for young women to think of marriage and to look for signs of whether they would be married in the coming year. A woman could learn not only this but also what sort of man her husband would be and what his profession would be.

For other people, particularly those in rural areas, who would have been farmers, it was the time to look for signs of what the next year would bring in terms of weather. A nice, sunny Christmas could mean good or bad weather later in the year, depending on which saying a person believed. Fortune telling on the subject of the coming year's harvests was also popular.

As it was for the Scandinavians, preparation was important to the Poles. Cleaning was the most important task, because it was thought that evil would invade any spaces left dirty. Tradition also stated that a man should be the first to cross the threshold into a house on Christmas Eve.

Russia

In Russia, one speaks of "Grandfather Frost." This figure, a secular (nonreligious) version of Saint Nicholas or Santa Claus, became popular after the Russian Revolution, during which the Communists took over. Celebrations of religion were not allowed under the Communist government, so the Russian people created a new Christmas figure that they named "Grandfather Frost."

Grandfather Frost and Santa Claus are generally acknowledged to be different people. There is currently a cooperation between the Russian Grandfather Frost and the Finnish Santa Claus in an effort to unite children around the world and to celebrate their unique heritages.

The Russians also have the legend of Babushka, which is very similar to that of Befana in Italy.

Sweden

Saint Lucia's Day (December 13), celebrated in a few of the Scandinavian countries but most closely associated with Sweden, has certain rituals that accompany it. Lucia decided at a young age to dedicate her life to God. Her mother had promised her to a nobleman, whom Lucia refused to marry. He was furious and reported her activities—she had been sneaking food to Christians who hid in underground tunnels to escape persecution—and she was caught and executed. The legend states that Lucia wore a wreath with candles on her head to guide her through the dark tunnels.

Saint Lucia (Lucia means "light") was an Italian saint, but her story spread throughout Europe. Famine had plagued parts of Europe, including Sweden, for years, and one year, a ship landed in a harbor with a woman in a white robe standing at the stern. She was believed to be Saint Lucia. When the Catholic saints fell out of favor with the Protestants in Sweden, they were replaced with new ones. Lucia was one, and she came to symbolize the end of hunger. Because her feast day is so close to Christmas, her celebration became closely connected to the holiday.

To commemorate Saint Lucia's Day, the eldest daughter in Swedish families rises early in the morning and dresses in a white robe with a red sash. A wreath with candles is placed on her head and she gives each member of the family food and drink. This tradition is also followed in areas in which Swedish people have settled.

Turkey

Turkey is generally a Muslim country, although there are members of other religions living there, so there are no official Christmas traditions. There are, however, traditions involving Saint Nicholas and other winter celebrations.

Saint Nicholas was from Turkey. He was born in Patara around A.D. 270 or 280 and spent most of his adult life in Myra (now Demre), where he was bishop. Every year, there is a Saint Nicholas Festival, which lasts for three days around his feast day, December 6. Many tourists come for this festival. Visitors can see Saint Nicholas Church and a statue of him, in which he appears much like the American Santa Claus, with a bag of toys and children all around. Of course, the Saint Nicholas in the statue is a tall thin man wearing the hooded robe of a bishop, not the suit of Santa Claus.

There is a celebration late in the month of December in Turkey, but this is to celebrate the coming new year, not Christmas.

United States of America

The American Christmas blends old and new traditions, from stockings hanging on the mantelpiece, home-made Christmas dinner with all the trimmings, to band concerts in the schools, carolers at the mall, and piles of gifts under a brightly lighted Christmas tree. Unique customs characterize each region, reflecting America's rich cultural inheritance from every corner of the world. Christmas is therefore the greatest melting pot of holidays. No other holiday celebrates the glorious diversity of America like the quaint New England Christmas in Massachusetts, the luminous Las Posadas procession of the Southwest, or the glitzy Hollywood Christmas parade.

Santa Claus, gift-giving, and the Christmas tree are permanent fixtures from coast to coast. But in terms of America's complete history, these traditions are young. Christmas as we know it in America was born in the late 1800s and did not become a national holiday until 1890. American immigrants brought Christmas to every corner of the new land from the places they left in Europe. Each nationality left its mark in a special way. During the holiday season American households are filled with warm, personal glimpses of history, each characterized by the special influences of the many nationalities that form this cultural melting pot, America.

Bibliography

STORIES:

Christmas Treasury, The. Philadelphia: A Running Press Miniature Edition™, 1998.

Church, Francis P. *Yes, Virginia, There Is a Santa Claus: The Classic Edition.* Illustrated by Joel Spector. Philadelphia: Courage Books, an imprint of Running Press, 2001.

Dickens, Charles. *A Christmas Carol: The Heirloom Edition.* Retold by Jane P. Resnick. Illustrated by Christian Birmingham. Philadelphia: Running Press, 2002.

Henry, O. *The Gift of the Magi.* Philadelphia: Running Press, Miniature Edition, 2001.

Hoffman, E. T. A. *The Nutcracker: A Young Reader's Edition of the Holiday Classic.* Adapted by Daniel Walden. Illustrated by Don Daily. Philadelphia: Running Press, Courage Books, 1996.

Thomas, Dylan. *A Child's Christmas in Wales.*
    Illustrated by Fritz Eichenberg. Philadelphia:
    A Running Press Miniature Edition™, 1993.

Twelve Days of Christmas, The. Illustrated by Don
    Daily. Philadelphia: Courage Books, an
    imprint of Running Press, 2000.

POEMS:

A Christmas Treasury: The Children's Classic Edition.
    Illustrated by Christian Birmingham.
    Philadelphia: Running Press, 1997.

Moore, Clement C. *The Night Before Christmas:
    The Classic Edition.* Illustrated by Christian
    Birmingham. Philadelphia: Running Press,
    1995.

CAROLS:

A Christmas Treasury: The Children's Classic Edition. Illustrated by Christian Birmingham. Philadelphia: Running Press, 1997.

The Family Treasury of Classic Christmas Carols. Illustrated by Sarah Gibb. Philadelphia: Courage Books, an imprint of Running Press, 2002.

RECIPES:

Becker, Ethan and Marion Rombauer Becker and Irma S. Rombauer. *Joy of Cooking Cookie Kit.* Philadelphia: A Running Press Miniature Edition™, 1997.

Beland, Nicole. *The Cocktail Jungle: A Girl's Field Guide to Shaking and Stirring.* Philadelphia: Running Press, 2003.

Clegg, Holly. *Trim & Terrific™ Cookbook: More than 500 Fast, Easy, and Healthy Recipes.* Philadelphia: Running Press, 2002.

Collister, Linda. *Chocolate: Basic Baking*. Philadelphia: Courage Books, an imprint of Running Press, 1997.

Lukins, Sheila and Julee Rosso. *Silver Palate Desserts: Recipes from the Classic American Cookbooks*. Philadelphia: A Running Press Miniature Edition™, 1995.

Seideman, Rob. *Real Cooking for Kids: Inside-Out Spaghetti, Lucky Duck, and More Recipes for the Junior Chef*. Philadelphia: Running Press, 2002.

Staib, Walter. *City Tavern Cookbook: 200 Years of Classic Recipes from America's First Gourmet Restaurant*. Philadelphia: Running Press, 1999.

Staib, Walter. *City Tavern Baking & Dessert Cookbook: 200 Years of Authentic American Recipes from Martha Washington's Chocolate Mousse Cake to Thomas Jefferson's Sweet Potato Biscuits*. Philadelphia: Running Press, 2003.

Von Klause, Kevin and Judy Wicks. *White Dog Café Cookbook: Multicultural Recipes and Tales of Adventure from Philadelphia's Revolutionary Restaurant.* Philadelphia: Running Press, 1998.

Wolf-Cohen, Elizabeth. *The Cookie Lover's Cookbook.* Philadelphia: Courage Books, an imprint of Running Press, 1998.

Betty Crocker Deluxe Pie Kit. Philadelphia: A Running Press Miniature Edition™, 2003.

The Gingerbread House Book. Illustrated by Leslie Wu. Philadelphia: Running Press, Miniature Edition, 2002.

CHRISTMAS TIPS AND CRAFTS:

The Gingerbread House Book. Illustrated by Leslie Wu. Philadelphia: A Running Press Miniature Edition™, 2002.

SANTA CLAUS AND CHRISTMAS TRADITIONS AROUND THE WORLD:

Felix, Antonia. *Christmas in America*. New York: TODTRI; Philadelphia: Courage Books, an imprint of Running Press, 1999.

Index